UNDERSTANDING CÉLINE

Essays by:
Wayne Burns
Bill Ott
John Leeds
Gerald J. Butler
Jerry Zaslove
William K. Buckley

Edited with an Introduction by:
James Flynn

Associate Editor:
C.K. Mertz

Genitron Press
Seattle, Washington

Library of Congress Cataloging in Publication Data

Understanding Céline.

    Includes Bibliographies.
    1. Céline, Louis-Ferdinand, 1894-1961--Criticism
and interpretation--Addresses, essays, lectures.
I. Flynn, J. (James), 1934-   . II. Burns, Wayne,
1918-   .
PQ2607.E834Z936 1984   843'.912   84-10281
ISBN 0-915781-00-X

ISBN 0-915781-00-X
Library of Congress No.: 84-10281

Copyright 1984 © by James Flynn

Published by Genitron Press
        P.O. Box 31391
        Seattle, Washington 98103-1391

Printed in the United States of America

This book is dedicated
to
Michael Horvitz

ACKNOWLEDGMENTS: The following selections in this volume are reproduced by permission of the authors and their publishers.

From *Recovering Literature*:

Bill Ott, "The Death of Des Pereires: Possibilities for Compassion in Céline's World," 2:1 (Spring 1973), 65-74.

Gerald J. Butler, "Céline's *Bagatelles pour un massacre*: The Expression of a Forbidden Passion," 8:1 (Spring 1980) 27-42; "The Meaning of the Presence of Lili in Céline's Final Trilogy," 10 (1982), 57-63.

Abbreviated versions of Wayne Burns' essay and Gerald J. Butler's section, "The Feeling For Women" were presented at the Céline section of the Modern Language Association annual meeting in December, 1983.

The contributions of William Buckley were written for this volume and were based upon earlier work: "A Bibliography of Critical Articles, Books and Commentaries on Louis-Ferdinand Céline and His Works: 1932-1973," *Recovering Literature* 3:1 (Spring 1974); and Stanford L. Luce and William K. Buckley, *A Half-Century of Céline: An Annotated Bibliography, 1932-1982*, New York: Garland Publishing, Inc., 1983.

My appreciation and gratitude are due to Gerald J. Butler, Wayne Burns and Jerry Zaslove for their comments and suggestions on earlier drafts of the

"Introduction." Naturally, I assume full responsibility for its contents which do not necessarily represent their views.

Evelyn Butler and Gerald J. Butler provided a thorough proof-reading of the manuscript and their care, patience and skill prevented the inadvertent reproduction of numerous errors. I would like to record my indebtedness to them. Hopefully this final version represents an accurate presentation of each author's work.

Céline's use of three dots as a punctuation device can lead to confusion in quoting his texts where omissions are necessary. Therefore, omissions from Céline's writings are shown by placing three dots inside brackets--(. . .)--while omissions from all other authors use the standard procedure of three unbracketed dots.

The cover for the book was designed and produced by Connie Wirtz whose patience and good humor survived through many revisions.

The support of Michael Horvitz was essential in the final realization of this project as a book. The depth of our appreciation is indicated by the dedication of this work to him.

Finally, the production of this volume was due in large part to the work of C. K. Mertz who is in every sense a co-editor and without whose efforts, assistance and perseverance it would never have appeared.

JHF

TABLE OF CONTENTS

INTRODUCTION

Louis-Ferdinand Destouches (Céline) was born on 27 May 1894 at Courbevoie, a suburb of Paris. He joined the French army in 1912 and in November 1914 he was wounded in action and was awarded the Méddaille Militaire for bravery. He entered medical school at the University of Rennes in 1919, qualifying as a doctor in 1924. His medical thesis for the Faculty of Medicine at the University of Paris was on "The Life and Work of Philippe-Ignace Semmelweis," the nineteenth century Jewish doctor who discovered that infection could be prevented by sterilization. For most of his adult life, Céline practiced medicine. He died on 1 July 1961 at Meudon, also a Paris suburb.

When he published *Journey to the End of the Night (Voyage au bout de la nuit)* in 1932, he adopted the pen-name of *Céline* which was one of his mother's Christian names, and it is by this pseudonym that he is generally known. The recent publication by Stanford Luce and William Buckley, *A Half-Century of Céline: An Annotated Bibliography, 1932-1982*, lists 19 major works, of which nine have been translated into English. Six of these works are novels, and his first two books of fiction--*Journey* and *Death on the Installment Plan (Mort à crédit)* (1936) have been translated twice, first by John

Marks in the 1930's and more recently by Ralph Manheim. English versions of these six novels are currently in print.

"Louis-Ferdinand Céline walked into great literature as other men walk into their own homes," Leon Trotsky wrote in his 1935 review of Céline's first novel, *Journey to the End of the Night*.[1] His second novel, *Death on the Installment Plan*--while it was not as well received at the time--underscored Trotsky's judgment; if anything, it surpassed his first effort. Céline continued to write and in fact completed a final manuscript version of *Rigadoon* on the morning of 1 July 1961, the same day that he died. If his later fiction does not surpass the achievements of *Journey* and *Death on the Installment Plan*, it is in no way unworthy of Céline's talent. Merlin Thomas, in his sympathetic and perceptive full-length study, claims that "there is a case for regarding [his last] three 'novels' as the supreme artistic achievement of Céline"[2] (210). Still, Céline is not widely known to English-speaking readers; his novels are seldom taught in either French or English departments in American universities and critical and scholarly discussion is scanty. Why is this?

Patrick McCarthy in his biography says that Céline has been "neglected because of his political opinions. He wrote anti-semitic pamphlets, sided with Hitler and fled to Germany in 1944. He belonged to an era that Frenchmen prefer to forget. Camus, Sartre and the writers of the Resistance dominated the post-war period. A curtain of silence was drawn over their opponents."[3] The problem with this statement is that it seriously misrepresents both Céline's role at the time and distorts the circumstances. Céline was not, in any usual sense, a

2

supporter of Hitler. He fled to Germany not as a collaborator in exile but simply to escape assassination by Resistance forces that under the circumstances were not inclined to make elemental distinctions let alone subtle ones. Nor was he what we would normally understand as an "opponent" of the Resistance writers.

Thomas echoes McCarthy's main conclusion about the political response to Céline's novels (but with important qualifications): "there are reasons why Céline . . . is less well known than he deserves. Political reasons." No doubt this is at least partly true, and Thomas' study presents in detail the political objections to Céline. Still, Céline was anything but a political partisan. In one way or another, he managed to antagonize political followers of almost every persuasion from the communists to the fascists. His greatest difficulties, however, resulted from his anti-semitic writings. These produced virulent attacks against him including a charge by Jean-Paul Sartre that "if Céline supported the socialist theses [anti-semitism] of the Nazis, it was because he was paid to do so."[4] This judgment was gratuitously slanderous—Céline's writing was never for sale in any such way, as Sartre must have known in his more rational moments—and such a charge introduces a question about Céline's motives in all his writings that should not be there. Nevertheless, as Thomas puts it, "it is abundantly clear that Céline had anti-semitic views over a number of years." But he goes on to say that "it was both shameful and irresponsible for Sartre" to claim that Céline was in the pay of the Nazis.

In his careful examination of the evidence, Thomas concludes that "despite his pre-war pamphlets, despite the undoubted anti-semitism, despite the pro-German sentiments voiced before the war, there is *no* evidence of collaboration with Germans during the war that has been substantiated" (171). Yet such charges resulted in Céline's being condemned *in absentia*--he was in the custody of Danish authorities from December 1945 to June 1951--by a French court in 1950 as a collaborator. This judgment imposed a one year's imprisonment in addition to fines and confiscation of half his assets. When Céline was amnestied in 1951, he returned to France and settled in Meudon.

The fact of the matter is that much of the controversy about Céline's anti-semitic views is basically irrelevant to reading his novels. One would have to make some extremely curious interpretations of the texts to find anti-semitic or fascistic themes in Céline's fiction. This is not to deny that many readers come to Céline's novels with a basic antagonism to his work based on his anti-semitic reputation. Nor is it to deny that political idealists can find plenty to be upset, outraged and disgusted with in the world as Céline shows it to exist. But the point that Céline's reputation as a novelist has been damaged due to his political beliefs, while true, is only part of the problem that readers and critics have had with his fiction. The objections of idealistic critics are founded upon much more than political standards. Finally, it is not only political values that are brought to risk in reading Céline, but all social, cultural and moral values. In the words of Wayne Booth, talking about *Journey*, "The better it is understood, the more immoral it looks" [5] (383). Moreover, if the picture of human life shown in these novels has political implications it is not due to anti-semitic polemics but to a basic incompatibility between

4

political ideology and human life as it is experienced in its day-to-day reality. What appears to be at least equally upsetting for readers, however, is that the whole range of accepted social and cultural values which support and yet go well beyond political idealisms of every sort is undercut. This negative function of the novels is opposed to every kind of domination over human beings; it becomes a relentless and implacable anarchism. It is at this point that one might usefully consider the themes of Céline's novels, in particular the early works.

The overall theme of Céline's early novels, *Journey to the End of the Night* and *Death on the Installment Plan*, is that the struggle of human life to realize itself reveals the deadly, dominating nature of the idealistic claims of society, culture, and civilization. In their common forms, these claims assert that human life must be directed by abstract values as expressed in moral, intellectual, political, economic and community standards; that such values are necessary for the proper organization of society and, subsequently, for the full realization of human life. All these claims for the necessity, rationality and desirability of social domination, Céline's novels undercut. What is exposed is not only the fact of human domination and its full meaning in terms of the individual human being, but equally all the domination's claims to legitimacy. Few critics have been willing to face the depth and severity of Céline's attack on social values as presented in his novels, preferring to attribute his vision to a basic disgust with human nature or a misanthropic element in his own psychological makeup. These positions are repeated time and again, often buttressed with psychological jargon, references to nihilistic traditions in literature or, for those who want to be sympathetic, excuses that in spite of it all Céline was a genius. Often his contributions to language, especially his stylistic innovations, are posited as his great achievement. In the end, however, such approaches represent little more than final, last-ditch efforts to preserve those cherished cultural and social values of domination that the novels so thoroughly undermine.

This negative, anti-idealistic theme is not exclusive to Céline's novels, although few other writers demonstrate its meaning with such relentless clarity, such sensitive understanding, and such full awareness for human life. Ortega y Gassett in his essay "The Nature of the Novel" points towards this theme as a central truth of literature in talking of Cervantes' work:

> The poetic quality of reality is not real-
> ity as this or that thing but reality as a
> generic function. Therefore it does not
> actually matter what objects the realist
> chooses to describe. Any one at all will
> do, since they all have an imaginary halo
> around them, and the point is to show the
> pure materiality under it. We see in this
> materiality a conclusive argument, a crit-
> ical power which defeats the claims to
> self-sufficiency of all idealizations,
> wishes and fancies of man. The insuffi-
> ciency, in a word, of culture, of all that
> is noble, clear, lofty--this is the sig-
> nificance of poetic realism. Cervantes
> recognizes that culture is all that, but
> that, alas, it is a fiction. Surrounding
> culture--as the puppet show of fancy was

surrounded by the inn--lies the barbarous, brutal, mute, insignificant reality of things. It is sad that it is shown to us thus, but what can we do about it! It is real, it is there: it is terribly self-sufficient. Its force and its single meaning are rooted in its presence. Culture is memories and promises, an irreversible past, a dreamed future. But reality is a simple and frightening "being there." It is a presence, a deposit, an inertia. It is materiality.[6]

In saying that "it is sad that it is shown to us thus," Ortega no doubt deliberately understates the case since the whole impact of his writing shows us that the recognition of this "materiality" is far beyond sadness, beyond even tragedy or disillusionment. He has followed Cervantes to a crack in the wall of life as it is defined for us, and looking through at what he has been shown, Ortega has recognized an abyss of social meaninglessness. Then he has had the courage to recognize the implications and truth of what he has been shown, neither denying the experience nor berating Cervantes for showing it to him. This vision eventually realizes that life does not match the terms of cultural ideology, and therefore in some basic way society is unable to deal with the material world that will not adapt itself to such designs. But rather than abandon the claims of its abstractions, society resorts to force. And this force contains the drive to domination; physical force and domination for insensient nature, political and economic force and domination in social relations, psychological force and domination of human relationships. When all these are combined, as they are in modern society, the result is a relentless drive toward total control, in short, totalitarian domination.

Yet, all of society's power, including its use of modern science and technology, cannot erase the gap between the desired cultural patterns that existence "should" follow and obey, and the antisocial qualities of materiality, including that portion of human beings that is not reduced to societal terms. Nor can society's claims answer the negation of a Cervantes or a Céline except to completely reject the vision of "materiality" and to assert ever more shrilly the claims of its ideology. It can push its power and domination to ever further reaches, even to nuclear annihilation. And it can sing its own praises for having "conquered nature." But in the end, nature is not conquered, and the wellsprings of human life that stand against domination are not conquered either. These wellsprings may be buried in the deepest recesses of unconsciousness, and the individuals themselves may be killed either through physical murder or the "soul murder" of their emotional, social and intellectual lives. There are always the death squads. But still human nature has not been conquered in the sense that human beings have been finally and totally transformed into the abstract terms of cultural ideology. We may be impressed with the energy of social life, and the claims that humans as jiggling puppets are a sign that nature has been overcome. But finally such responses are invested in the grossest kind of delusion, regardless of how much they are supported by the claims of society or by our own willingness to enter totally into the act and become puppets who with our social roles dance on the strings of economics, politics, religion, fame, or social ideology. No matter how fast the tune is played, nor how much light is focused on the little stage, nor how hard the puppets dance, nor how carefully we refuse to look about, the "materiality" of life tells us, if we can recognize it at all, that our little puppet show is a lie. From the depth of our own illegal and immoral feelings to the infinite indifference of the universe, the message everywhere echoes the same critique of our little puppet show: it is a sham, it is a lie, it is a fake, it is a fraud, it is a waste of a person's life.

Once we have been where Ortega has been, and we have seen something of what he has seen, then we must either reject entirely the vision of our artist guides or conclude that society's abstract "truths" *about human experience* are lies. They lead us away from our real chances for life and not toward them. The further we go into human experience as it is shown to us in genuine novels, the blacker these lies appear since we see more clearly with each step the human costs, not only the great pain, sorrow and suffering that are generated by the social lies, but also the lost chances for an individual human life.

It is not easy to understand how and why the cultural perspective operates as it does. A useful analogy might be made to Freud's analysis of dreams where he makes a distinction between manifest and latent content which is basic to understanding both the function of "dream work" and the repressed human condition underlying it. The manifest content of dreams condenses, mystifies and distorts the deepest aspirations of the human being, the striving to express his desires in a concrete relationship with the material world around him, including his social world. The standards of the conscious mind come from the ideology of the social structure which in our time is based almost entirely on economic power and domination. A primary function is to allow the dreamer to continue sleeping. In condensation, numerous distinct and individual experiences, feelings, longings, impulses are reproduced in a single common pattern. The latent content must be derived from clues of the manifest dream work. Yet it is only in the unveiling of the latent content that a complex and more complete "truth" about the individual and his experiences in life can be found. In this sense, the description of the latent content of dreams can be said to be more "true" than the manifest content. And it should be noted that it is also less abstract, less mystical, less symbolic, less organized, and less acceptable to the cultural censors of consciousness.

In terms of this analogy, it might be said that society's purpose is to insist upon the manifest dream as the only reality, to keep us in the dream world of culture by denying the deepest individual experiences and by substituting standardized or abstracted symbols, myths, rationalizations, and even feelings. In other words, to turn the human being into a thing, like other things, that can be created, managed and controlled in the economic system. To see and understand the latent content of the cultural dream, the social lie, is implicitly to deny the value of this dream world and all its claims to represent "reality." Such is the work of genuine fiction, to awaken the reader from his slumber through life, or as D. H. Lawrence has stated it, to recognize and respect "man alive" rather than the spectres we have become to each other and even to ourselves by becoming things in our cultural life. But, as Lawrence goes on to observe, "the dead are not dead for nothing. Who buries his own

10

sort? The dead are cunning and alert to pounce on any spark of life and bury *it*, even as they have already buried Cézanne's apple and put up to it a white tombstone of Significant Form."[7]

In modern existence almost all abstract and idealistic "truths" (white tombstones of Significant Form) are quickly turned to the service of the social lies, if not directly then through revision and interpretation. This is the case for our greatest thinkers—for the works of Marx and Freud, great and truthful as they are in themselves. It is even easier for most of modern sociology, psychology, economics, history, and literary criticism which are created to serve the social lies and the whole structure of modern life upon which these lies rely. Perhaps the most discouraging part of this is found in the commitment, energy and enthusiasm that people bring to furthering the ends of dominating thought. This is not to say that nothing critical can be said about the conditions of modern life. Recent works by Christopher Lasch in such books as *The Culture of Narcissism* and *Haven in a Heartless World*, and Russell Jacoby in *Social Amnesia*, provide illuminating critical analyses of the position of man at the current time. But these books and the approaches they take apparently have very little influence in bringing about either social awareness or the possibility of change. Meanwhile, the overwhelming bulk of both academic and popular work remains firmly committed to supporting the status quo, i.e., the system that is in large part responsible for diminishing human life to the "interfacing" of mechanical things.

Part of the problem is that even the best of the work done by social scientists has a flat and abstract quality to it; it lacks the sustained immedi-

11

acy of what is experienced by the human being. This is one result of a view of life that understands human beings as symbolic elements or units of measure that can be categorized. Something of the reductive force of these processes is understood even by their most relentless practitioners. Freud, for example, has been accused of applying a mechanistic or biological typography to his discussion of the human psyche. Most often this charge has been brought by so-called "humanists" who have been eager to substitute categories of social values which are at least equally abstract, and where, in turn, they eliminate almost entirely the awareness that human relationships are the creative source of history. (e.g., Jung, Adler, Horney, Sullivan, etc.). In contrast to these abstract, if well-intentioned approaches, Freud's work is distinguished by his "being there," by his full human interaction with the subjects of his case studies and his intellectual ideas. The complete opposite of this human element can be seen in someone like B.F. Skinner and the behaviorists to whom human beings are entirely mechanical-biological things as if, for example, they were to be manipulated like the contents of a bank account. Most of modern social science has adopted the view of the observer as instrument and the human being as abstract subject. Therefore, their work tends to reduce itself to considerations of representative case histories, typical types, and truncated examples; all of which may be illustrative, and even on occasion moving, but in the end subservient to the rhetorical terms of the presentation. This rhetoric is predicated on a particular kind of perspective. It looks upon life and things from the outside, and it is prepared to consider types of data, patterns of arrangement, representative evidence from which abstract theories can be made or tested. This view from the outside can be very powerful, whether it is looking "into" the mysteries of space or those of the human psyche. But it is always a stranger to the inner, felt quality of what it is examining, and to the human relationships.

All this changes dramatically in Céline's novels. Ferdinand, the I-narrator, is no mere example or representative of modern man. He is, instead, a fully realized fictional character, as complex, feeling and responsive as any "real" human counterpart. And as Ferdinand journeys through his fictional world, it too takes on a full and complex existence that makes it as "real" as any we ourselves are likely to encounter. In fact, Ferdinand's world is remarkably like our own, the last fifty years apparently having served to extend and expand the significant features without witnessing any notable improvements that would negate either his experiences or the understandings he is driven to realize.

The difference between the social awareness of these novels and the analyses of social science is that through Ferdinand we come to understand modern life in a wholly new and intimate way. And this is a way in which we have to abandon, or at least set aside during our reading, the detached outside perspective which looks upon human beings and their relationsips as if they were objects. Instead we are on the inside of human experience, looking out. Of course Ferdinand is capable of seeing outside himself, as when he and little Robert become peeping toms to watch the sexual antics of Madame Gorloge and the workman Antoine. In fact, Ferdinand is something of a voyeur throughout. However, there is a crucial difference between this seeing and that reported from the scientific or instrumental perspective. While the outside-objective perspective seeks to detach the person who is doing the viewing, or turns him into an instrument, in the case of Ferdinand the complex human being is fully there, fully recognized in our reading, and in full interaction with the object being seen. And when this full human component is added, everything takes on a completely different meaning and importance. The outside-objective perspective is not only turned upside down, but its greatest limitations are revealed. For what becomes vitally important is not the "thingness" or abstract qualities of the objects that are seen, nor the instrumental qualities of the observer, but the interaction, the relationship, the living moments of experience and recognition.

Perhaps a small example will be helpful. Ferdinand the stock boy at Berlope and Son is not merely exploited labor--although he most assuredly is that too--but he also makes us feel and understand what exploited toil is in truly human terms. It is the stupifying drudgery of meaningless work and long hours, the helplessness in the face of oppression by the bosses, even the sacrifice of human contact in a system that pits all against all. Ferdinand's valiant attempts to deal with his job fall short. He cannot, in the end, cancel out his inclinations for human contact nor his feelings of human compassion. And then he is fired outright, on the whim of Lavelongue who thoroughly enjoys his minor kingdom of domination. Throughout it all, Ferdinand is subjected to the endless harangues of his parents and the ultimate indignity of a completely hypocritical sermon from Lavelongue who even ends by singing his own praises for having done his dirty work.

"Ten years from now he himself . . . I can assure you . . . will come to me and say: 'Monsieur Lavelongue, you did the right thing. You are a good man! Thanks to you, I found out what's what!'" (151). Ferdinand's mother agrees and exits thanking Lavelongue. This is by no means the most dramatic case in which Ferdinand is an "exploited" worker, merely one of the first. But in every case, exploitation as experienced through Ferdinand attains a new meaning as compared to exploitation as observed from the outside. It is no longer just a fact. Our understanding no longer has meaning as an event from which we are detached and therefore to which we can respond only with sentimental platitudes. Rather, the totality of the case, which includes the whole range of Ferdinand's feelings, overcomes our detachment. We become personally involved with a sense of compassion that not only condemns the fact of this exploitation but undercuts all our abilities to rationalize it or categorize it, be these attempts in terms of sentimentality or of economic and political "understanding."

Once we have entered into Ferdinand's life and his world in this way, we have established a pathway of a kind which also leads back from the novel to our own world. Ferdinand comes into our world, and his experiences, vision of life, and conscious understanding are added to our own, transforming it. If we see some of Ferdinand in other people, or even begin to see others as Ferdinand sees them, then the stage is set for us to doubt the claims of our social domination, to reject its rationales as expressed in its ideology, to seek another way to understand the life we are leading and its meaning. And this new way of understanding life is not based upon other, newer, or more justifiable abstractions

such as *Justice, Love,* or *Human Decency.* At this
point, those interesting and important writings of
the social scientists can be understood in a new
light; they take on a new critical importance. In
other words, the representative element of things
attains a new meaning, one that is so personal and
different from the "representative" element of the
outside-objective view that the very word contains a
different and more inclusive meaning. It is true
that the most important portions of this new meaning
are almost entirely negative. Descriptions of society begin to provide evidence that unmasks the social
lies, once we are no longer limited to the deadend
of outside-objective reality. Nor should we be
driven away from this vision of reality by the
charge of "negativity," since the object of doubt,
denial and rejection is not a truth, but only at
very best a kind of partial truth masquerading as
the whole thing. What does our world need more than
this kind of negativity? What do we need less than
a new positive program based on the structure of old
lies and designed to create more power and domination over human beings? Personally, I can not see
that any new plan based on the outside-objective
perspective and imposed on human life in this way
can ever lead to the liberation of either individuals or society. At its very best, a new organization of social life might give some people a better
economic or political deal within the structures of
domination.

In the case of Céline's novels, while he provides a detailed and extensive critique of society
that undercuts almost every claim to truth and legitimacy, he does not offer us yet another, albeit
superior, pattern for our lives. On the contrary,
he helps us deny and destroy the meager, dream-

producing patterns of society. He offers us a chance to see the latent content of living, not a new promised land. He offers an escape from spectre-land. Where one might escape to, I do not know, nor does Céline purport to tell us. We might expect that it would be a "journey to the end of the night," to use his poetic language.

Such a perspective on the relationship between civilization, the human being and art necessarily implies a different concept of individuality than that currently fashionable in contemporary versions of quantified, behavioristic, humanistic or therapeutic social science. It is directly opposed to these pseudo-sciences; the ones that have been popularized to the status of common-sense wisdom, as well as those that are the exclusive domain of the professional experts. For one thing, it rejects the common but simplistic premise that people exist as autonomous beings with integrated, personal characters. It denies that they can by themselves confront their social circumstances and resolve the dilemmas of modern life. It does not offer easy personal solutions such as those peddled by the advocates of self-improvement, positive-thinking, adaptation to social norms, or gestures of rebellion. Lawrence's "man alive" survives, if at all, only in the deepest recesses of modern man; for the most part we remain "spectre" to ourselves because the bulk of our makeup is so thoroughly penetrated and shaped by the social circumstances of civilization. Under the conditions of modern life, it is impossible to talk seriously of the autonomous individual as a citizen of modern civilization, or to assert that the citizen-individual holds within his own power the ability to shape a satisfying social life for himself. All this, Céline saw and under-

stood clearly, and presented in his novels. Therefore, the objects of Céline's attacks on the social
lies are not only economic or political but personal. The anti-human elements of modern life exist
not only in social institutions but within modern
man.

In his "blackening" of Ferdinand (providing him
with a full complex human nature), Céline not only
establishes his character's reliability, as Wayne
Burns demonstrates in his essay, but he reveals the
depth and viciousness of our social processes. In
his novels, Céline spares neither Ferdinand nor any
other character. This is not nihilism, as so many
critics have claimed, but an illuminating revelation
about the conditions of modern life and the extent
that they have overtaken human beings. To see it as
nihilism or self-hatred is to succumb to the most
banal interpretation of the individual. It is at
the same time, to deny the most awful and important
aspects of civilized life as we know it. In short,
it is a classic case of repression.

The great difficulty of reading novels at the
current time exists in the fact that we, all of us--
I certainly don't exclude myself--are so thoroughly
caught up the process of social-psychological domination. To one degree or another, we accept the
social lies. Its aspirations are our own; personal
success is a lofty perch in the social structure of
domination. We all want to reach the top. For the
most part, we cling to various versions of domination because we are convinced that these social lies
are all there is and all there can be. We claim one
version is better than another, more equitable, more
humane, more efficient, or whatever else we can come
up with to justify it and ourselves. We cannot
imagine another kind of life, and we delude our-

selves into thinking that there is some hope in the improvement of social lies--in political, economic, social schemes. We deeply believe that without these lies there would be nothing, a void for each of us individually and for the social life of mankind. As we cling to the social lies, we resist what the novel asserts, not just intellectually, but with a major portion of our emotional energy.

Contextualist reading is the only way I know that we can approach the latent truth of life as presented in genuine novels, such as Céline's. This is not the place to go into an extended description of what contextualist criticism is or how it applies specifically to novels. For readers who are not familiar with this term, I refer them to the works of Stephen Pepper and Wayne Burns, in particular *The Panzaic Principle* and *Journey Through the Dark Woods*.[8] *Recovering Literature: A Journal of Contextualist Criticism* has published essays on contextualist theory and criticism of specific literary works for more than a decade. I hope that a very brief summary of contextualism will suffice here.

Contextualist criticism bases its aesthetic on the quality and vividness of the experience which characterizes the work of art. In other words, it is based on characteristics that are specifically human, *i.e.*, issuing from the capabilities of human interaction with other human beings and with material existence. The root of this standard for making aesthetic judgments can be contrasted to others that are dogmatic (either moral or cynical), or those based on standards of normality and similarity, or on patterns of organization. These alternative ways of understanding art are detailed by Pepper, and they can only be pointed to in this essay. But the difference between these approaches and contextualism might be summarized as the difference between various versions of the outside-objective perspective and the involved perspective. It might be said to be the difference between a survey of work, even one with a "Marxist" interpretation, and Céline's account of Ferdinand's experiences with work. According to Wayne Burns, the measure of aesthetic quality is in the "illumination" of experience that a novel or other work of art provides. Or as Pepper puts it: "The more vivid the experience and the more extensive and rich its quality, the greater its aesthetic value." Such an aesthetic sides with those aspects of literature which oppose the sentimental reruns of manufactured feelings, the stock responses of sexual, racial, economic, political and social causes, the patterned sensations of melodrama, whether they are presented in the terms of international diplomacy or the latest horror movies. In short, a contextualist aesthetic recognizes the full, complex human element in literature and it articulates the latent meaning of individual life as opposed to all the claims to truth made by the social lies, the "claims to self-sufficiency of all idealizations, wishes and fancies of man."

What must be kept clear is that these experiences and illuminations are of a different kind from the sensations and sentimentality that characterize so much of modern life. They are not in any way the equivalent of "consciousness raising" which is based upon one or more programs of further socialization. At best such efforts lead to vapid self-congratulations for attaining an agreement with the banal common-sense "truths" of the social lies. Nor do these artistic illuminations lead to a solipsistic and narcissistic detachment from social life. The life of human beings is, after all, realized in its interaction with other human beings and with the material world. And society itself cannot be seen as a "thing" but must be recognized as the complex expression of human interaction. While the rationale and authority of our society may come from its ability to turn human life and effort into things, its final power comes from its ability to control, reorder, and process human action. In its most recent forms, the very psyche of human beings has been penetrated and shaped by social power. The processes by which the integrity of modern man has been taken over by social values, perspectives and responses to life means that there is no safe refuge. No amount of self-improvement, self-realization, self-motivation, or adaptation that merely asserts in more vigorous and effective ways the social lies can erase the problem; at most it can only repress it more effectively.

To attempt to read genuine novels as symbols of other truths, as technical accomplishments, as versions or demonstrations of the scientific findings of sociology, economics, or psychology, in other words, as verification of "isms" (Marxism, Freudianism, Catholicism, patriotism, socialism or even anarchism)--all such attempts must be seen as contrary to the evidence of genuine novels. To substitute one social lie for another may indeed lead to improvements, political or other, but it will not answer the novel in the terms with which it is speaking to us.

These claims may seem to be in themselves doctrinaire. But actually they are not. It is not my claim that there is only one true reading of a novel, nor that all the knowledge of other disciplines is irrelevant to understanding novels. On the contrary, a full reading of any genuine novel must account for the circumstances that surround that reading, and it can be an intensely personal experience. At the same time, the novel itself has its own existence, and it must be allowed its own integrity which can only be respected and understood through a close textual reading. To assert that the novel itself should be changed in our reading of it to fit our preformed perceptions would be to deny what is basic to a very real form of human contact. Yet in most cases novels are not easy to understand. It would be foolhardy indeed to ignore or deny the contribution of any form of knowledge that can aid us in our attempts to read novels and understand the human life they illuminate. What I am claiming--and in this I merely echo D. H. Lawrence's assertions-- is that for readers of the novel the only course is to follow the novel itself; to recognize that the novel is not inferior to philosophy, psychology, science, religion or any other form of thought; to realize that the truth of the novel is not a valid-ation of these other forms of human thought, but rather that its claims to valid knowledge of human life as it is revealed by our greatest novelists is not surpassed in any other form. Lawrence makes these claims for the novel repeatedly, and in "Mo-rality and the Novel," he puts it in terms that are both provocative and crystal clear:

Now here we see the beauty and the great value of the novel. Philosophy, religion, science, they are all of them busy nailing things down, to get a stable equilibrium. Religion, with its nailed-down One God, who says *Thou shalt, Thou shan't*, and hammers home every time; phi-losophy, with its fixed ideas; science

with its "laws": they, all of them, all
the time, want to nail us on to some tree
or other.

But the novel, no. The novel is the
highest example of subtle inter-related-
ness that man has discovered. Everything
is true in its own time, place, circumstance, and untrue outside of its own
place, time, circumstance. If you try to
nail anything down, in the novel, either
it kills the novel, or the novel gets up
and walks away with the nail.[9]

In another essay, "Why the Novel Matters," Lawrence again claims for the novel the ability to
overcome the limitations of abstract ideals. "And
being a novelist, I consider myself superior to the
saint, the scientist, the philosopher, and the poet,
who are all great masters of different bits of man
alive, but never get the whole hog."[10] It is in the
alive or genuine novel, Lawrence claims, that human
experience is seen in its fullest sense, where
"time, place and circumstance" are recorded as they
are lived, and where, therefore, the abstractions
that lead to the social lie are properly accounted
for in terms of what they mean to an individual
life.

What I have written in this introduction so far
is in itself quite abstract, although hopefully in a
different sense from what I have characterized as
the social "abstractions." I realize that I have
dealt more with an approach to Céline rather than an
actual reading of his fiction. The essays in the
remainder of this book are concerned more directly
with the texts themselves, the most extensive criticism being that provided by Wayne Burns in his

consideration of *Journey*. This approach to reading
Céline, which insists that the core of his fiction
is to be found in its anti-social assertion of human
life and that this connects to the life and society
of the reader, implies a number of practical difficulties. And these practical concerns are by no
means trivial. In one way or another, they can
eventually come down to the question: "But if I
accept all of this—Céline and your approach and
these readings—what am I to do about my own life?
My B.A., MBA or Ph.D. program? My girl friend, boy
friend, wife, husband, child, parent, friends? My
job?" If I were a Catholic priest, I would have an
answer: "you should do this and that, and obey the
ten commandments, and say your prayers, trust in
God, etc." If I were an analyst, I might listen
patiently, even for years, ask many perceptive questions, and when you had worked out your psychological difficulties or adapted to your circumstances, I
would release you from your treatment. If I were a
Marxist revolutionary, I would devise a list of
actions, attitudes and goals for you. If I were
your employer, I would tell you to work hard; if I
were your college president, I would tell you to
study hard. But in the end I, as myself, can offer
no such answers. The very best I can do is to
recommend Wayne Burns' *Journey Through the Dark
Woods* which is the description of his teaching of
literature for more than 40 years. In particular,
Chapter 6 discusses many of the practical concerns
that students have had over the years, and how these
have been connected to the reading of fiction.

It should be clearly stated, however, that Burns
does not offer solutions to either these practical
problems nor to the theoretical questions they im-
ply. If this is a fault then it is an inevitable

fault that proceeds from the conditions of civilized life itself. I am reminded of Freud's conclusion to *Civilization and its Discontents*:

> Thus I have not the courage to rise up before my fellow-men as a prophet, and I bow to their reproach that I can offer them no consolation: for at bottom that is what they are all demanding--the wildest revolutionaries no less passionately than the most virtuous believers.
>
> . . . .
>
> Men have gained control over the forces of nature to such an extent that with their help they would have no difficulty in exterminating one another to the last man. They know this, and hence comes a large part of their current unrest, their unhappiness and their mood of anxiety. And now it is to be expected that the other of the two 'Heavenly Powers', eternal Eros, will make an effort to assert himself in the struggle with his equally immortal adversary [Death--the instinct of destruction]. But who can foresee with what success and with what result?[11]

Freud's "inability" to offer consolation or to foresee a successful result to the strivings of civilization has not been taken to heart by those who have followed him. For the most part he has been attacked for these "failures" and new self-apppointed prophets have arisen to offer both the consolations of psychological therapy and the promise of social success through politics. Of course they have had to deny the essential discoveries of Freud in order to assume their status as prophets; as they and their ilk must deny the discoveries of Céline in order to continue offering the whole range of society's consolations and promises. And it must be admitted that to see human life in our times without the promises of consolation now or future social success is to make a tremendous demand on the reader.

It is not the claim of this book and these essays that a final and complete understanding of Céline's novels has been achieved, nor even that such an attempt would be possible or desirable. But each essay here implicitly accepts the task of reaching towards such an understanding as the goal of criticism, and each writer goes as far as he can to reach this goal with the subject he has outlined for himself. While these essays are not in any sense a final answer to our need to understand Céline, I feel that they help us to read Céline with a fuller awareness and understanding. For that reason, they are included here.

James Flynn
Seattle, Washington
January, 1984

FOOTNOTES

1. Leon Trotsky, "Novelist and Politician," *Atlantic Monthly*, 156:4 (Oct. 1935), 413.
2. Merlin Thomas, *Louis-Ferdinand Céline* (New York: New Directions, 1979), p. 210.
3. Patrick McCarthy, *Céline* (London: Allen Lane, 1975), p. 7.
4. Jean-Paul Sartre, *Anti-Semite and Jew* (New York: Grove Press, 1962), p. 41.
5. Wayne Booth, *The Rhetoric of Fiction* (Chicago: Univ. of Chicago, 1961), p. 383.
6. Jose Ortega y Gassett, "The Nature of the Novel," *Hudson Review*, 10 (1957), 30-31.
7. D. H. Lawrence, "Introduction to These Paintings," in *Phoenix: The Posthumous Papers of D. H. Lawrence* (London: Heinemann, 1961), pp. 569-570.
8. Wayne Burns, *The Panzaic Principle* (Vancouver, B.C.: Pendejo Press, n.d.); *Journey Through the Dark Woods* (Seattle: Howe St. Press, 1982).
9. D. H. Lawrence, "Morality and the Novel," *Phoenix*, p. 528.
10. D. H. Lawrence, "Why the Novel Matters," *Phoenix*, p. 535.
11. Sigmund Freud, *Civilization and its Discontents* (New York: Norton, 1962), p. 92.

JOURNEY TO THE END OF THE NIGHT: A PRIMER TO THE NOVEL

Wayne Burns

A Note on Translations

Since there are always problems in discussing a translated novel I feel that I should make it clear from the start that I am discussing, not *Voyage au bout de la nuit*, but *Journey to the End of the Night*. And since my French is by no means good enough for me to decide which translation (the Marks or the Manheim) better represents the original I have chosen the Marks--in part because I am more familiar with it, having used it in my classes over the years; in part because I consider it a somewhat better novel. But the qualitative differences between the two are for the most part not that consequential. In almost every passage that I quote from *Journey* I could substitute Manheim's translation for Marks' without seriously affecting what I am trying to say. In the footnotes I have included page references to both translations.

*Louis-Ferdinand Céline walked into great
literature as other men walk into their
own homes.*

-Trotsky

*What throws me into a rage, you see, is
the insensitivity of men--the malady of
the world is insensitivity.*

-Céline

*There's pity in people for the blind and
infirm; they really have got love in reserve. I'd often felt the presence of
this love in reserve. There's any amount
of it. No good saying there isn't. Only
it's a pity people should still be such
sods, with so much love in reserve. It
stays where it is, that's what. It's
stuck away inside and it doesn't come out,
doesn't do them any good. They die of
love--inside.*

-Céline

*Here it is! It's love about which we
still dare not speak in this hell as if
one could compose quatrains in a slaughterhouse. Love impossible today.*

-Céline[1]

Not very many writers have gone as far as Céline
in their denial of morality and rhetoric--or what
Wayne Booth calls "civilization." Genet, in his
play, *The Balcony*, may seem to go further, in that
he presents a world in which there is nothing but
rhetoric, in which there is no essential difference
between what goes on in the whorehouse (called "The
Balcony") and what goes on in the world outside, in
which a plumber playing at being a judge is indistinguishable from judges on the bench, in which
Irma, the madam of the whorehouse, is indistinguishable from the queen on the throne, except that Irma,
given the chance to assume the throne, makes a
better queen than the queen.

Now and again the characters try to break
through their roles, and the rhetoric which justi-
fies those roles, to some kind of reality. But they
cannot: they have lost all sense of themselves as
well as all sense of reality; they have become role
players for whom rhetoric is the only reality.
There are no more people, only physical shells
filled with the simulacrums of feeling dictated by
their social roles. When Carmen, Irma's protege in
The Balcony, tries to convince herself that she
wants to leave the Balcony to be with her daughter,
Irma (and the play) is relentless in showing her
that her feelings are not real, only self-induced
sensations deriving from the rhetoric of mother
love. In Irma's words: "Your precious pink cat-
house, your soulful whorehouse. . . ."

The essentials of Genet's dramatic argument, as
it connects with experiential reality, can hardly be
disputed--at least not by anyone who recognizes the
old Hollywood actor who is now acting out his old

Hollywood roles as president of the most powerful
country in the world. And if Genet had developed
his argument with more understanding and compassion,
with more of an eye to its complexities than to its
possibilities for theatrical sensation, he might
conceivably have created something more than a bril-
liant *tour de force*. But in his attempt to show
everything, including mother love, as unrelieved and
unmitigated rhetoric, Genet falls into a kind of
reverse rhetoric of his own. To say that everything
is rhetoric may, in effect, be tantamount to saying
that nothing is, and may in fact tend to enforce the
moral, as in my judgment the play actually does,
that since everything is rhetoric no one who is sane
has any choice but to capitulate to it and accept it
as reality--the only true reality. And so the play
ends with Roger, the idealistic revolutionary, cas-
trating himself, in an act of romantic defiance that
is finally an act of ritual submission which permits
the Chief of Police to find his fulfillment in his
tomb of 2000 years.

ii

In this brief criticism, it should be obvious, I
have not attempted to do full critical justice to
The Balcony. My interest in the play is only as it
provides a basis for understanding Céline's *Journey
to the End of the Night*. And I shall also, to a
lesser extent, be drawing upon the work of various
novelists in an effort to show how certain aspects
of their fiction relate to or contrast with *Journey*
--once again without attempting to do anything like
full justice to their aims and achievements. Consequently it may seem at times as if I am using these

31

writers as whipping boys for Céline, as if I am
playing fast and loose with their work in an effort
to defend Céline's. Needless to say that is not my
intention. But if I observe in passing that Dickens' Pip, for example, falls into a kind of rhetoric
that Céline's Ferdinand avoids, I can hardly, in an
essay as brief as this, stop to justify my observation. I have to presume that it will be taken in
the spirit in which I am offering it. Nor can I
take time to add that I nevertheless consider *Great
Expectations* a great novel. That too, I trust, can
be understood without specific acknowledgment. In
comparing Céline with other writers my aim is to
clarify his work, not to denigrate theirs, and I can
only hope that in trying to fulfill this aim I have
not sacrificed my critical integrity to my enthusiasm. Céline is, I believe, the greatest novelist of
the twentieth century, and *Journey to the End of the
Night* is one of his greatest novels, second only to
Death on the Installment Plan.

iii

The great difference between *Journey* and *The
Balcony*, on a philosophical level, is that in *Journey* there is no ultimate submission to rhetoric.
Although Céline, writing some twenty-five years
earlier, sees as clearly as Genet what people have
been reduced to, he also sees that not everyone,
everywhere, has totally succumbed. And that leaves
him free to create characters who are not mere role-
players, who can in some ways at some times break
through the rhetoric in which they are enmeshed to
experience feelings of tenderness--even love. Céline's Molly, a whore who works in a whorehouse in

Detroit, would be as lost and out of place in *The Balcony* as she would be in a graduate seminar on existential drama. She spends her nights screwing the customers, not acting out kinky charades or debating illusion versus reality with the madam of the house; and she knows, with her body as well as her mind, where reality is and what it does to her own and other people's feelings. While it may seem at this point that I have mistaken Céline's realistic variation on a type (the whore with a good heart) for a round or three-dimensional character, I really have not. I am not arguing that Molly belongs alongside Moll Flanders, or even that she is entirely convincing; I am merely arguing that, in context, she is sufficient, as a character, to lend conviction to her expressions of feeling.

And what is true for Molly is true for nearly all the other characters in *Journey*. Céline does not intend them to be "round"--in E.M. Forster's sense of "round." For his purposes he is, like Dickens, content with types, and for the most part, they are Dickensian types. Bébert, in everything but his playing with himself and perhaps his curiosity about neighborhood violence, could be straight out of a Dickens novel. He is the young innocent boy who is, despite his illness and his grumpy aunt, playful and friendly and utterly charming. Everyone loves him, including Ferdinand; and when he dies, the neighbors, who are usually at each others' throats, cease their meanness long enough to express their genuine sadness. Yet if Bébert is, in all outward respects, a sentimental Dickensian figure, he nevertheless conveys the feelings that Céline, through Ferdinand, intends him to convey. Céline, in short, works the same kind of magic as Dickens in presenting his types. The main difference is that in characterization, as in almost every other aspect of *Journey*, Céline works his magic through Ferdinand, his I-narrator--in ways at once more simple and more subtle than his critics, accustomed to the technical complexities of modern fiction, have been prepared for. In a Jamesian sense Céline's handling of point-of-view is entirely straightforward: what is not straightforward, what is infinitely subtle, is how, at his best (and he is at his best throughout the greater part of *Journey*) he defines and redefines and dirties and defends Ferdinand in ways that validate his every word, feeling, response, thought, and experience, and turn him into one of the most reliable I-narrators in fiction--a man without pretense who never postures, never resorts to self-justifying rhetoric.

iv

In making this statement I am fully aware that others before me have seen Ferdinand quite differently. Wayne Booth, in his influential *Rhetoric of Fiction*, after citing *Journey* as one of his prime examples of the "unreliable narrator," goes on to argue that neither Céline nor his narrator can ever be trusted, that Ferdinand is "vicious," Céline "evil":

> Though Céline has attempted the tradi-
> tional excuse--remember, it is my charac-
> ter speaking and not I--we cannot excuse
> him for writing a book which, if taken
> seriously by the reader, must corrupt him.
> The better it is understood, the more
> immoral it looks. It is immoral not only

34

in the sense that Céline cheats, though that is important: the world he portrays as reality contains no conceivable explanation of how anyone in that world could bring himself to write a book--even this book. More important, if the reader takes its blandishments seriously, without providing a judgment radically different from Céline's, the result of reading the book must be not only to obscure his sense of what is wrong with such an action as clouting a woman's face just to see how it feels but finally to weaken his will to live as effectively as possible. Taken seriously, the book would make life itself meaningless except as a series of self-centered forays into the lives of others.[2]

Booth's moralistic splutterings would hardly be worth repeating if they were not representative of what so many critics have been saying for the past fifty years. Céline is laying bare their values, which they equate with "civilization's values," and what he reveals apparently drives them into the state they accuse him of being in--a state in which they simply cannot see Ferdinand as anything but an incarnation of "evil," the novel itself as "corrupting" or "degrading."

Although Booth, to his credit, does try at times to do more than splutter, reading *Journey* is for him, in the guise of "our reader," an unremitting ordeal marked by one "appalling problem" after another, beginning with the problem of Ferdinand's moralizing:

The reader cannot help wondering whether Ferdinand's moralizing, of which there is a great deal, is to be taken seriously or not. Is this Céline's view? Should it be mine, at least temporarily, so that I can go along sympathetically with this hero? Or is it simply "life seen from the other side," as the epigraph has promised? Even assuming that the reader knows nothing of Céline's personal life, he must find it hard to believe, after a hundred or so pages of the following kind of thing, that Céline is merely dramatizing a narrator who is completely dissociated from him:

> You don't lose anything much when your landlord's house is burnt down.
> Another landlord always comes along, if it isn't always the same one--a German or a Frenchman or an Englishman or a Chinaman--and you get your bill just the same. . . . Whether you pay in marks or francs, it doesn't much matter.
> Morals, in fact, were a dirty business . . . [p. 48].
> . . . .
> When one's been able to escape alive from a mad international shambles, it says something after all for one's tact and discretion [p. 102].
> It was then that one saw the whole of the white man's revolting nature displayed in freedom from all

constraint, under provocation and
untrammelled; his real self as you
saw it in war. . . . reality, heavy-
smelling pools of slime, the crabs,
the carcasses and scum [p. 103].

Are these Céline's views? If not, what do
they tell us about Bardamu? If his view
of the white man's "real nature" is incorrect, we have no clues from Céline about
the correct alternative.[3]

Everything Booth says here, I submit, is either
silly--or dishonest. Of course Ferdinand's comments
are to be taken seriously. Of course they are
Céline's; or what amounts to the same thing, they
are the novel's. All this Booth knows very well.
His pretending to wonder is merely a rhetorical ploy
on his part: an attempt to discredit Ferdinand's
moralizing without having to confront it--by quoting, out of context, passages which he then dismisses with high-toned expressions of moral dismay.

What Booth really fears, as he elsewhere acknowledges, is that "the non-professional reader,"
left on his own, may not be properly dismayed.
Ferdinand's remarks on landlords, for example, are
undeniably true, in a factual sense, as anyone who
has paid rent can immediately recognize; and his
concluding note ("Morals, in fact, were a dirty
business . . .") merely emphasizes that morals, in
justifying the collection of money, as in justifying
so many other things, become a dirty business. Any
number of moralists have said this over the years,
in words far more emphatic than Ferdinand's--includ-
ing Christ himself when he drove the moneychangers
from the temple:

37

And Jesus went into the temple of God,
and cast out all them that sold and bought
in the temple, and overthrew the tables of
the moneychangers, and the seats of them
that sold doves, and said unto them, It is
written, My house shall be called the
house of prayer; but ye have made it a den
of thieves.[4]

The search for Christ figures in unlikely places
has lent itself to all kinds of ingenious critical
games--none of which I wish to play. My point is
simply that Ferdinand's words and actions do at
times come close to being Christ-like--as in the
passage in which he describes the feelings he has
when he is obliged to collect fees from his patients, or go hungry himself:

And my colleagues go on blithely talking
about "fees"! As if the word were enough
in itself and explained everything. . . .
I could not help crying "Shame!" myself,
and there was no way out of that. Everything can be explained away, I realize
that. But it does not alter the fact that
the man who has taken five francs from
poor, disgruntled wretches is a scoundrel
for the rest of his days. In fact, it was
from this time on that I have known myself
to be as dirty a blackguard as any. It's
not that I lived wildly and wickedly on
their five and ten-franc payments. No,
indeed. Because the landlord got most of
it, anyway. But even so, that's no excuse. One would like it to be an excuse,
but it isn't quite. The landlord's lower

than dirt, of course; that's all there is
to that.[5]

To just about all doctors, then or now, Ferdinand's
words and actions would certainly qualify him as
nutty or saintly if not Christ-like, even though a
number of doctors might to some extent share his
feelings, and even though, in their own defense,
which they would elevate into a defense of medicine,
they would almost certainly invoke the Grand Inquis-
itor's argument. Ferdinand too is acquainted with
this argument ("Everything can be explained away, I
realize that") yet he refuses to take refuge in it.
More than that he refuses to hide behind the landlord ("That's no excuse") in a remark that further
qualifies the passage which Booth quotes earlier.
Here as elsewhere Ferdinand refuses to exonerate
himself. His words and actions may at times be
saintly, or even Christ-like, but he makes certain
the reader understands that he is no saint, that he
is "as dirty a blackguard as any . . . a scoundrel
for the rest of his days."
     To anyone who has not read the novel, who has
merely read what I have written thus far, it may
seem that Ferdinand is posturing, that he can't
really see himself as a "scoundrel for the rest of
his days," that sooner or later he will, like all
hero-narrators, seek to differentiate or justify or
excuse himself. But he never does. From first to
last he is, if anything, harder on himself than on
anyone else. His one significant difference, his
one great strength, is his power to see and hear and
understand and express his own and other people's
sufferings and infrequent joys on their journey to
the end of the night; and he uses this power, not to
justify himself but to justify his going ever fur-

ther in his efforts to see and hear and understand. In his own words (after he has heard the man and the woman in the house across the way using their little girl to get themselves steamed up sexually):

> I simply stood there and listened as always, as I did everywhere. Still, I think I somehow gained strength listening to this thing, strength to go on further, an odd sort of strength, and next time, I felt, why, next time I would be able to go deeper and hear other cries that I had not heard yet or which I had not been able to understand before, because there seem always to be some cries beyond those which one has heard, cries which one has not yet heard or understood.[6]

Although Ferdinand goes on to give a full account of the episode that provoked the cries he has heard, he refuses to permit himself or the reader to revel in its possibilities for sexual titillation. Here as elsewhere in the novel there is no trace of pornography. (Over the years I have noticed that students in my university classes who get at least a mild sexual charge from, say, *Lady Chatterly's Lover* or *The Tin Drum*, draw an absolute blank with *Journey*.) When Ferdinand plays the voyeur it is never to indulge his or the reader's penchant for sexual excitement; it is to make the reader hear the cries, as he himself hears them, in all of their unrelieved horror.

It is to this end of rendering the cries that Céline wrote *Journey*. And it is likewise to this end that he shaped Ferdinand as he did, and made him the hero-narrator. Ferdinand is not Céline: he is Céline reshaped and redirected to serve Céline's primary end in the novel--to make the reader hear cries he has never heard before; to make him realize that there is no end to these cries (in either time or circumstance), for they are cries which cannot be remedied by religion or philosophy or morality--much less by the paltry palliatives of social reform or even social revolution.

Everything about Ferdinand, from the way he feels and thinks to the way he responds to people and situations, is amazingly consistent--in relation to what Céline is trying to achieve with and through him. In many ways, indeed, Ferdinand's consistency is like that of the popular heroes and heroines of nineteenth-century fiction; or, on a serious level, that of Jane Eyre who (as I-narrator) pits her moral rectitude against every experience in life that threatens it without, on a conscious level at least, budging a single inch. The difference is that Jane Eyre is adhering to a recognized moral code, sanctioned by religion and society, whereas Ferdinand is not adhering to any moral code whatsoever, much less a sanctioned one. Nor is he, like Hemingway, for example, adhering to a code of his own. He has no use for codes. His adherence is to his own feelings, his own sensibility, his own sense of what people are doing to him and one another--in the name of moral and social rectitude.

Other writers too have created I-narrators remarkably true to their own sensibilities--with Dostoevski's underground man being perhaps the most remarkable, as well as the most extreme, since his sensibilities are so acute, his feelings of insecurity so powerful, that in order to survive at all in the world he can permit no one outside himself to exist except as a reflection of himself. For a few seconds with Lisa he perhaps responds to someone else as more than a threatening reflection--only to retreat in terror and vicious reprisals when he realizes what is happening. Ferdinand, on the other hand, although he remains true to his sensibilities, has no fear of them, no need to keep them constantly in check. When he finds himself falling in love with Molly he too, like the underground man, senses that this feeling is too much for him, that it somehow threatens the life to which he has committed himself. Yet, unlike the underground man, he has no compulsion to deny what he is doing, and what it means:

> I was very fond of her, of course, that's certainly true, but I was fonder still of my own obsession, of my longing to run away from everywhere in search of something, God knows what. (. . .)
> . . . .
> I was always rather thinking about something else, about not wasting time, or tenderness, as if I wanted to keep it all for something grand, something sublime and later on, but not for Molly, and not really even for that. As if Life were going to take away from me and hide from me, while I was devoting all of myself to kissing Molly, what I wanted to know about it, about Life itself beyond all this

blackness; and then I shouldn't have
enough fervour left and in the end I
should have lost everything through being
weak, and Life, the one and only mistress
of all true men, would have tricked me as
she had tricked every one else.[7]

Although Ferdinand is being ironical here, at
his own expense, he nevertheless knows that he cannot escape his obsession. And Molly knows this too.
She knows that he is, in her words, "sort of ill
with this desire . . . always to be discovering
something new. . . ." And when he finally decides
to leave she sees him off--loving him still but
refusing to let him tell himself that he will come
back:

> The train came in. I wasn't so sure
> what I wanted to do once I saw the engine.
> I kissed Molly with all the fervour I had
> left in my wretched carcass. I was sad
> for once, really sad, sad for everybody,
> for myself, for her, for all men.
> Maybe that is what one is looking for
> throughout life, that and nothing more;
> the greatest misery there is to feel, so
> as to become oneself truly before death.
> Years have gone by since that depar-
> ture, many years. . . . I have often
> written to Detroit and to every address I
> could remember, where they might have
> known her and might have traced her. I
> have never had any answer.
> The house is shut now. That's all I
> have been able to find out. Good, admira-
> ble Molly, I should like her, if she ever

reads these lines of mine, to know for certain that I have not changed towards her, that I love her still and always shall, in my own way; that she can come to me here, whenever she may care to, and share my bread and my furtive destiny. If she is no longer beautiful, ah, well, no matter! The more's the pity, we'll manage somehow. I've kept so much of her beauty with me still, so warm, so much alive, that I've enough for both of us, and it will last another twenty years, long enough to see us through.

Surely I needed to be very mad to leave her, and mad in a cold-blooded, dirty way. All the same, I've held on to my soul till now and if tomorrow death came to take me, I know I should not be as heavy, or as ugly, or as hard, as the others are, because of all the kindness and the dreams Molly made me a present of during those few months in the United States.[8]

Of course it can be argued that this passage lapses into autobiographical sentimentality, that Céline has, in fact, entered the novel in his own person to express his own feelings for the Molly he knew in real life. (Probably Elizabeth Craig, to whom he dedicated *Journey*.[9]) Yet if this is a serious lapse, coming as it does at the climactic moment when Ferdinand finally sacrifices his own and Molly's love to his obsession, the lapse cannot erase the preceding pages in which Ferdinand has revealed, through ironical understatement that bears no trace of sentimentality, the full meaning of his "obsessive need"--a need which is nothing less than that which Joyce's hero expresses, in more grandiose language, in *A Portrait of the Artist as a Young Man*, the difference being that Ferdinand is not setting out "to forge the uncreated conscience" of his race but to discover "Life itself beyond all this blackness." And to accomplish this, the ultimate end of his journey, Ferdinand knows that he has to leave Molly and return, alone, to what he calls his "greasy adventuring."

vi

Ferdinand's adventurings begin with his enlistment in the cavalry in 1914. Completely innocent, "a virgin to horror," he becomes ever more terrified as he encounters the blood and violence and brutality and stupidity of war. For him there is no meaning in anything he does or anything anyone else does—no meaning except death. And he refuses to accept the meanings that everyone from Colonel Entayes to Major Pincon to his mother try to provide—the meanings that previous novelists have also tried to provide when, even as they have condemned war, they have lauded the fellowship that the soldiers feel, or the courage they show, or their devotion to the ideals of protecting their loved ones, or their country, or their freedom, or their culture. Ferdinand will accept none of this: to him it is all rhetoric, and he refuses, as thoroughly in his way as the good soldier Schweik in his, to have anything to do with it:

> I came to the conclusion that even if
> the Germans were to arrive where we were,
> slaughtering, pillaging and setting fire

45

to everything, to the hotel, the apple
fritters, Lola, the Tuileries, the Cabinet
and all their little friends, the Coupole,
the Louvre and the big shops, even if they
were to overrun the town and let hell
loose in this foul fair ground, full of
every sordidness on earth, still I should
have nothing to lose by it and everything
to gain.[10]

Once Ferdinand has, thanks to his wounds, es-
caped from the front lines, he encounters a rhetoric
still more virulent--a rhetoric that he dismembers,
piece by piece, without ever, like Genet in *The
Balcony*, falling into a compensatory rhetoric of his
own. While some of his remarks, like those he
occasionally directs at Lola and Musyne and the
nurses are undeniably bitter, his bitterness is
direct and scathing, not rhetorical. When, for
example, he refers to himself as "a little nobody"
he is not speaking rhetorically, not asking for the
reader's sympathy. He is describing himself exactly
as he sees himself--exactly as he appears in the
novel. The one time that he threatens to become
something more, by telling bigger, more epic-sound-
ing lies about his war experiences than any of his
fellow patients in the hospital, he ends up as the
butt of a wonderful farce at the Comedie Francaise.

vii

On his voyage to Africa and in Africa itself,
after he has managed to get completely free of the
army, Ferdinand encounters, in the colonials and in
colonialism, still another version of "the white

46

man's revolting nature displayed in freedom from all constraint, under provocation and untrammeled; his real self as you saw it in war. . . ." And while he never wavers in his severity, never succumbs to rhetoric, he does strike a deeper and more compassionate note in recording the plight of the natives, most tellingly in his account of the rubber trader:

> Our Corocoro friend trafficked in crude rubber which was brought from the bush and sold to him, in the form of moist balls, by the sackfull.
>
> As we stood there, never tired of listening to him, a family of rubber tappers came timidly up and hovered about his doorstep. The father was at their head, a wrinkled old man wearing a little orange-coloured loin cloth and dangling his long cutlass in his hand.
>
> The poor savage didn't dare come in. So one of the native assistants called out to him, "Come on, nigger! Come along in! We no eat black man!" Thus addressed, they managed to make up their minds. They trooped into the glittering store at the back of which our Corocoro patient was raving.
>
> The black, it seemed, had never seen a shop before, or any whites either, maybe. One of his wives followed him, with lowered eyes, carrying balanced on the top of her head a great pannier full of raw rubber.
>
> The assistants brusquely snatched at her pannier to weigh its contents on the scales. Poppa native didn't understand

the business of the scales any more than
the rest of it. His wife didn't dare
raise her head. The other members of the
black family waited outside, with very
goggling eyes. They were made to come in,
all the children and everybody, so that
they shouldn't miss anything of the show.

It was the first time they'd come all
together like that from the bush towards
the white men and their town. They must
have all been working away for a very long
time to collect all that rubber. So that
the result of the deal was naturally of
great interest to the whole family. It
takes a long time to sweat rubber into the
little containers you hang on the trunks
of the trees. It often takes over two
months to get a small cupful.

When the weighing had been done, our
scratching friend took the gaping Negro
behind the counter and worked out in chalk
what was due to him and stuffed a few
pieces of silver into the hollow of his
hand. Then, "Get out," he said to him,
just like that. "There's your money!"

All his little white friends squealed
with laughter, he'd put the deal over so
well. The Negro stood there unhappily
before the counter, with his little orange
covering round his loins.

"Don't understand money, do you, bo?
Don't know nuthin, eh?" the most irre-
pressible clerk, who was anyway probably
accustomed to these peremptory transac-
tions, shouted at him to wake him up.
"You don't parly French, do you? Still a

gorilla are you? What do you savvy then, tell me? Kouskous? Mabillia? You're a clod, ain't you? A bush ape—a damn great clod."

But the Negro stood before us, holding the coins in his fist. He'd have bolted if he'd dared. But he didn't dare.

"What you buy with your dough then, nigger?" put in the scratcher at just the right moment. "I haven't seen quite such a mug as this for a long time, I must say," he observed. "It must have come from way back. What d'you want? Give me that stuff!"

He snatched the money away from him and in its place shoved into the palm of his hand a large bright-green handkerchief which he nimbly extracted from a drawer in the counter.

The Negro hesitated to leave with his handkerchief. Then the scratcher went one better. He certainly knew all the tricks of a roaring trade all right. Waving the great square of green cloth before the eyes of one of the little black kids: "Don't you think that's pretty, you little bug, you? Haven't seen a handkerchief like that before, have you, my pretty one; have you, my dungheap, my little black-belly?" And without more ado, he tied it round the kid's neck, dressing him completely.

The backwoods family now gazed at their little one adorned by this great green cotton thing. . . . There was nothing more to be done about it now that the handker-

chief had come into the family. There was
nothing left but to accept it, take it,
and go away.

So they all began to back gradually out
and through the door. Just as the father,
who was last, turned to say something, the
toughest of the assistants, who wore
shoes, helped him out with a great kick on
the behind.[11]

Later on, in discussing Milton Hindus's criticism, I shall have more to say about this passage,
which, as I read it, breathes compassion in almost
every line. The natives, as Ferdinand sees them,
are the ultimate victims of a colonial system that
is rotten from top to bottom, and he spares neither
those at the top nor those at the bottom:

The natives after all have to be bludg-
eoned into doing their jobs—they've still
got that much self-respect. Whereas the
whites carry on on their own; they've been
well schooled by the State.

The wielder of the lash gets very tired
of his job in the end, but the white man's
heart is brimful of the hope of power and
wealth and that doesn't cost anything; not
a thing. Let's hear no more about Egypt
and the Tartar tyrants! In the supreme
art of urging the two-legged animal really
to put his back into his work, these classical exponents are the merest conceited
amateurs. It never entered the heads of
the antique school to give the slave a
"Mister" before his name, to get him to
vote now and again, to buy him his newspa-

per; above all, to put him in the front
line so as to rid him of his baser passions![12]

Now this is not, as so many readers thought at
the time the novel was published, Communist rhetoric. It is not, in any ordinary sense, rhetoric at
all. Ferdinand is not speaking from reason or prejudice with an intent to persuade; he is speaking
from hatred—a hatred that goes so deep and so far
back that he can hardly put it into words; a hatred
that springs from the fears and torments he endured
as a child from the hands and words of the one
person he loved most, or wanted to love most, his
mother; a hatred that boils up in him with unbear-
able urgency when he first sees his "unhealthy little colleagues at work," and spills directly into
his description of them:

> They harassed the black dock hands
> quite frantically. They were full of
> zeal, no one could dream of denying that,
> and they were just as vacant and bloody-
> minded as they were zealous. Employees
> worth their weight in gold, in fact, care-
> fully picked men, as enthusiastic and
> unreasoning as one could wish. Sons such
> as my mother would have liked to bear,
> dead keen on their jobs. What would she
> not have given to have had just one such
> son, of whom she could be truly proud
> before all the world, a really *legitimate*
> son![13]

Céline has once again entered directly into the
novel. Of that there can be little doubt. But in

this instance Ferdinand can bear the burden that Céline has placed upon him. The hatred comes through as Ferdinand's; and since it is a hatred that nearly everyone has felt, at least to some degree, it is a hatred to which nearly everyone responds. And its effect is to turn the entire African section of the novel into a realistic version of Kafka's *In the Penal Colony*.

Yet there is one significant difference. Ferdinand does encounter a few people who in some measure redeem the human race: his young black guide, "the good woman at the pagoda," and Sergeant Alcide, who, for all his being a part of the colonial system, has given "almost without noticing it . . . these years of hardship, the annihilation of his wretched life in this tropical monotony, to a little girl who was vaguely related to him, without conditions, without bargaining, with no interest except that of his own good heart. He was offering this little girl far away tenderness enough to make a world anew."[14] These lines, with a few minor changes, could come straight from a Dickens novel--as could Alcide himself, up to the point that Ferdinand reveals Alcide's system for bilking the native soldiers in his command. That would have been too much for Dickens. Yet it provides Ferdinand with just the element he needs to distinguish Alcide's "good heart," his tenderness, from the moral or rhetorical kind.

If this distinction is difficult to comprehend it is because, in our society, our culture, we invariably tend to see "tenderness" or "a good heart" in relation to duties or obligations. To many liberal-minded people, for example, what a policeman has to do in the line of duty may on occasion seem objectionable or even cruel, in which case they will usually try to excuse his actions by

saying that he is just doing his job. But at the
same time, if the policeman is good to his children,
these same people will say that he has a good heart
--when, in point of fact, he is once again just
doing his duty, his job. His obligations may differ
but his motives for killing a criminal and being
good to his children may well be the same, and if
they are, he does not have "a good heart." Alcide
does what he does for his niece "without conditions,
without bargaining." The feelings he has for this
little girl have nothing to do with conscience or
morality: they are as spontaneous as the tenderness
he feels for the flowers around his hut.

viii

By this time, roughly a quarter of the way
through the novel, Céline has endowed Ferdinand with
every characteristic, every quality, he needs to
carry through his mission; and, equally important,
has established him, within the framework of the
novel, in a position which enables him to overcome
the resistances that his mission is bound to provoke. If, as Wayne Booth acknowledges, the reader
is going to understand the novel at all, he has no
choice but to identify with Ferdinand; and because
Ferdinand is so compelling the reader's identification forces him, again quoting Wayne Booth, "to
succumb morally as well as visually." "Yet regardless of how much we may reason about it, we have, in
the course of our reading this book, been caught.
Caught in the trap of a suffering consciousness.
. . ."[15] While this tribute may be something of a
backhander, it is, coming from Booth, an amazing
tribute nevertheless--one that Céline himself would

certainly have relished. For in succumbing to Ferdinand's consciousness Booth has entered the state that Céline is always trying to get his readers into--the state in which, quoting Merlin Thomas, "the reader begins to have the curious sensation that there is someone inside his own head who is reading to him willy-nilly."[16] Or as Céline himself puts it, in his *Entretiens avec le Professeur Y*, "Not just in his ear! . . . no! . . . in the intimacy of his nerves! right inside his nervous system! inside his own head (. . .) as though someone is playing at will on the harp of his very nerves."[17]

From this state, this "trap," Booth draws back in horror--to repudiate, in the name of art and morality, everything that he has experienced:

> And then we draw back. At least if we are lucky enough not to be entirely vulnerable to this kind of rhetoric, we draw back and repudiate what we have been told. It is *not* an honest picture, it is not a realized picture at all. These things have not been "judged and given each its appointed place in the whole scheme," and as Katherine Mansfield said about Dorothy Richardson's unjudged accumulations of detail, "they have no meaning in the world of art." That it includes a vision of sordidness no more makes it honest than if the sentimental identification with the hero were based on a complete denial of evil.[18]

Here, finally, Booth sums it all up. He draws back and repudiates what he has been told because it is neither an honest nor a realized picture. He

54

knows it is neither honest nor realized because it does not correspond to what he and Katherine Mansfield and (if I may include a few names from his footnotes) Edmund Fuller and Norman Podhoretz and Harold C. Gardiner have, in their seminal wisdom, recognized as honest and realized.[19] Actually, however, the names he cites are of no consequence. He could line up critics from Aristotle to T. S. Eliot and it still wouldn't matter--unless one is prepared to accept Booth's premise: which is that he (and all those right-thinking people with him and behind him) know what an honest and realized novel will say and be and do before the novelist writes it; that it is therefore up to the novelist to fulfill their expectations.

The truth is, as I along with many others have been arguing for some forty years now, that great fiction has never fulfilled the expectations of the Wayne Boothians--though, with time and effort, they have usually managed to work out interpretations of the great novels that bring them into seeming accord with their own expectations--the way Booth, in his reading of *Remembrance of Things Past*, for example, renders Marcel's world "compatible with our experience of life, time, memory, and art."[20] With some novels, however, this kind of compatibility is more difficult to achieve. Or it may even be impossible--as it is for Booth in his criticism of *Lady Chatterley's Lover*: "if we finish the book with a sense of embarrassment . . . it is ultimately because no literary techniques can conceal from us the confused and pretentious little author who is implied in too many parts of the book."[21] At this point my own inclination is to retort in kind, by describing the pretentious little critic I find implied in Booth's remarks. And this is the same critic, not surprisingly, I find implied in his criticism of *Journey*, the main distinction being that he moves from condescension to outright condemnation. *Journey* terrifies him; it makes him shout with pain, and then try, in self-defense, to blot out everything that the novel expresses.

Booth could hardly respond in any other way. To him as to all those critics who share his beliefs *Journey* really is a trap. For if they succumb to Céline's vision, the way Booth apparently found himself on the verge of succumbing, they will never again be able to see themselves or the world as they now see it, never again be able to feel secure in their uprightness, never again be able to say in full confidence: "These things have not been 'judged and given each its appointed place in the whole scheme.'"

ix

A full scale example of this type of criticism is Milton Hindus's "Céline: A Reappraisal," in *The Southern Review* (Winter, 1968). Although Hindus might perhaps object to being identified as a Wayne Boothian, since he was at one time an ardent admirer of Céline's work, his article has, at its center, a comparison of the African section of *Journey* with Gide's *Travels in the Congo* that follows the Wayne Boothian line from start to finish. To begin with, Gide's remarks on the tropical heat are "balanced . . . good weather is the rule rather than the exception in his pages"--as in the sunset he describes on December 17:

The evening was splendid, as all the
last evenings have been. The sun, when it
is still a good height above the horizon,
'turns into a mandarin orange,' as Morel
says. It loses both heat and radiance and
becomes an orange-red mass which the eye
can contemplate without being dazzled.
This is the delicious hour when a helmet
is no longer needed. Exactly above that
point of the horizon that is still colored
by the dying sun, a very fine crescent
moon makes its appearance.[22]

Céline's description in *Journey*, according to
Hindus, is by contrast "a kind of screaming melodrama, very effective and memorable, especially to
people who have no first hand ideas of the original
model":

Sunsets in this African inferno were
amazing. They never failed. A tragedy
each evening like a vast assassination of
the sun. An incredible piece of tomfool-
ery. But it was too staggering for the
admiration of one man alone. For a whole
hour the sky preened itself in great mad
streaks of scarlet from end to end, and a
green light flared out of the undergrowth
and swirled upwards in flickering clouds
towards the first stars of the night.
After that the whole horizon turned grey,
then red once more, but this time a tired
and shortlived red. That then was the
end. The colours all fell back in strips
like paper streamers at a carnival. This

happened every day at the stroke of six
o'clock.[23]

After characterizing this description as "hallucinatory . . . merely the evidence of 'a singular
sensibility,'"[24] Hindus then proceeds, once he has
characterized other descriptions in the novel in a
similar light, to extend his argument still further
by suggesting that Céline "is doing the same thing
in portraying the white man's exploitation of the
blacks in Africa."[25] Gide's treatment of social
injustice, Hindus argues, "differs from Céline's as
much as his sunsets differ from Céline's melodramat-
ic versions. . . . His [Gide's] treatment . . . is
muted and restrained *and all the more convincing as
a result*."[26] And Hindus apparently finds Gide's
treatment even more convincing because he has been
"charged with the responsiblility of an official
investigation in the French Congo."[27] In Hindus's
words:

> In his journal entry of October 21,
> 1925, he [Gide] retells the story of an
> atrocity involving a Sergeant Yemba and
> the administrator of Boda as it was given
> him by a native chief, Samba N'Goto, who
> witnessed an incident in which hostages
> for native resistance--men, women and
> children--were ruthlessly shot, knifed,
> and burned alive. It is truly a Goya-like
> tableau of man's inhumanity to man, but
> Gide presents it frankly as hearsay evi-
> dence. His report had a moderating ef-
> fect, we are told, both on governmental
> agencies and the administration of power-
> ful private corporations.[28]

It seems impossible that anyone with any intellectual pretensions whatsoever could suggest that Gide's treatment is convincing because it "had a moderating effect . . . on governmental agencies and the administration of powerful private corporations."[29] Yet this is what Hindus suggests, on his way to setting up a contrast between Gide's account of "a trading market in rubber" with Ferdinand's account of the rubber-trader which I quoted above. Hindus quotes the passage at length--to conclude:

> No one can say, of course, that such a scene did not actually take place or that the narrator of *Journey* did not see it take place, but on the face of it it reads very much like one of the hearsay atrocities in Gide--an exceptional, colorful incident which, isolated and unbalanced by any instances of more humane conduct, makes of Africa as of every other continent Ferdinand visits an unrelieved nightmare of cruelty and exploitation. No wonder that Leon Trotsky and the writer for *Pravda* found this picture of degradation to their taste and could describe it as an accurate rendition of "what is." This is the outline of western imperialism which is the one Moscow has striven to make the world buy for two generations now.[30]

Criticism so crass, not to say vicious, would hardly require comment if Ferdinand's account were in any sense political. But it is not. What the rubber-trader and his black assistants do to the black family is what people in power, whether they be colonial traders, or agents of any political persuasion, invariably do to the poor and the help-less--even though, as in the present instance, the force they use may not be overt. Except for the final kick in the ass there is no physical violence, and the natives are so child-like in their innocence that they have little if any sense of the equally vicious if less direct violence they are encounter-ing. But Ferdinand knows, and through him the read-er understands the gratuitousness of the cruelty that is visited upon the family--as they are robbed, not only of their rubber and their money but of their self-respect. It is like a bear-baiting, with the bear replaced by people who have no way to fight back. The long cutlass that the father dangles might as well be made of cardboard.

Although Ferdinand's sympathy for the native family is everywhere evident in his account--from his first reference to "the poor savage," to his description of how long and hard they had worked to gather the rubber, to their dismayed acceptance of "this great green cotton thing"--his compassion never becomes obtrusive. Nor does his hatred for their tormentors. He permits the words and actions to speak for themselves. Which they do--with an understated eloquence that culminates in his final two paragraphs:

> The whole little tribe, in a group, stood silently on the other side of the Avenue Faidherbe, under a magnolia tree, watching us finish our drinks. You'd have said that they were trying to understand what had happened to them.
>
> It was our "Corocoro" friend's party. He even played his gramophone for us.

There wasn't anything you couldn't find in
his shop. It reminded me of the supply
trains in the war.[31]

x

Ferdinand's compassion runs like a groundswell
through the entire novel. In some form or another
it is always there, even in those passages in which,
for dramatic reasons, Céline, in his own words,
covers Ferdinand with shit. "My use of 'I' isn't at
all daring," he says in his *Entretiens avec le
Professeur Y*, "I only employ it with great care!
. . . with infinite prudence! . . . I always coat
it completely, taking every precaution, with
shit."[32] At times, indeed, it may seem as if Céline
has so coated Ferdinand with shit that he can no
longer fulfill his dramatic function--as in the
scene in which Ferdinand is so overwhelmed by the
moralistic playacting of a dying girl's mother that
he is incapable, as a doctor, of taking the action
that might save the girl's life:

> I hazarded the suggestion that the girl
> should be removed at once to the hospital
> to be operated on immediately.
> Alas, what a mistake! I had played
> straight into her hands, providing her
> with the perfect answer, the one she had
> been hoping for.
> "What a disgrace! To the hospital,
> Doctor! What a disgrace for us! That is
> all that was needed--the last straw!"
> There was nothing more I could say.
> (. . .) While she invoked heaven and

hell, howling with misery, I hung my head
and discovered a little pool of blood
forming under the girl's bed and a trickle
threading slowly along the wall towards
the door. A drop fell regularly from the
mattress. Plop. Plop. The towels were
scarlet now between her legs. (. . .) But
to pull myself together was really more
than I could do.

I had been so long overcome by depres-
sion myself. I'd been sleeping so badly,
that in this chaos I was no longer in the
least interested as to whether any one
thing happened before anything else. I
only reflected that it was easier to be
listening to this mother's wailings sitting down than standing up. It doesn't
take much to give you satisfaction when
you have become really resigned. Besides,
what strength of will would have been
necessary to interrupt this wild creature
just when she "didn't know how she was
going to save her family honour!" What a
game! And how she yelled!³³

For all his excuses Ferdinand's resigned inef-
fectuality remains inexcusable. He himself knows
that it is: "I ought to have tried, of course.
Tried to do something. It was my duty to, as they
say." Yet even as he feebly acknowledges his obligations he is, with a qualifying "but," lapsing into
his old stupor: "But I was too comfortable sitting
down and too uncomfortable standing up."³⁴
To maintain any kind of sympathetic identification with Ferdinand at this point is terribly difficult, as Céline well knows. He is, in his own

words, employing his "I" with great care, coating it completely with shit; and he is doing this for a very good reason. A more sympathetic Ferdinand, a Ferdinand with the courage to confront and overcome the wailings of the mother, would have turned this tragic episode into just another version of the good doctor overcoming the hysterically moralistic mother and saving the life of the girl. And while this version might be modified and made somewhat sadder by having the girl die, the effect would still be much the same: the doctor would still have overcome the mother, and done all he could to save the girl.

In Céline's version, on the other hand, there is no hope, no sense that somehow something is being done. Because the mother is absolutely impregnable in both her rhetoric and her rectitude the effect of her theatrical moralism is absolutely unmitigated. Her deadly play-acting comes through in all its horror: her mournful tremolos fill our own as well as Ferdinand's little shrunken world. Morals is not only a dirty but a bloody business.

Yet if Céline, through Ferdinand, refuses to ameliorate the horror, he also refuses, again through Ferdinand, to excoriate the mother. For that too would provide a way for the reader to distance or even dismiss the mother's actions as those of a monster, and therefore unconnected with the way ordinary mothers treat their daughters. As Ferdinand presents the mother, however, she is no monster. What she does is monstrous but she herself is not a monster; she is a mother, like so many other mothers, who is jealous of her daughter: she "guessed her daughter's animal superiority over her and jealously disapproved by instinct of her gift for tremendous delights, for enjoyment to her innermost depths."[35] Furthermore she is a mother who

63

finds in conventional morality the justification she needs for going into "an hypnotic state of nervous imbecility" in which she can thrill to her own play-acting as it leads to the death of her daughter. Nor is her performance all that unusual: "People move from one piece of play-acting to the next."[36]

In offering this final devastating observation Ferdinand is not, like Irma in Genet's *The Balcony*, speaking cynically. He is speaking sorrowfully. There are all kinds of ways of saying "There but for the grace of God go I," and here as elsewhere Ferdinand is saying it with so much fellow-feeling, so much sadness, so much compassion, that we as readers should be able to hear the cries he hears the way he hears them. If we cannot it may be because we find his resignation, or, as it is usually designated, his pessimism, more than we can bear. In the present instance the possibility that Ferdinand may, for all his inexcusable behavior, be right; that whatever he does or does not do the mother is "never going to stop complaining and waxing indignant;" that, consequently one might "as well hold one's peace"[37]--all this may be too much to accept. Yet the novel leaves us no choice: either we must close the book or recognize that the horror we have experienced is neither remediable nor stoppable, that people will go right on moving "from one piece of play-acting to the next."

xi

Although writers have been working variations on "all the world's a stage" for centuries, the horror that Ferdinand brings to his words about play-acting gives them a meaning they have never had before.

It's almost as if they are being spoken for the first time. The shock of recognition they bring is, I believe, that great. And Céline leaves his readers none of the escape routes that other writers, by design or inadvertence, have built into their expressions of despair.

In *The Balcony*, for example, Irma brings down the final curtain by speaking directly to the audience: "You must now go home, where everything--you can be quite sure--will be falser than here." Yet the effect of these words, spoken as they are by the absolute mistress of dramatic illusion, is merely to encourage the people in the audience to extend the titillations of the play to their own humdrum lives. In the words of *The New Yorker*, quoted on the back cover of the play, "[*The Balcony*] satisfies to a degree hitherto unknown our contemporary appetite for violence, perversion, and squalor."[38] Nor does it matter, for the moment, that intellectually the play attempts, and perhaps does, much more than this. As D. H. Lawrence long ago pointed out, in his much quoted letter to Aldous Huxley, apropos of Huxley's efforts in *Point Counterpoint* to write a Lawrentian novel:

> Intellectual appreciation does not amount to so much, it's what you thrill to . . . if you can only palpitate to murder, suicide, and rape, in their various degrees--and you state plainly that it is so--*caro*, however are we going to live through the days? Preparing still another murder, suicide, and rape? But it becomes of a phantasmal boredom and produces ultimately inertia, inertia, inertia and final atrophy of the feelings. Till, I suppose,

comes a final super-war, and murder, suicide, rape sweeps away the vast bulk of
mankind.

The distinction Lawrence draws here applies directly
to *The Balcony*: like so many other modern works in
the same vein--from the most serious to the most
popular--it thrills to, and encourages its audience
to thrill to, what it presumably intends to explore.
   While the violence Lawrence speaks of is also
present in *Journey*, Ferdinand neither thrills to it,
nor permits the reader to thrill to it. If, in
presenting the mother's killing of her daughter, he
makes certain the reader hears as well as sees the
blood dripping from the daughter's bed, his aim is
not to drench the reader in blood but to show that
the murderer refuses to see it or hear it. Hence
there is nothing for the reader to thrill to: he
can only see the mother, in her self-righteous play-
acting, doing what people do.
   For the reader the horror never stops, the cries
never cease. Yet Ferdinand provides no religious or
philosophical or political or social assurances to
cushion the shock of his revelations. There is no
better world to come, here or hereafter; no hope of
individual fulfillment through science or art or
devotion to a cause, or even through man-woman or
any other kind of love, although he does come close
to this with Molly. Nor is there any comfort to be
derived from appeals to fate, or destiny, or rolling
a rock up a hill. The best that people can be is
what Molly and Alcide and Bébert and a few others
are. As for the rest they too have to be seen "as
they are--that is to say as skeletons, nothing but
ciphers, which nevertheless you will have to love,

cherish, defend, and encourage as if they really existed."[39]

Pessimism so complete and unremitting, and yet so humane, has seldom if ever been expressed in fiction. In his later work Tolstoy comes close, particularly in *The Death of Ivan Ilych*, generally conceded to be one of the grimmest treatments of life and death ever written. And if Tolstoy had not provided his protagonist with a religious answer, through the simple faith of Gerasim, *Ivan Ilych* would anticipate Céline. But Gerasim is always there in the novella, and he is there in such a way that he holds up not only the dying Ivan Ilych's feet but the reader's. So that neither Ivan Ilych nor the reader experiences the sense of life and death that Céline conveys.

Thomas Hardy's pessimism also comes close to Céline's. But Hardy places his characters against natural backdrops (the heath, the woods, or even the cosmos) in such a way as to provide a philosophical perspective that to some extent lessens the impact of their individual experiences. It is not until *Jude the Obscure* that Hardy brings his characters to the point where Jude can curse the day he was born; and even then Jude's curses are those of a tragic hero, and therefore to some extent distanced and rendered less shocking by the conventions of literary form.[40]

In *Journey* there is no such distancing. Ferdinand's curses are not directed at God or the gods or even at society or social systems; his curses are for everyone and everything that torments him and the few decent people he finds around him. The best that Ferdinand can do, by way of modulating the cries that he hears, is to try, through poetic invocations, to place them within a compassionate human perspective—as he does when he finally realizes that he cannot prevent the mother from killing her daughter:

> As well hold one's peace and look out through the window at the grey velvet of evening beginning to cover the street opposite, house by house,—first the little ones and then the others; the tallest at last are taken too, and people scurry about among them, more and more slowly, doubtful and dim, hesitating across from one side of the street to the other before going off into the darkness.
>
> Further away, far beyond the town walls, strings and clusters of little lights were dotted about the shadows like nails fastening forgetfulness across the town, and other little lights there were twinkling among the green ones,—spangles of red light, as if lots and lots of boats, a whole fleet come from far, were waiting there all of a shimmer for the great gates of the Night to open before them.[41]

xii

At this juncture I should perhaps acknowledge that I have thus far been discussing the novel primarily in terms of what takes place in, roughly, the first three hundred pages. And while there is no radical break at any specific point the novel does begin to undergo a gradual change when Robinson and the Henrouilles begin to assume prominent roles.

Robinson has of course been there right along, making brief appearances in the war, in Paris, in Africa, and in America. And Ferdinand has, from the beginning, looked upon him as a man more forceful and enterprising than himself. When he arrives in New York, and is feeling lost and helpless in the Gay Calvin hotel, he can think of nothing better than finding Robinson:

> I would redouble my efforts to find Robinson, that is, as soon as I felt strong enough again. Robinson wasn't at all like me! Oh, no, not Robinson. He, at any rate, was a man of guts. A real fine fellow! He was certain to know already all the ins and outs, all the tricks of the trade over here. Maybe too he had some way of laying hold of this certainty, this peace of mind, which I so badly needed. . . .[42]

But Ferdinand soon discovers, once he gets to Detroit, that Robinson has "not got on in the states either," and from this point onwards his attitude towards Robinson begins to change--until, at Rancy, he actually dreads meeting him again:

> And he'd be along here for sure, and I would have to get all mixed up in his affairs again. As it was, everything now brought his dirty presence back into my mind. Even the people I could see through my window (. . .) To kill others and to kill themselves, that's what they wanted; not right off, of course, but bit by bit, like Robinson, with anything that came to

69

hand,--old sorrows, fresh griefs, still
nameless hatreds.[43]

Although Ferdinand tries to explain why he develops such a strong aversion to Robinson at just
this moment there is no denying that his efforts are
less than convincing. Céline's intention, it would
seem, is to justify the new turn that Ferdinand is
about to take in his journey to the end of the
night. And by having Ferdinand express his dread,
not only of Robinson's "dirty presence" but of his
penchant for "killing," Céline is employing Dickensian foreshadowing, a stratagem common to nineteenth-century fiction, to lead into the depths of
murder into which he is about to send Ferdinand--not
this time on his own but as Robinson's witting and
unwitting accomplice.

What I am suggesting here is of course to some
extent speculative. I am presuming that Ferdinand's
journey, as Céline envisages it, cannot be complete
unless it brings him to what is generally acknowl-
edged to be the ultimate degradation--deliberate
murder. Yet Céline knows that he cannot turn Ferdinand himself into a murderer. To do so would be a
drastic violation of Ferdinand's character--a violation that would threaten the integrity of the entire
novel. So rather than trying to enlarge or reshape
Ferdinand, Céline provides him with a partner of
sorts in his old acquaintance Robinson--a partner
(he can hardly be called a friend) who is incapable
of human feeling and love and therefore capable of
murder for hire. In this way Céline places Ferdinand in a position to enter into depths of human
degradation that he could never explore alone. Robinson acts, Ferdinand reacts.

Before Robinson actually appears at Rancy Ferdinand has already become involved with the Henrouilles, the penurious husband and wife who have
"never in fifty years . . . spent a penny, either of
them, without regretting it," and who are now trying
to get Henrouille's mother, with Ferdinand's help,
committed to a convent or a madhouse. But when
Ferdinand meets the old Henrouille he finds her
wonderfully alive—and sane:

> This gay glance of hers enlivened ev-
> erything in the shadows round with some-
> thing young and blithe about it, a minute
> but sparkling enthusiasm of a kind we no
> longer possess. Her voice, which was
> hoarse when she shouted, sounded sprightly
> and charming when she talked normally;
> then she made her words and her sentences
> frisk about and skip and come bouncing
> merrily back, as people could with their
> voices and everything in the days when not
> to be able to tell a story well or sing a
> song when necessary was considered feeble,
> deplorable and stupid.
> Age had covered her, like an old, sway-
> ing tree, with jaunty branches.
> She was a gay old Henrouille; discon-
> tented and grimy, yet gay. The bleakness
> she had lived in for more than twenty
> years had affected her spirit not at all.
> On the contrary, it was from the outside
> world that she had shrunk in self-defence,
> as if the growing cold and all the fright-
> fulness and death itself were to come to

her from there, not from inside. From inside herself she seemed to fear nothing. She seemed certain of her own head as of something definite and solid and understood, understood once and for all.[44]

And when Ferdinand, still tempted by "the thousand franc note . . . [he] could so easily pocket just by signing that certificate of madness," continues to talk to the Henrouilles, the old lady bursts in on the three of them and assaults Ferdinand with a verbal barrage that sends him scurrying for cover:

"Blackguard!" she yelled straight at me. "You can go now, I've told you so already--get out! There's no point in your staying here. I'm not going to any madhouse, I tell you, and I won't go to the convent either! You can talk and lie as much as you like--you won't get *me*, you rascal! These rogues will go before me, these fleecers of an old woman! And you too, you scum, you'll go to gaol, let me tell you, and pretty damn quick!"
I was out of luck all right. Just when there was a thousand francs going begging at one fell swoop! I left at once.
When I was back in the street she leaned out over a little balcony to shout after me, far in the darkness that was hiding me. "You cad! You swine!" she yelled. The echoes rang with it.[45]

The old Henrouille, after routing Ferdinand so easily, actually goes to visit him at his consulting room, where she amuses herself by asking him if he really does think she is mad. "It was sort of an amusement for the old lady." It is there that she meets Robinson, becomes friendly with him, and invites him to meet the Henrouilles, who then offer Robinson 10,000 francs to kill the old lady by planting dynamite in a rabbit hutch near her little house. These developments Ferdinand himself remains unaware of until, quite by chance, he meets Robinson late one night, "loaded with all sorts of planks," on his way to the Henrouilles to build the rabbit hutch.

Ferdinand is not, however, very surprised to learn what the planks are for: "Just rather more sad than before, that's all." Nor does he try to dissuade Robinson; instead he lapses into a soliloquy justifying murder: "The impulse to murder which had suddenly come over Robinson seems to me to be more in some way an improvement on what I'd noticed till then, in other people, who were always half-hating, half kindly, always irritating, in the indecisiveness of their attitude." Then, by way of conclusion, Ferdinand observes: "Decidedly through having followed Robinson in the dark as far as this, I had learned a number of things."[46]

But what has he learned? For the first time in the entire novel I, for one, am left with the feeling that Ferdinand himself has fallen victim to rhetoric, that Céline, in trying to bring his I-narrator to the ultimate depths (via Robinson) has merely brought him to moral debate about the ultimate depths. For there is no acknowledgement anywhere, on Ferdinand's part, that a person is to be murdered, and that the person is the old Henrouille whom he has found so alive and so charming. The closest he comes is in reporting Robinson's efforts to cheer him up:

He tried to cheer me up by giving me
several good reasons for not bothering
about the old woman, who hadn't much longer to live anyway, whatever happened; she
was much too old as it was. He'd just be
arranging for her departure in fact, and
that's all.[47]

To this Ferdinand's only response is: "all the
same, as dirty businesses go, it really was a very
dirty business." And only the first three words of
this response apply directly to the old Henrouille:
the statement about the "dirty business" applies to
the plans for the murder. These plans (which Robinson has adapted from a grisly story that Ferdinand
once told him) Ferdinand recounts in full, right
down to the "explosion . . . they were going to let
her have. . . . Slap in the middle of the face
. . .," and then concludes, in a remark that comes
close to being flippant: "There were no two ways
about it, that was the hell of a story I'd gone and
told Robinson."[48]
    Ferdinand's callousness is hardly lessened by
the fact that, as things turn out, it's Robinson who
gets the explosion slap in the middle of his face.
Nor is it much lessened by the fact that the old
Henrouille not only survives the attempt on her life
but glories in the drama of it all:

She had had a very narrow escape, but
she wasn't really as outraged as she made
out. It was put on. This unsuccessful
attempt on her life had really rather
thrilled her, brought her out of the dim
tomb she had been shut up in all these
years at the end of that damp garden. At

74

her age, now an exciting sense of vitality
had returned and taken possession of her.
She gloated over her victory and with joy
at having a means of going for her beastly
daughter-in-law as long as she lived.
She'd got that now. She wanted *me* to be
told every detail of this abortive attempt
at murder and of how it had all taken
place. (. . .) She was enjoying herself
enormously. She wished to astonish *me* by
her superiority to what had happened, to
confound the whole lot of *us*, to humiliate
us, in fact. [my italics][49]

Whatever sympathy Ferdinand feels for the old
Henrouille—and it never comes to very much—soon
disappears in his concern for "me" and "us." The
real question, however, is why he chooses to link
himself with Robinson and the Henrouilles in this
way. Once again Céline seems to be manipulating
Ferdinand, this time in a desperate attempt to place
him in a position where he can go all the way into
the dark with the three conspirators: "For the
moment, what *we* had to do was patch up the wound
. . . and see to it that the old woman didn't com-
promise *us* all with her damned blabbing . . . she
had got *us* on the run, and that's all there was to
it. . . . [my italics][50] And when Ferdinand finally
tries to account for his own role in the conspiracy,
the best he can do, after conceding that he himself
has not "committed any actual crime," is to maintain
that he nevertheless feels himself to be guilty:

Right among the reefs as *we* were, the
slightest hesitation would wreck the lot
of *us*. Everything would split asunder,

crack, be shattered, sink and be washed
ashore. Robinson, the old lady, the bomb,
the rabbits, his eyes, the incredible son,
the cutthroat daughter-in-law, *we* would
all be washed up there amid all *our* wick-
edness and *our* secrets under the gaze of
thrilled, inquisitive people. Not that I
had committed any actual crime. I hadn't.
But I felt myself to be guilty, nevertheless. I was guilty, at any rate, of being
willing in my heart of hearts that this
should go on. And of not now seeing any
reason why *we* shouldn't all go wandering
off together, deeper and deeper into the
night. [my italics][51]

Here and throughout their "wandering off together" Ferdinand's guilt seems terribly contrived.
It's as if, by this time, Ferdinand has become so
fully defined that he can no longer be manipulated
in the way Céline is attempting to manipulate him--
by turning him into a fellow conspirator. Why Céline makes the attempt is clear enough, but so is
his failure. Ferdinand never becomes a credible
conspirator; and his lack of credibility affects the
entire conspiratorial sequence, which takes on a
"literary" quality that sets it apart from the rest
of *Journey*. At times, indeed, Céline's treatment
suggests that he may be trying to insert his own
version of *Crime and Punishment* into the middle of
the novel.

Once past his conspiratorial phase Ferdinand
again assumes his old self: at the dispensing clin-
ic, at the Tarapout Theatre, at the student boarding
house--in his encounters with Protiste, Matrodin,
Parapine, Tania, and Pomone. His account of his
months at the Tarapout (where, in the stage show, he
plays the part of a "Pasha" in the midst of twenty
chorus girls) is at once loving and funny and sad
and compassionate--as the cries of the girls quiver
beneath the gay songs they are singing:

But this was the worst of all--it was a
gay song, theirs, which wasn't gay. And
there they were, these girls, swaying as
they sang, trying to make it come off. My
God, really I must say it was awful; it
was as if we were spreading ourselves in
unhappiness and sadness. . . . That's it.
Roaming around in the fog in lamentation.
It quivered in their wailing song, they
made one older every minute. It seemed to
trickle from the scene itself: in panic.
Yet they went on and on, my little compan-
ions. They did not appear to understand
what an awful evil effect their song was
having on us all. . . . They mourned their
whole life, twirling away there, grinning,
beautifully in time. . . . When the thing
comes to you like that, so distinctly,
from such a distance, you can't be making
a mistake, you can't resist.
Unhappiness was everywhere, in spite of
the comfort of the stalls; it was on us,
on the blackcloth; it was drenching the

whole world round us. They were artists,
oh, yes, they were complete artists. An
utterly sordid misery surged up from their
song and dance without their wishing to
prevent it or even understand it. Only
their eyes were sad. Eyes are not enough.
They were singing the defeat of life and
they didn't see it. They thought it was
only love, nothing but love; they hadn't
been taught the rest of it, little dears.
. . . A little bit of the blues was what
they were meant to be singing! That's
what they thought it was! When you are
young and don't know, you think it's all
only unhappiness in love. . . .

> *Where I go, where I look . . .*
> *It's only for you . . . ou* . . .
> *Only for you . . . ou . . .* 52

Tania, one of the chorus girls whom Ferdinand
befriends, has immersed herself in just such a delirium of love for her boy-friend, and when he dies,
and Ferdinand tries to comfort her, the two of them
walk slowly up towards Montmartre. "In the little
square there," feeling that they have "come to the
end of the world," Ferdinand goes into a delirium of
his own--a wholly different kind of delirium in
which he calls up the people in his past with a
tenderness that, in most instances, he has been
unable to express in his more direct and tough-
minded role as I-narrator:

> There, close at hand on the Place du
> Tertre, was where the dead began. We had
> a good place to see them from. They were

passing over Dufayel's, that is to say, to the east of us.

All the same, you have to know how to see them--from inside and almost closing your eyes--because the great draughts of light from the electric signs make it awfully difficult to see them, even through the clouds. I realized at once that the dead would have taken Bébert to themselves; we even made a little sign to each other, Bébert and I, and then, quite close to him, we signalled to the very pale girl from Rancy who had had her miscarriage at last and was there now, all empty inside.

There were lots of old patients of mine here and there, and women patients whom I had long since forgotten about and many others,--the Negro on a white cloud, all by himself, who was the fellow they had thrashed rather too thoroughly, over there, I remembered him from Topo--and old Grappa too, that old soldier himself from the wilds! I had thought of them from time to time, I'd certainly thought of Lieutenant Grappa and the flayed Negro and my Spaniard, the priest; he too had come along with the dead that evening to pray in heaven, and there was his gold crucifix getting in his way as he hopped from cloud to cloud. He got caught up with his crucifix in all the dirtiest, yellow clouds, and all the time I recognized many more of the departed, more and more of them. . . . So many that one really is ashamed of not having had time to see them while they

were living here by one's side year after
year. . . .

You never have the time, it's a fact,
except to think of yourself.

So all these blighters had turned into
angels, without my knowing anything about
it! There were clouds and clouds full of
angels now, very odd-looking ones and
disreputable ones in all directions.
Jaunting around, high up over the town! I
looked for Molly among them; now was my
chance, my dear, my only friend Molly--but
she hadn't come with them. She probably
had a little heaven all to herself, close
to the Lord God; she'd always been so
kind, my Molly. . . . I was happy not to
find her with all that riff-raff--because
that's what these dead men were, scamps,
just a lot of scapegrace ghosts that had
been gathered together this evening over
the town![53]

XV

One untoward effect of Ferdinand's delirium is
to remind him of Robinson: "That jaunt of the night
before had left me with an odd feeling of remorse.
The thought of Robinson had come back to plague me.
The fact was that I had actually left the fellow to
his fate."[54] Following this sentimental preamble,
Ferdinand sets off to join Robinson in Toulouse,
where, thanks to the machinations of the Abbé Protiste, Robinson, now half-blind, has not only been
reconciled with the old Henrouille, but also acts as
her partner in the strange business of exhibiting

mummies in a cave. That Ferdinand is more than a little intrigued by these developments is understandable enough, and Céline offers still further justification by having Ferdinand once again declare his ultimate purpose in following Robinson:

> To go to Toulouse was again a foolish thing to do. Thinking it over, I realized as much. But by dint of following after Robinson in his adventures like this, I had developed a taste for this shadiness racket. Even back in New York that time, when I wasn't sleeping well. I had begun worrying whether I couldn't go along a bit further with Robinson, and further yet. You delve deeper into the night at first and start to panic, but you want to *know* all the same, and after that you don't come out of the depths of the darkness. But there are too many things to understand at one fell swoop. Life's much too short. You don't want to do any one an injustice. You have your scruples, you don't want to jump to conclusions, and above all you are afraid of having to die before you have done hesitating, because then you would have come into the world for no purpose whatsoever. And that really would be hell.[55]

Here, in the final three lines, is Céline's answer to all those critics who have questioned his purpose as man and artist. And the rest of the passage constitutes an eloquent restatement of Ferdinand's avowed purpose in following Robinson: a restatement which might be convincing if Robinson were convincing. But he is not. Despite Céline's continued attempts to make him into an interesting and significant figure, he remains what Ferdinand later calls him--"a poor fish."

During his convalescence Robinson spends hours talking with Ferdinand--to reveal among other things, the one youthful experience that he has never been able to overcome:

> While in his bandaged state, Robinson told me about his early life. He had started in a shop. His parents had made him an apprentice to a high-class milliner. One day when he was delivering some goods, a lady-customer invited him to taste of a pleasure he had previously experienced only in the imagination. He had never gone back to his employer, he was so dreadfully ashamed of what he had done. To go to bed with a customer was certainly still in those days an unpardonable thing. The lady's crêpe-de-chine chemise had had an extraordinary effect on him. Twenty years later he could still remember that chemise exactly. The rosy scented limbs of that frolicsome young woman in an apartment full of cushions and fringed curtains had provided Robinson with grounds for endless depressing comparisons for the rest of his life.
>
> Many things had happened since, though. He had been all over the world, he had gone through whole wars, but he never properly got over this vision. (. . .) childhood was something he couldn't bear to bring himself to think about, it had

been so very far from enjoyable. After
the business of the lady-customer he could
remember nothing, even in odd corners of
it, that didn't dishearten and sicken him,
like a house full of smelly horrible
things, old brooms, old washtubs, fussing
women, and clouts over the head.[56]

All this helps to explain why Robinson hates
women: "I can get along all right without women--
with their fat thighs, their Cupid's-bow lips and
those stomachs of theirs which always have something
growing in them, either a baby or a disease."[57] And
it also helps to explain why he seems to have no
feelings whatsoever--only nerve-end sensations when
he experiences pain. But nothing that is said, here
or later, by either Ferdinand or Robinson, accounts
for his single-minded pursuit of money--to the point
of attempted murder, and finally murder, since he
eventually kills the old Henrouille. At times Ferdinand does speak quite scathingly in characterizing
Robinson, as, for instance, when he declares him to
be "as obstinate as a mule--a real case of persecu-
tion mania . . ."; or when he tells Robinson
straight out: "You really have no thought for anything beyond money. . . ."[58] Yet such observations
do little more than underline the obvious. More
promising are those in which Ferdinand frankly owns
that something is missing in Robinson: "I came to
the conclusion that really he wasn't a very attractive person, Robinson. There are some animals so
made that it isn't any good their being simple and
unfortunate and all; one's aware of it, but one just
can't bear them all the same. They've something
lacking. . . . Here's Robinson, I reflected, whom I
once took for an adventurous sort of bloke, and he's

really only a poor fish, cuckold or not, blind or not. . . ."[59] In these reflections Ferdinand at long last seems on the way to a full recognition of the "disgusting . . . poor fish" that he himself has shown Robinson to be.

Unfortunately, however, Ferdinand offers these reflections only to withdraw them a few pages later: "I set out to define Robinson's temperament, as if I myself really knew what he was like, but I realized immediately that I didn't know Robinson at all-- aside from one or two rough indications of his character. No more than that."[60] Now this declaration sounds more than a little disingenuous, coming as it does after Ferdinand's previous remarks. And his further efforts to excuse himself are likewise difficult to accept in the way they seem to be intended:

> It's astonishing how difficult it is to conceive of what will make one human being either more or less likeable to others. . . . Yet one wants to help him, to stick up for him--and one just babbles. . . . You open your mouth, and it's pitiful. . . . You're absolutely lost.
>
> It isn't easy in our day to play the La Bruyère. The whole subconscious mind slinks away from you as you approach.[61]

All this may be true enough. But its specific application is another matter. Ferdinand, who seems to be speaking directly for Céline, is not merely declaring himself incapable of exploring Robinson's subconscious; he is declaring himself incapable of drawing the most obvious common-sense inferences from his own observations and reflections. Of course it can be objected that I am being unduly critical, that quite possibly Céline, speaking through Ferdinand, really does feel incapable of defining Robinson's temperament. But why then subject Ferdinand (and the reader) to page after page of Robinson's maudlin maunderings? The answer, I am indeed sorry to say, seems to be that Céline, by leaving the maunderings undefined, hopes that they will somehow lend depth and significance to Robinson's zombie-like responses.

xvi

This is not to say that the Toulouse section is a total loss. It has some good things in it (*e.g.,* the scene in which Ferdinand observes the waitresses going after one another) and in a lesser novel the section as a whole might be considered quite acceptable, even good. But it fails to measure up to the earlier parts of *Journey*. And the final section in Baryton's asylum, prior to the climactic scenes, is not a great deal better--primarily because Robinson once again shows up to divulge and act out his fears of Madelon, the girl to whom he had become engaged at Toulouse.

When Robinson is not present there are some excellent passages--with Parapine (the distinguished medical researcher who lost his position at the Bioduret Joseph Institute because of his fascination with little girls' legs) and Baryton (the eccentric Dickensian doctor who owns and operates the asylum) and the certified loonies of various description who inhabit it. Ferdinand is immediately at home in the madhouse, and he makes the most of his situation, as assistant to Baryton, in showing how slight the distance is that separates the inmates from their keepers. Baryton's discussion of Parapine's madness (in which he distinguishes between just ordinary madmen and "madmen who're in agony over the set forms of our civilization"[62]) reveals more about Baryton's madness than Parapine's, and in doing so provides an ironical portrait of Ferdinand himself.

Then, in the "sulky, sombre, timorous atmosphere" of the madhouse Sophie appears--to give Ferdinand another opportunity to express his love of a beautiful woman's body: "A desperate task . . . There's none more difficult, hazardous. Compared to this vice of seeking after perfection in shapes, cocaine's nothing but a hobby for stationmasters."[63] Yet however lecherous Ferdinand portrays himself his words and actions are not those of a roué.   Through loving the woman's body--Sophie's, Tania's, Molly's, even Madelon's--he comes to love the woman herself. Much as Céline would have disliked having Ferdinand compared with Mellors (Céline once described *Lady Chatterly's Lover* as " a gamekeeper's miserable prick for six hundred and fifty pages"[64]) Ferdinand's attitude towards women is essentially Lawrentian in that he comes to the woman herself through her body. Ferdinand's lyrical description of Sophie's powers runs to three full pages--with these lines at their center:

> We admired her aliveness by our side,
> if she merely rose and came to our table
> or walked away again. . . . She enchanted
> us. And each time she performed these
> simple gestures, we were overcome with
> joy--and surprise. In some way, we seemed
> to gain in poetry just in admiring her
> being so utterly beautiful, so much more

unselfconscious than we were. . . . The
rhythm of her life was drawn from other
sources than ours. Ours were jangling
rhythms, sickly and sad. . . . This happy
impulsation, at once precise and gentle,
which animated her from the waves of her
hair to her ankles, troubled us; it
charmed us but it made us uneasy, that is
the word--uneasy.

Our cross-grained knowledge of the
things of this world rather resented, even
if instinct did not, the fresh delight of
this creature--knowledge ever present,
fundamentally afraid, taking refuge in
life's depths, accustomed to accept the
worst, self-enured to it.

Sophie had that winged, supple and
balanced carriage which one so often finds
in the women of America, the bearing of a
people of the future, whom life carries
ambitiously and lightly towards new forms
of enterprise. . . . A brigantine of tender gaiety headed for the Infinite.

Parapine, who wasn't, you'd have said,
at all given himself to any particular
lyricism over matters of attraction, would
smile to himself as soon as she went out
of the room. . . . The simple fact of
contemplating her did your soul good.
. . . Especially mine, in justice be it
said, which longed for it so much.[65]

What happens here is what happens in the bargeman's
scene in *The Rainbow*--as Sophie's body, in a perfect
exemplification of what I have elsewhere defined as

the Panzaic principle, gives the lie to "our cross-grained knowledge of the things of the world."

Unfortunately, however, the woman of this passage never reappears in the novel. Céline cannot permit her to reappear: he is committed to having Ferdinand and Sophie follow Robinson in "the Madelon business," and he cannot afford to have a Panzaic Sophie on the premises. So he transforms her into a good-hearted girl from Central Europe who forwards the plot by advising Ferdinand "to make it up" with Madelon, at the same time reminding him that he has "been thoroughly brutal and horrid to her"--a reference to the episode, made so much of by Wayne Booth and other critics, in which Ferdinand slaps Madelon:

> As long as I can remember, I had always wanted to clout a face possessed by anger, as hers was, just to see what happens to an angry face if you do. That, or a fat cheque, is what you need so as to see an instant change come over all the passions which dodge around in a person's head. It's as lovely to watch as a sailing ship going "about" on a high-running tide. The whole mind answers to the new shift in the wind. That's what I wanted to see.
>
> For twenty years at least I had been pursued by this desire. On the street, in cafés, in all the places where people, with greater or less aggressiveness, fretful and bragging, fly at each other's throats. But I had never dared, for fear of being slugged myself, and above all for fear of the shame which follows coming to blows. But here was the opportunity for once, magnificent.

"Are you going to get out?" I asked
her, just to make her angrier still, to
bring her to the proper pitch.

She no longer knew who I was when I
talked to her like that. She started to
smile, abhorrently, as if she were finding
me very ridiculous and negligible. . . .
Biff! Bang! I landed two slaps across
her face which would have been enough to
shake a house.

She tottered and fell flat across the
broad pink divan on the opposite side of
the room, against the wall, her head in
her hands. Her breath came in little
gasps; she moaned like a little dog that's
been too thoroughly thrashed. Then after
that she seemed to think a while and suddenly she jumped up, lithe and supple, and
was out of the door without even turning
her head. I had seen nothing. It hadn't
been any good.[66]

According to Wayne Booth Ferdinand is "clouting
a woman's face just to see how it feels"[67]--though
clearly that is not what the passage says. For one
thing Ferdinand never once uses the word "feels."
He wants to "see," not "feel," what happens to the
angry face (a "fat cheque" would have served the
same purpose.) But there is no need to quibble,
since what is most remarkable here, I should say, is
that Ferdinand has had this desire for twenty years,
and never till this moment acted on it--despite all
that he has been through. As for his attributing
his reticence to fear, that hardly accounts for his
not having slapped any women or children in the past
twenty years. In this as in so many past instances

Ferdinand is demeaning himself; he is presenting himself as an utterly spineless coward in order to remove any trace of manly self-justification for his actions. What can hardly be denied, even so, is that the scene remains, like so many of the scenes in *The Balcony*, a sensational *tour de force*.

Also sensational, and completely out of character, are Ferdinand's attempts to suggest that his real motive in following Sophie's advice and trying to placate Madelon is to get the four of them in bed together. Not that Ferdinand would be averse to such an arrangement; it's just that he would never have made such a fuss about it. But Céline is by this time winding up for his climactic scenes and he has to latch on to any motivation that will lend credence to Ferdinand's maneuverings.

xvii

The final section of *Journey* opens at the Batignolles fair, with Madelon not only refusing to be appeased by Ferdinand's attempts at reconciliation but also showing increased impatience with Robinson --until, in the taxi on the way back from the fair, she launches into a frenzied inventory of her wrongs, accusing Robinson of scorning her love and at the same time letting him know that Ferdinand has seduced and mistreated her: "Cuckolding your friends and then striking their girl friends." Then, getting still more worked up, Madelon insists that Robinson leave with her or she will tell the police that he murdered the old Henrouille. And when that threat fails she accuses all three of being sexual degenerates: "Why do you bother with pretexts? You've tried everything and you're bored, that's all it is! Only now you've not even got the courage of your vices. Your own vices frighten you."[68] Whereupon Robinson really cuts loose:

"Oh, yes, I have!" he exclaimed. "I've plenty of courage and I daresay quite as much as you have! Only--if you really want to know the whole of it . . . why, it's every darn thing that repels me and disgusts me now. Not only you! Everything! . . . Love especially. . . . Your love along with every one else's. . . . All this sentimental monkey-business you're so fond of--d' you want me to tell how that strikes me? It seems to me like making love in a lavatory! Now do you understand? . . . And all this sentiment you rout out to keep me glued to you affects me like an insult, if you'd like to know. . . . And on top of that, you don't even suspect as much because it's you who're such a numbskull because you don't realize things at all. . . . And you don't even guess that you make one sick. . . . It's enough for you just to repeat all the drivel people talk. . . . You think that's quite all right. . . . That's quite enough, you think, because other people have told you there's nothing greater than love and that it would always work with every one and that it lasts for ever. . . . Well, as far as I'm concerned, you know what they can do with their love. . . . D' you hear me? It doesn't catch on with me, my good girl, that stinking love of theirs! . . . You're out of luck!

You're too late! It no longer works with
me, that's all! And that's what you go
getting into such tempers about. Do you
have to make love in the middle of all
that's going on? And seeing the things
one sees? Or maybe you don't notice anything? No, I think it's that you just
don't care. . . . You play at being sentimental when really you're as tough a little animal as any one. . . . You don't
mind eating rotten meat? Helping it down
with that Love sauce of yours?[69]

Coming from anyone else these words might be
devastating; coming from Robinson they are more than
a little puzzling, since he has already shown himself to be devoid of feelings, and more particularly, where women are concerned, sexual feelings.
More than that he has shown himself to be devoid of
any concern for anyone or anything except making
money. It's almost as if Céline has forgotten who
is speaking, or expects the reader to forget. As it
is there seems to be no way of telling how the words
are to be taken--as defensive rhetoric on Robinson's
part in which he tries to deny his own deficiencies
by attacking the rhetoric of love and marriage, or
as new-found wisdom that Robinson has arrived at in
some mysterious way. Or perhaps, at this stage, the
words are merely there to drive Madelon to murder.

The three pistol shots that Madelon fires point-
blank into Robinson's stomach do not kill him immediately. His death agonies take place in the asylum, with Ferdinand and Parapine in attendance, and
with Ferdinand expressing his feelings of grief in a
threnody that, in and of itself, does full justice
to the title of the novel:

At such moments it's a little embarrassing to have become as poor and as hard as one has. One lacks almost everything that might be of use in helping some one to die. One has nothing left inside one but things that serve the purposes of everyday life,--a life of comfort, one's own life, a damned insensibility. On the way you've lost confidence in things. You've chased and harried all the pity you had left in you carefully, right to the back of your system, a dirty little ball. You've pushed pity to the lower end of your bowels, with the rest of the refuse. That's the best place for it, you tell yourself.

There was I, standing by Léon's side so as to be of help to him, and never have I felt so awkward. I couldn't manage it. . . . And he couldn't find me. . . . He tried to and he just gaped. . . . He must have been looking for some other Ferdinand, one of course much greater than me, so as to die, or rather, for me to help him to die, more quietly. He made efforts to discover whether there hadn't been perhaps some improvement in the world. He was going over it all, poor wretch, in his mind, wondering whether men hadn't changed just a bit for the better while he had been alive; whether he hadn't sometimes, without meaning to, been unjust toward them. But there was nobody but me, really me, just me, by his side,--a quite real Ferdinand who lacked what might make a man greater than his own trivial life, a love for the life of others. I hadn't any of that, or truly so little of it that it wasn't worth showing what I had. I wasn't death's equal. I was far too small for it. I had no great conception of humanity. I would even, I believe, have more easily felt sorry for a dog dying than for Robinson, because a dog's not sly; whereas, whatever one may say, Léon was just a bit sly. I was sly too; we were all sly. . . . All the rest of it had fallen by the wayside and even those facial expressions, which are still some use by a death-bed, I'd lost as well. I had indeed lost everything along the road. (. . .)[70]

Except for a few shockingly false and sentimental lines (Robinson never once wondered, in the sense Ferdinand implies, about whether or not men were changing for the better, or about whether or not he had been unjust to them) the passage as a whole never falters. Robinson is there, not as a great or a good or even an average man, but as "the poor fish" who is nevertheless a fellow human being and therefore deserving of more than Ferdinand or anyone else can give. And Ferdinand's upbraiding himself for his own lack of pity and love, though it may in some respects seem Christ-like, never falls into the rhetoric of the Christ-like. Wayne Booth, in his criticism, mistakes the sense as well as the tone of the passage, particularly in his comments on "sly." In saying that "a dog's not sly" Ferdinand is merely stating an observed fact--a fact that Céline, in *Castle to Castle*, turns into poetry in his elegiac tribute to his dog Bessie--and his statement of fact is not intended to suggest that

94

human beings are lower than dogs--only that they are
sadly different from dogs in having a sense of death
which they can never escape or overcome.

When Robinson's body is removed to police head-
quarters Ferdinand, in following along behind, tries
to lose his way--"so as not to find myself face to
face with my own life." Yet he meets himself at
every turn: "My aimless pilgrimage was over now.
Let others carry on the game. The world had closed
in. We had come to the end. . . . As we had at the
fair! . . . Being sorrowful isn't all; there ought
to be some way of starting the music up again, of
discovering a further poignancy. . . . But not for
me; let others carry on."

All this makes eloquent sense--until he observes: "And yet I hadn't gone as far in life as
Robinson had . . . I hadn't made a success of it;
that much was certain. I hadn't acquired one single
good solid idea like the one he'd had to get himself
severely manhandled like that." What Ferdinand can
possibly mean here I, for my part, am at a loss to
know. What was Robinson's "one single good solid
idea"? In what sense had he gone further--by mur-
dering or getting himself murdered? Or in saying
"no" to Madelon? Yet Ferdinand continues on--as if
what he is saying should be quite clear:

> . . . How many lives should I have had
> to live to get myself an idea stronger
> than anything else in all the world?
> There was no way of telling! It was all
> no good! My own idea, the ideas I had,
> roamed loose in my mind with plenty of
> gaps in between them; they were like lit-
> tle tapers, flickering and feeble, shud-

dering all through life in the midst of a truly appalling, awful world.

Perhaps it was going a bit better now than it had twenty years ago; it couldn't be said I hadn't made some little progress, but even so there was never any chance of my managing, like Robinson, to fill my head with a single idea, some really superb idea that was definitely stronger than death, nor of my ending up, just because of my idea, exuding joy and insouciance and courage--a lush demigod![71]

Is this actually the way Ferdinand sees Robinson, or is he by this time so overcome with grief that he is in a kind of delirium? That is the suggestion, at any rate, with which he ends the succeeding paragraph: "The fever had come, after all." And if everything Ferdinand says about Robinson's courage and his "superb idea" can be attributed to fever, then perhaps the entire passage can be read as delirium. Yet even so Ferdinand's glorification of Robinson creates difficulties--the same difficulties, really, that have been there right along. Robinson, by Ferdinand's own showing, is a hopelessly and sadly mixed up slob and whenever Ferdinand tries, even in delirium, to endow him with superior attributes his efforts invariably seem contrived. When Céline, in a letter to Milton Hindus, boasted that he could "make alligators dance to Pan's flute,"[72] he was claiming little more than the greater part of *Journey* bears out. It is only with Robinson that his magic fails him.

Yet if Robinson never dances, these final scenes are still powerful enough to provide a fitting climax to the novel--primarily because Ferdinand himself comes through so magnificently. From his threnody on Robinson to his visit to police head-quarters and "the *estaminet* by the canal" his words are those of a man who has come to understand and accept his lot as a human being in this world--together with all the other human beings. As he and Sophie and Parapine leave the bar alongside the canal, just before dawn, the world is beginning to move again:

Towards the end of the night the lock gates begin slowly to open. After that the whole countryside comes to life again slowly and starts to work. The banks of the river come apart from it very gently. They leave, they lift themselves up from the water between. The day's work steals out of the shadows. You begin to see everything again, all very simply, all hard. Winches close by, fences, timber yards yonder, and far away on the road men, too, returning from still further distances, coming towards us. They strag-gle into the grey light in little chilly groups. To start the day, they splash their faces with the morning light as they walk up past the dawn. They go on. All you can truly see of them is their pale, simple faces; the rest of them's still in the night. They'll all of them have to die too, some day. How will they take it?

They plod on up towards the bridge. Beyond it, little by little, they're lost in the flatness of the land and still more of them follow after these have gone,-- more men, paler each time as the day rises

up all round. And what are they thinking?
(. . .)

Far away, the tugboat hooted; calling
across the bridge, the arches one by one,
a lock, another bridge, further, further
away. . . . It was calling to itself every
boat on the river, every one, the whole
town, and the sky and the country and us,
all of it being called away, and the Seine
too, everything,--let's hear no more of
all of this.[73]

Up to this final point I have neither questioned
nor quarrelled with Marks' translation, and I hesi-
tate to do so even now. But the final words of this
passage are the final words of the novel, and if
they are translated the way Marks translates them
(Let's hear no more of all of this.") they bring the
novel to a close on a note of desolation, even
disgust, that seems wholly unwarranted. Merlin
Thomas, in his *Louis-Ferdinand Céline*, offers a
different translation ("And there's no more to be
said.") which seems to be much more in line with
what the novel has been saying.[74] For if Ferdinand
is weary he is not in despair. He knows now where
the end of the night is and he (along with others)
must continue on his journey towards it.

xviii

Because this is a primer concerned with clari-
fying Céline's primary intentions in *Journey*, I have
tried to avoid bringing my own critical theories
directly into the discussion--more particularly my
theories of the Panzaic.[75] This reticence has been

all the easier for me because *Journey* is so thoroughly Panzaic (in the sense that Trotsky, without using the word, demonstrates in his now famous review) that to discuss the novel in Panzaic terms is very nearly, but not quite, supererogatory--as I hope to show in a separate essay.

In this same essay I also plan to discuss many aspects of *Journey* that I have either passed over or merely touched upon in this primer. In everything from his ideas (or lack of them) to his "comic lyricism," Céline is forging a new fictional medium, and the full measure of his achievement in *Journey* can hardly be realized without further consideration of what he is and is not attempting in his fiction--with as much emphasis on the "not" as on the "is," and with due regard for what he himself has to say about his own theories and practices. "I ain't got no ideas! not a one . . ." he says in his *Entretiens avec le Professeur Y,* "and I find nothing more vulgar, more common, more disgusting than ideas! . . . the impotent are bursting with ideas! and the philosophers!"[76]

Everything Céline is trying to express, he says again and again, comes from his nerves, his visceral reactions, in spite of or in contradiction to what he and others may think or believe. And he is trying to use words to force his own visceral reactions directly into his reader's consciousness: "The emotion of spoken language through writing." What Céline achieves through this directness in *Journey* I have already, in a few instances, tried to suggest. But much more needs to be said. Ferdinand's words have to be read the way they would be heard by someone to whom he was speaking. A part of Wayne Booth's difficulty with *Journey,* for example, derives from the fact that he either cannot or will not read Ferdinand's words as if they were being spoken, and for this reason misses or mistakes both their tone and the emotion they are intended to convey.

Céline's ultimate aim, as he explains it in his *Entretiens*, is to get his readers into what he calls his emotive subway: "Never the briefest stops any place! no! to the end of the line! nonstop! into emotion! . . . by emotion! nothing but the end of the line: right into emotion . . . from beginning to end!"[77] Although Céline did not publish *Entretiens* until 1955 he first adumbrated this concept of the emotional metro in 1944 (in a letter to Claude Janet[78]) and he may well have been thinking along the same lines much earlier—without realizing the full implications of what he was attempting. For in *Journey* he does not yet have his emotive subway on rails. He uses his famous three dots, which in his view of the subway serve the same purpose as railroad ties, only sparingly; and he is generally more reliant on conventional literary techniques than in his later works. Yet if in *Journey* his emotive subway is careening along without rails in the first three hundred pages it nevertheless goes "right into emotion . . . from beginning to end" to express "cries beyond those which one has heard, cries which one has not yet heard or understood."

Then, with the advent of Robinson as Ferdinand's alter ego, the subway begins to sputter and slow down. The cries become weaker and weaker, finally to be superseded by Robinson's whinings, which are only redeemed, in so far as they are redeemed, by what Ferdinand makes of them. It's almost as if, around page three hundred, Céline begins to lose his energy, or his nerve—as if, in his inexperience (*Journey*, it must never be forgotten, is his first novel) he begins to worry about where his emotive subway is taking him, and perhaps begins to feel that he has to return to a more conventional literary form that will lend itself to a more conventional ending.

To substantiate this interpretation of *Journey* in a full-scale critical study I shall, I realize, have to take into account the work of previous scholars and critics far more than I have in this primer. And since criticism, as I understand it, can never be separated from critical theory, I shall also have to define my own contextualist theory of fiction, and then try to show how it validates the more controversial aspects of my criticism—including, for example, my criticism of Robinson, in which I acknowledge discrepancies between Céline's aims and achievements that, to formalist critics with a belief in unity or wholeness as the final measure of fictional art, would destroy the aesthetic integrity of the entire novel.[79] But I, as a contextualist, have no obligation to see *Journey*, or for that matter any other novel, in these restrictive terms. Great novels are invariably marred by serious weaknesses of one kind or another—with some of the greatest having some of the greatest weaknesses. In *The Craft of Fiction* Percy Lubbock, after acknowledging *War and Peace* to be perhaps the greatest novel ever written, goes on to concede that it nevertheless breaks in two. And similar criticisms can be levelled against great novels of the past from *Don Quixote* to *Vanity Fair*. Robinson could be even more of a liability than he actually is and *Journey* would still be a twentieth-century successor to these novels.

FOOTNOTES

1. The first quote is from Trotsky's famous review of *Journey* in *The Atlantic Monthly* (October 1935), p. 413; the second is from a letter to Milton Hindus; the third from *Journey* itself; the fourth from Céline's interview with Merry Bromberger (L'Intransigeant), in *Cahiers Céline*, I (Paris: Gallimard, 1976), p. 31. The second and fourth quotes I have taken from J. H. Matthews, *The Inner Dream: Céline as Novelist* (Syracuse: Syracuse University Press, 1978), pp. 54, 68.

2. Wayne C. Booth, *The Rhetoric of Fiction* (Chicago: University of Chicago Press, 1963), pp. 383-384.

3. Booth, pp. 380-81.

4. Matthew 12:20.

5. I shall give page references to *Journey* by citing Marks' translation first, then Manheim's: Marks, p. 263; Manheim, p. 228.

6. Marks, p. 265; Manheim, p. 230.

7. Marks, pp. 228, 230-31; Manheim, pp. 197, 199.

8. Marks, p. 235; Manheim p. 203.

9. Céline was still trying to find Elizabeth Craig some fifteen years later.

10. Marks, pp. 48-49; Manheim, p. 43.

11. Marks, pp. 135-37; Manheim, p. 117-118.

12. Marks, p. 138; Manheim, p. 119.

13. Marks, p. 131; Manheim, pp. 113-114.

14. Marks, p. 160; Manheim, pp. 137-38.

15. Booth, p. 383.

16. Merlin Thomas, *Louis-Ferdinand Céline* (London, 1979), p. 89.

17. *Entretiens avec le Professeur Y* (Paris: Gallimard, 1955), as translated by Merlin Thomas, pp. 89-90. Thomas uses parentheses to distinguish an ellipsis from Céline's three dots.
18. Booth, p. 383.
19. Booth, p. 379.
20. Booth, p. 291.
21. Booth, p. 81.
22. Milton Hindus, "Céline: A Reappraisal," *The Southern Review* (Winter 1968), p. 84.
23. Marks, p. 168; Manheim, pp. 144-45.
24. Hindus, p. 85.
25. Hindus, p. 86.
26. Hindus, p. 86.
27. Hindus, pp. 86-87.
28. Hindus, p. 87.
29. Hindus, p. 87.
30. Hindus, p. 89.
31. Marks, p. 137; Manheim, p. 118.
32. *Entretiens avec le Professeur Y*, as translated by Merlin Thomas, p. 85.
33. Marks, p. 259; Manheim, pp. 224-25.
34. Marks, p. 260; Manhiem, p. 225.
35. Marks, p. 260; Manheim, p. 225.
36. Marks, p. 258; Manheim, p. 224.
37. Marks, p. 260; Manheim, p. 226.
38. Jean Genet, *The Balcony* (translated by Bernard Frechtman), Revised Version (New York, 1966).
39. Marks, p. 213; Manheim, p. 185.
40. Hardy's strange and little known final novel, *The Well-Beloved*, is even more deeply pessimistic than *Jude*. In my "And There Shall Be Burning Instead of Beauty: A Study of Hardy's *The Well-Beloved*," (*Paunch*, [April 1977], pp. 131-173), I trace the pessimism that runs through Hardy's novels--to conclude:

But none of Hardy's novels, not even *Jude*, goes quite so far as *The Well-Beloved* in denying the possibility of love. Jude can say, "And I here. And Sue defiled!" while he dies a slow death, but his cry of agony is in itself a kind of affirmation of the continuing possibility of love--if not for himself and Sue, perhaps for others. In *The Well-Beloved*, however, there is no longer even this possibility. . . .

But what is most terrible, finally, [in *The Well-Beloved*] is what happens to the sixty-one-year-old Pierston. . . . [In the end] his defenses collapse, and he collapses with them, to become the most embittered of all Hardy's heroes, and certainly one of the most embittered in all literature --comparable, say to Gulliver of Book Four. For Pierston not only denies the possibility of love, and with it art and beauty; he goes still further, to deny even the memory of love, or of art, or of beauty; and he finds contentment only in reducing himself and Marcia to a state of sexless, loveless decrepitude.

41. Marks, pp. 260-61; Manheim, p. 226.
42. Marks, p. 204; Manheim, pp. 176-77.
43. Marks, p. 268; Manheim, p. 232.
44. Marks, p. 253; Manheim, pp. 219-220.
45. Marks, p. 256; Manheim, p. 222.
46. Marks, p. 307; Manheim, p. 266.

47. Marks, p. 308; Manheim, p. 266.

48. Marks, p. 308; Manheim, p. 267.

49. Marks, pp. 319, 321; Manheim, pp. 277, 278.

50. Marks, pp. 322-23; Manheim, pp. 280-81.

51. Marks, p. 329; Manheim, p. 286.

52. Marks, pp. 360-61; Manheim, p. 313.

53. Marks, pp. 364-65; Manheim, pp. 316-17.

54. Marks, p. 368; Manheim, p. 318.

55. Marks, pp. 379-80; Manheim, p. 329.

56. Marks, pp. 324, 328; Manheim, pp. 281, 285.

57. Marks, p. 313; Manheim, p. 271.

58. Marks, pp. 313, 389, 392; Manheim, pp. 272, 337, 339.

59. Marks, pp. 389-90, 392; Manheim, pp. 337, 339.

60. Marks, p. 395; Manheim, p. 342.

61. Marks, p. 395; Manheim, p. 342.

62. Marks, p. 418; Manheim, p. 361.

63. Marks, p. 475; Manheim, p. 407.

64. In *Bagatelles pour un massacre*, as translated by Merlin Thomas in his *Louis-Ferdinand Céline*, p. 106.

65. Marks, p. 476; Manheim, pp. 407-08.

66. Marks, pp. 472-73; Manheim, p. 405.

67. Booth, p. 384.

68. Marks, p. 497; Manheim, p. 424.

69. Marks, pp. 497-98; Manheim, p. 425.

70. Marks, pp. 500-01; Manheim, pp. 427-28.

71. Marks, pp. 504-05; Manheim, p. 431.

72. Quoted by Erika Ostrovsky, *Céline and his Vision* (New York, 1967), p. 60.

73. Marks, pp. 507-08, 509; Manheim, pp. 434, 435.

74. Merlin Thomas, p. 62.

75. Wayne Burns, *The Panzaic Principle* (Vancouver: The Pendejo Press, 1968). See also my *Journey Through the Dark Woods*, (Seattle: Howe Street Press, 1982).

76. Quoted by J. H. Matthews, p. 223.
77. Quoted by J. H. Matthews, p. 226.
78. Quoted by Merlin Thomas, p. 81.
79. I shall also have to acknowledge what Céline himself said in an interview with Merry Bromberger (*Cahiers Céline*, Vol. I, Paris, 1976, p. 31):

> Le voilà! C'est l'amour dont nous osons parler encore dans cet enfer, comme si l'on pouvait composer des quatrains dans un abattoir. L'amour impossible aujourd'hui. Robinson le cherche comme chacun, avec l'argent, cet autre bien indispensable. Il finit enfin par trouver un coin tranquille, des rentes, une petite femme qui l'aime. Pourtant, il ne peut pas rester là. Il lui faut partir quand il a le bonheur bourgeois sous la main, une petite maison, une épouse câline, des poissons rouges. Il se dit qu'il est fou pour être comme cela. Il s'en va. Madelon le poursuit. Elle ne croit pas qu'il soit fou et lui le comprend aussi. Il n'est seulement pas assez égoiste pour être heureux. La petite l'assaille. Elle ne comprend rien. Lui, pour en sortir et sortir de lui-même, voudrait être heroïque dans son genre. Mais il ne sait pas comment.
>
> A la fin, dans le taxi, il trouve. Il dit à Madelon que ce n'est pas elle mais l'univers entier qui le dégoûte. Il le dit comme il peut et il en meurt.

My good friend Gerald Butler (San Diego State University) just recently called my attention to this statement, which he has included, with his own translation, in a paper for the Céline section of the MLA (1983) entitled "The Feeling for Women in Céline and his American Imitators":

Here it is! It's love of which we do not venture to speak yet in this hell, as if one could compose quatrains in a slaughterhouse. Love impossible today. Robinson looks for it like everyone, along with money, that other very indispensible thing. He finally ends up finding a peaceful corner, an income, a little woman who loves him. However, he cannot stay there. He has to leave when he has the good bourgeois life in hand, a little home, a cajoling wife, goldfish. He tells himself he's crazy for being like that. He goes away. Madelon pursues him. She doesn't believe he is crazy and he knows it too. He is only not egotist enough to be happy. The little girl assails him. She understands nothing. As for him, in order to go away from her and from himself, he wishes to be heroic in his way. But he does not know how.

In the end, in the taxi, he finds out. He tells Madelon that it is not her but the entire universe that disgusts him. He says it as he can and he dies because of it.

Had I been aware of Céline's statement earlier I should have included it in this primer. And I shall certainly take it into account in the critical study I am projecting. But I do not see how Céline's words can in any sense redeem his failure with Robinson; if anything they accentuate it--by showing how far the Robinson he presents falls short of his intentions.

THE DEATH OF DES PEREIRES: POSSIBILITIES FOR COMPASSION IN CÉLINE'S WORLD

Bill Ott

To attempt to analyze Courtial des Pereires' suicide in *Death on the Installment Plan* in such a way as to discover why he chose to kill himself would necessarily require a thorough examination of a very big character in an even bigger book. Rather than oversimplify this enormous topic by attempting to funnel it into term paper size, I will instead discuss how the scene in which Ferdinand discovers des Pereires' body, and the subsequent events relating to that discovery, function both in terms of the novel, and in terms of Ferdinand's development as an individual.

After Ferdinand has been informed by the postman of des Pereires' suicide, he and Irene "shake a leg" down to the foot bridge where the body has been found. Once he has examined the situation, seen that Courtial's head is now "like hash on a skewer," and noticed that Irene is virtually paralyzed by the spectacle, Ferdinand announces simply, "So then I decided to do something." In context, this declaration is perhaps one of the most crucial single statements Ferdinand makes in the course of the entire book. That is, he had decided much earlier,

before his trip to England, that involvement in any
form with other people could lead only to suffering,
both his own and others'. His attempts to hold
jobs, first as a clothing store apprentice, next as
an assistant to Gorloge the jeweler, both developed
in him the awareness that any attempted intimacy,
whether of friendship, as with André, or of sexual
passion, as with Madame Gorloge, leaves one inevitably vulnerable to deceit. It is, therefore, hardly
surprising in light of these incidents that Ferdinand decides, upon his arrival in England, that he
is through talking. The last thing he wants to know
is how to speak a new language--the more ways you
know how to talk, the more ways you have of getting
burned. Once in England, Ferdinand discovers
through his encounter with Nora that suffering seems
inevitable even where deceit does not play an active
role. At least on the surface, Ferdinand and Nora's
intimacy leads directly to Nora's suicide. While
this notion actually oversimplifies the tremendously
complex Nora-Ferdinand episode, I intend only to
suggest that in the mind of a young boy, already
convinced that intimacy breeds suffering, Nora's
suicide can not help but seem to be the result of
their relationship.

Until his meeting with des Pereires, then, Ferdinand encounters nothing to change his mind about
human affairs. While one may sense in him a growing
conviction throughout the des Pereires episode that
the price of human compassion may after all not be
too high, it is not until the suicide scene that
such a conviction is actually displayed. Throughout
his escapades with des Pereires, Ferdinand necessarily plays a subordinate role. He is the mender
of his teacher's balloon, the keeper of the shop.
While a definite camaraderie and ultimately an inti-

macy develops between the two, it is always with des
Pereires as master, Ferdinand as protege, as assistant. (Their excursions with the balloon illustrate
this pattern perfectly. While there is a definite
sense of teamwork as des Pereires lectures and as
Ferdinand picks pockets, it is always Ferdinand who
cleans up the mess while des Pereires retires to the
local pub.) What is significant, then, is that in
his relationship with des Pereires, Ferdinand's
decisions are never really his own. While he grows
more and more to like what he is doing, he still
does what he is told. In a sense, therefore, his
"apprenticeship" with des Pereires provides for
Ferdinand a kind of temporary hiatus from having to
make decisions, from deciding once and for all
whether compassion is worth the price of vulnerabil-
ity. With des Pereires' death, however, Ferdinand
can no longer accept the decisions of his teacher.
The hiatus is suddenly over. In this context,
therefore, the simple statement, "So I decided to do
something" becomes much more than it seems. What
Ferdinand has decided to do is to once again become
vulnerable, to place compassion before safety.

To be compassionate in a world of little compassion, however, is no easy task. Immediately after
informing us of Ferdinand's decision to do something, Céline makes it all too clear what he is up
against: "We tug a little harder . . . It wouldn't
come loose . . . We weren't getting anywhere . . .
It was stuck too solid . . . Especially the ears
were welded fast . . . The whole thing made a solid
block with the ice and gravel" (526). Death, in
other words, is not an idea. For Ferdinand to show
compassion both for his dead friend and for his
friend's wife, it is necessary for him to not only
acknowledge, but to deal with the hash stuck to the

gravel, with the inevitable physicality of human
life. Both Ferdinand's readiness to face the hash,
as well as the other people's repugnance of it, are
made clear in the remainder of the scene. Unable to
budge des Pereires' body, Ferdinand goes to a neigh-
boring farmhouse for help. In response to his re-
quest for assistance in carrying des Pereires, the
lady of the house, Mrs. Arton, makes it clear that
she "wouldn't think of touching it" (526). Signifi-
cantly, throughout this scene Ferdinand refers to
des Pereires as "him," Mrs. Arton as "it." What she
refuses to accept, in other words, is that the hash
on the road is human. Ferdinand's contrasting ability to address that hash as "him," on the other
hand, becomes proof of his ability to do what she
will not do, to accept the humanity of hash. Mrs.
Arton's fear not only of touching "it," but even of
seeing "it," then, becomes a fear of being forced to
admit that "it" is actually "him," that hash is
indeed human. To understand this scene fully it is
necessary to ask why she is so concerned with des
Pereires' body. After all, the whole community,
Mrs. Arton included, were dedicated to running des
Pereires out of their village. He does their job
for them, and they become petrified with fear. Why?
Obviously it is not the simple fact of des
Pereires's death that scares them. The literal
cause of their fear, as Mrs. Arton illustrates, is
the hash stuck to the gravel, the untouchable, un-
seeable "it." But, again, why? How does des
Pereires' becoming hash threaten the Mrs. Artons of
the world? The answer, I believe, comes from the
already mentioned fact that to admit that des
Pereires is hash is to admit that hash is human.
Even Mrs. Arton knows enough to realize that she,
too, like des Pereires, is human. Therefore, by

looking at des Pereires, by acknowledging his body as "him" and not "it," she inadvertently acknowledges as well that she has the potential to becomes "like hash on a skewer." Mrs. Arton, in other words, is an excellent example of the proposition that compassion requires a realization that, as Ferdinand puts it later in the novel, "We are all a bunch of entrails." That is, Mrs. Arton's lack of compassion for des Pereires, Irene, and Ferdinand, her failure to offer them her assistance, has been seen to stem directly from her reluctance to face the dead body, and in doing so, to face her own physicality. Regardless of the cruelty she must inflict in the process, Mrs. Arton will not let her illusion be shattered. She must at all costs believe that she has no entrails.

That Mrs. Arton's refusal to help Ferdinand is based finally on her unwillingness to admit her own physicality is made even more evident when, as a ploy, Ferdinand threatens to spread the rumor that she was responsible for des Pereires' death. Immediately panicked at this suggestion, Mrs. Arton agrees to let Ferdinand use her wheelbarrow to move the body. Again we must ask why. Certainly she was not actually afraid of being implicated in a crime. Even if she had murdered des Pereires, the local police force would never have chosen to believe an eccentric troublemaker (Ferdinand) rather than a hardworking housewife (Mrs. Arton). Her fear, therefore, can only stem from the consequences of Ferdinand's threat, not the threat itself. That is, were Ferdinand to make his accusation, the police would at least be obligated to question Mrs. Arton; thus bringing her out of her so efficiently barricaded cottage, and forcing her to become involved in, or at least talk about, an incident which she is

trying very hard to ignore. It would have the
effect, in other words, of rubbing her nose in the
hash. In this sense, then, her capitulation to
Ferdinand's threat becomes an inevitable outgrowth
of her need to deny her physical self.

Perhaps the most frightening aspect of this
scene is the dehumanizing effect Mrs. Arton's conception of being human has on her behavior. In
giving Ferdinand the wheelbarrow she instructs him
"to positively bring it back that same day . . .
rinsed, cleaned . . . and scrubbed with javel water"
(528). What she is saying is that Ferdinand must
not only remove, but literally rekill, any lingering
signs of des Pereires that might remain on her
wheelbarrow. The absolute absence of feeling revealed in her comments is utterly staggering. Her
fear of being forced to face the givens of being
human is so powerful as to make it possible for her
to demand that Ferdinand see to it that any sem-
blance of his closest friend be thoroughly sani-
tized, thoroughly sterilized out of existence. Even
the vision of the dead man's wife, hovering over her
husband's body and screaming hysterically, does not
manage to crack the armor that, in keeping Mrs.
Arton from her entrails, keeps her as well from the
power to feel. It is significant that at this point
in the scene Ferdinand describes the Artons as "sav-
ages." His description is wonderfully appropriate.
It is not, as some would surely contend, the hyster-
ical, shabbily dressed Irene and the hash stuck to
the gravel which suggest savagery. On the contrary,
Ferdinand's epithet is more rightfully deserved by
the Artons who, in failing to acknowledge their own
humanness, are incapable of humanity to others. In
a world of disinfected wheelbarrows, Céline seems to

be saying, the possibilities for compassion are necessarily limited.

If Mrs. Arton's demands concerning the wheelbarrow cause us to doubt whether or not compassion is achievable in this world, then Ferdinand's behavior throughout this scene serves to offset Mrs. Arton, and to continually rekindle our hopes. Perhaps the clearest statement of Ferdinand's capacity for compassion occurs earlier in the scene while he is still trying to solicit Mrs. Arton's aid. After unsuccessfully pleading with her, Ferdinand finally becomes furious and exclaims:

> What are you afraid of? Good God, it's
> not a dog . . . he hasn't got rabies . . .
> It's not a calf . . . he hasn't got hoof-
> and-mouth disease . . . He's killed him-
> self and that's that . . . He was perfect-
> ly healthy . . . He hasn't got the glan-
> ders . . . The least we can to is shelter
> him in the barn for awhile . . . till they
> can come and take him away . . . Before
> the traffic starts up . . . They'll run
> him over. . . . (527)

What Ferdinand has said is simply that a man has died. "He's killed himself and that's that"; so seemingly obvious a notion, yet so very difficult for most people to let themselves understand. Men become hash; even those without the glanders. What so infuriates Ferdinand, in other words, is Mrs. Arton's insistence that somehow a mutilated corpse must have hoof-and-mouth disease, or at the very least must be treated as if it did; that nothing which looked like hash could possible be the remains of a perfectly healthy man. Ferdinand's refusal to

dehumanize his friend, whether alive and formed or
dead and deformed, is again evident by his continuing to address des Pereires as "him." In addition,
Ferdinand's concern with the possibility of the
corpse being run over is as indicative of his capacity for feeling as was Mrs. Arton's ultimatum about
the wheelbarrow indicative of her absence of feeling. That is, certainly no amount of traffic could
deform des Pereires' corpse any more than it is
already deformed. Ferdinand simply does not want
anything or anyone running over his friend, even if
it can no longer do des Pereires any damage. Inter-
estingly, this scene, as well as a later incident
where Irene makes a pillow to place under what is
left of des Pereires' head, bear striking similarity
to the segment in Kafka's "The Metamorphosis" where
Gregor's mother attempts to convince Grete to leave
the furniture in Gregor's room. In all three cases,
of course, the utilitarian value of the action under
consideration is absolutely nil. The gestures--
Ferdinand wanting to move des Pereires out of the
road, Irene giving her husband the pillow he no
longer needs, and Gregor's mother wanting to leave
in place the now useless furniture--are all infinitely humanizing, however, as they reflect a continuing sense of compassion for the individual,
regardless of whether he has become a "placenta," or
in Kafka, a dung beetle. It becomes evident, therefore, through both Ferdinand's violent reaction to
Mrs. Arton's coldness and through his desire to move
des Pereires out of the road, that he is indeed
capable of doing the "something" he set out to do
when he first saw his friend's body. While the fact
of des Pereires' suicide is one of the novel's
darker moments, then, Ferdinand's reaction to it is
one of the brighter moments. The fact that later in

the book Ferdinand actually says "we are all a bunch of entrails" can come as no surprise after this reaction. Without the essential knowledge of what it means to be human which that statement reflects, it would have been impossible for Ferdinand to do what he does and say what he says in this scene. That is, in his declaration that des Pereires was perfectly healthy before he shot himself, Ferdinand freely acknowledges what Mrs. Arton can never acknowledge, that he, being also healthy, is no different from des Pereires; that he too is potentially hash. As we have noted that Mrs. Arton's lack of feeling stems from her refusal to accept her own humanness, so we see that Ferdinand and Irene's abundance of feeling stem from their willingness to accept that same humanness. What Céline suggests in this scene through Ferdinand and Irene, and by contrast through Mrs. Arton, then, is that it is finally possible to get around the disinfected wheelbarrows; that the general absence of compassion in the world does not necessarily make it impossible for the individual to be compassionate himself.

As Ferdinand and Irene are soon to discover, the fact that it is possible for some individuals to have feelings in an unfeeling world does not mean that those individuals will not find themselves encountering continual harassment. Nearing the end of their four mile trek with des Pereires' body delicately balanced in Mrs. Arton's precious wheelbarrow, Ferdinand notices that the police are already waiting for them. When they arrive, the sergeant announces that in addition to suspicion of murder, they have committed a felony by moving the body. What Ferdinand and Irene are forced to confront in the form of the police, in other words, is nothing more than an institutionalized and more powerful Mrs. Arton. It stands to reason that a society of Mrs. Artons, most of whom are equally emphatic in their refusal to accept their own humanness, would develop institutions designed to protect their common illusions. To do its job properly, of course, it becomes necessary for the institution doing the protecting to somehow stifle any individual who either directly or indirectly threatens the stability of the mass illusions. Such is certainly the role of the police in their investigation of des Pereires' suicide. That is, what really bothers the investigating officers is not that des Pereires has killed himself, but rather that Ferdinand and Irene have touched the corpse. The sergeant points out sternly that because the body was moved he will be unable to make out his report. It is apparent, in other words, that the legal and bureaucratic machinery in operation here is devised so that the desired response to the presence of a corpse is Mrs. Arton's: ignore "it" until someone whose job it is to do such things can get rid of "it." Had Ferdinand left des Pereires stuck to the cement and in the way of the traffic he would have obeyed the law. It is the function of the police in this novel, then, to help the Mrs. Artons barricade themselves from their humanness. By being able to accept that humanness, and thus to act toward des Pereires with compassion, Ferdinand has inadvertently threatened to contaminate with the smell of human hash the sterilized shells in which the Mrs. Artons live. To pose such a threat is to be a criminal. It is inevitable, therefore, that the law, in protecting Mrs. Arton, will always stand in the way of human feeling. Finally, Céline tells us, to feel compassion is to be an outlaw.

The day and a half following des Pereires' death becomes in the novel a detailed examination of the price one is required to pay for compassion. Ferdinand and Irene are subjected not only to the direct police investigation, but to the circus atmosphere which that investigation creates. Their farm becomes a kind of tourist attraction, with people lining the fences and overflowing into the garden in hopes of getting a glimpse of the "murderers." It is significant that it is those same villagers who, like Mrs. Arton, were nowhere to be found when Ferdinand was attempting to move des Pereires, who are now stampeding to get a look at the corpse, or at least at the presumed slayers. The difference, of course, is the presence of the police, the implication that crimes have been committed. While helping clean up the hash was unthinkable, the prospect of gathering round to watch Ferdinand and Irene suffer is thoroughly titillating. Ferdinand comments particularly on the "whole slew of grandmothers . . . right against our windows . . . They fastened onto the shutters . . . They croaked louder than anybody else" (564). What is happening in this scene is what D. H. Lawrence has described as our fascination with "murder, suicide, and rape." In the context of the novel, thrills have become a substitute for emotions, for feelings. What Céline is saying by implication here is that all men must have some source of emotional life. If the expression of human feeling is made impossible by the refusal to accept one's humanness, the vicarious experience of substitute sources of emotion becomes necessary. Thrilling at des Pereires' murder, therefore, is ironically the result of being unable to come to terms with his, and ultimately with one's own, entrails. That the grandmothers lead the charge is only natural when one remembers that it is they who need thrills the most. After all, their ability to feel has been dead (or at least dulled) longer than that of their children or their grandchildren.

This process by which feeling is killed in men, and which leads ultimately to thrill-craving, is illustrated perfectly in another event which takes place during this two-day nightmare. When the police come to investigate, they find the remnants of des Pereires' "boarding school"—a group of teenagers who in the course of their stay on the farm have become totally self-sufficient, totally independent individualists, not to mention efficient thieves. Naturally, the police call in an ever ready social worker who sees to it that the group is deposited in a welfare home. What is significant about the incident is Ferdinand's futile attempts to explain to the kids what is happening. They simply can not understand. The idea of being forced to do anything by an absolute stranger is totally incomprehensible to them. They decide it must be a gag. As Ferdinand observes, "They weren't used to being treated like kids anymore . . . They were too emancipated . . . They'd forgotten about obedience and those kinds of things" (537). What has happened is that des Pereires and Ferdinand have ironically done exactly what they convinced the kids' parents they would do, e.g., create a "new race." Having grown up in an environment over which the Mrs. Artons and her institutionalized counterparts (police departments, schools, and welfare agencies) have no control, the kids are able intuitively to accept their humanness. This acceptance is evident, for example, when Ferdinand notes that even seeing "the old man with his face blown off" does not convince them they they are being taken away; that, as Ferdinand puts it, "the jig is up." For the kids, in other words, the sight of des Pereires' body does not inevitably mean what Ferdinand knows it to mean, *e.g.*, police, investigations, "sight-seers," and all the other forms of institutional harassment. On the contrary, for Dudule and the rest of the remaining nine "brats," des Pereires' corpse means only what Ferdinand earlier tried in vain to make it mean for Mrs. Arton: "He's shot himself and that's that." While the kids know and are able to deal with the fact that men become entrails, they are unable to even comprehend the world of disinfected wheelbarrows. In addition to their reaction to des Pereires, the ability of the kids to accept their humanness is evident by their idea of a good time. That is, some of the novel's most contented moments occur when the more ingenious and dexterous of the kids have managed to steal enough food to make possible an enormous feast. At these feasts, the kids, Ferdinand, des Pereires, and Irene all literally gorge themselves, retire to the corners to vomit, and gorge themselves some more. What is remarkable about these banquets is not the ravenous hunger of the participants (all of whom, after all, have been near starvation), but rather the joyous abandon with which they appease that hunger. Totally at ease with their bodies, they happily eat and vomit at will, enjoying the latter because it makes possible the former. Such abandon-ment would certainly not be possible in formal soci-ety, for in that setting vomit is only just this side of "hash."

Because the "brats," as Ferdinand likes to call them, have so completely managed to avoid constric-tions of any kind, it becomes all the more dismaying when the social worker finally does catch up with them, when they are at last made to "fall in." What Céline is doing here, it seems to me, is asserting that absolute escape from the Mrs. Artons, from those who would sterilize out of existence our humanity and our compassion, is inevitably impossible. If compassion is achievable, as it is for Ferdinand, it must be so in spite of, and not in the absence of, the dehumanizing forces which surround us. The cops, or in the kids' case, the social workers, are always right around the bend. Just as Ferdinand and Irene lugged des Pereires' body for miles only to find the police waiting for them when they finally made it home, so the nine kids are given the rare opportunity to become feeling human beings only to be eventually snared in the social worker's institutionalized net. Ferdinand knows only too well what will happen to them. As the social worker leads them off to the welfare office, he says flatly:

> Balls! Balls! I knew the score . . .
> Getting older is a crummy trick . . . Kids
> are like years, you never see them again.
> We locked up Dudule's dog with the old
> bag. The two of them cried together. He
> yammered the hardest. That day, honestly,
> take it from me, was one of the rottenest
> in my whole life. Balls! (539)

The "crummy trick" to which Ferdinand alludes is illustrated perfectly by what has happened to the kids. Not only does getting older mean coming closer to actual death, it means as well the process by which our capacity to feel is slowly but efficiently destroyed. The kids have just begun the journey on which this destruction process is to be initiated. As Ferdinand points out, you never see them again. Never again will any of the brats have the power to feel, to be human, which they now possess. That some of them may somehow manage to survive, as Ferdinand has done, can only be partially comforting at best. What Ferdinand is telling us in this passage is that many of those kids have begun an inevitable process which leads first to Mrs. Arton, and ultimately to the thrill-craving grandmothers, to what Lawrence foresaw as the total atrophy of the feelings. In this context, Céline's title becomes a working metaphor which captures perfectly the essence of Ferdinand's "crummy trick." That is, for most people, living is a process through which one gradually, as if on installments, loses his power to feel. As living without the power to feel becomes a kind of death, it follows that life becomes in effect "death on the installment plan." Ferdinand has given us the only satisfactory response to this process: "Balls."

From the discovery of des Pereires' body to the departure of the kids, then, Céline has presented in microcosmic form a picture of what it means to express compassion in the world as he finds it. With Ferdinand's initial declaration to "do something" the stage is set for a kind of ultimate confrontation between a compassionate individual and a compassionless world. The outcome of that confrontation is inevitably a draw. While Ferdinand proves that the individual is at least still capable of feelings, it also becomes evident that everything possible will be done to limit his capacity to feel, or at least to subject him to continual harassment. Perhaps the best sense of what is left for the individual comes from Ferdinand's reflections on saying goodbye to Irene. He says: "We'd been sharing the bad luck for a long time now . . . This time it had really laid us out . . . That was pretty well to be expected . . . There wasn't much more to say" (562). While institutionalized un-feeling has made bad luck "pretty much to be expected," in other words, it has not been able to keep individuals from sharing that bad luck with other individuals. Céline contends ultimately that as long as we can continue to make this sharing process possible by effectively hiding from the Mrs. Artons and the police and the social workers, we will continue to be able to live.

"POSSIBILITIES FOR COMPASSION":
AN ALTERNATIVE READING

John Leeds

It is so difficult to say anything definitive about Céline. It is difficult because Céline arranged it that way. In saying that "to feel compassion is to be an outlaw," Bill Ott succumbs naturally, excusably, to the critical impulse toward definition. But I think that Céline was aware, above all, of the fluidity of life, of life's constantly remaining one step beyond the grasp of rational formulation.

"Great instinctive disorder is the father of fertile thoughts" yells Courtial, in the midst of a two-page diatribe which is as close as Céline comes in either *Death on the Installment Plan* or *Journey to the End of Night* to an out-and-out statement of novelistic theory. In pursuit of great instinctive disorder Céline denies himself the more conventional means of art. The foremost of these is plot. Neither *Death* nor *Journey* has, properly speaking, a plot. Plot is an aesthetic imposition upon life, meant to seduce the reader into thinking that life points in one philosophic direction or another. That device is unacceptable to Céline. He gives us, rather, a series of episodes connected the way such

125

episodes actually are in life, by circumstance and chance.

Along with plot, Céline abandons the notion that there is any sort of underlying order, moral or rational, to life. Avoiding at all times what is specious and presupposed, he builds his novels solely on the perceptions of the young man Ferdinand. Céline is able to see the world because he is not interested in the excavation of meaning. He is interested in the intersection of two grand disorders—the individual personality and the life of the race. Even the most abstract passages in *Journey* are the temporary assertions of a single personality. This disorder is a form of emancipation.

What I am getting at is that I think Ott's analysis proceeds from a morally absolute, typically un-Célinian, sort of stance. To say that "institutionalized un-feeling has made bad luck 'pretty much to be expected'" is to establish a simple one-way causal connection, uncharacteristic of Céline, and certainly never so stated by Ferdinand. Bad luck is the condition of Ferdinand's life, a given, without beginning or end. There is nothing "behind" it. It would be more true, I think, to say that bad luck gives rise to institutionalized un-feeling, than the other way around.

I sympathize with the desire to read this way, to see a "compassionate outlaw" doing battle with bureaucratic insensitivity. It is a very unpleasant thing which Céline does to us, keeping us constantly off balance, granting us no dry moral ground on which to stand. The temptation is therefore to adopt the moral stance which seems closest to what Céline is getting at. But as soon as one does that, the surface is cracked, the gaze broken, the point lost. Ott says that "the stage is set for a kind of

126

ultimate confrontation between a compassionate individual and a compassionless world." I find that
romantic and inaccurate. Trotsky is much more to
the point in his discussion of the "organic" nature
of the corruption which Céline exposes: "In the web
of connections, favors, mediations, masked semi-
bribes, there are thousands of transitional forms
between civic virtue and capital crime." Just so,
there are thousands of transitional forms between
complete compassion and utter inhumanity. It is
impossible to exist in the culture without being
implicated, at various times to various degrees, in
the corruption. Corruption is the life-blood of the
culture. Ott concedes that compassion will not be
achieved "in the absence of . . . the dehumanizing
forces which surround us," and yet continues to
speak of "effectively hiding from the Mrs. Artons."
There is an artificial good-guy bad-guyism at work
here, whereas Céline's books are charged with the
ambiguity of life.

Céline's most overtly compassionate characters
and his most clearly drawn outlaws are not, in fact,
one and the same. Uncle Edouard, the angel of
Ferdinand's youth, "understood these sensitive
things perfectly . . . He didn't talk about them,
that's all . . . Uncle Edouard wasn't only good at
machinery . . . That would be the wrong idea . . .
He was very sensitive, there's no denying it." But
he is an outlaw in no sense of the word. Uncle
Edouard is an entrepreneur, thoroughly modern, conventional in his habits, in love with technology.
Céline makes the point explicitly in what I think
are the most ravishing few pages in either novel.
In the last three pages of the Topo section, he
describes a man of stunning compassion, but one we
have seen kicking his subordinates for no reason and

stealing their pay with tobacco. "And only yesterday I hadn't taken much account of Alcide, I had
even despised him a little." Far from being an
outlaw, Alcide is the author of "the Alcide system
proper . . . up-to-date and hypocritical." Far from
fleeing the institution, he is seeking to extend his
stay in it twice as long as necessary. "Suddenly he
slept, with the candle burning. In the end I got up
to study his features by its light. He slept like
anybody might. He looked quite ordinary. It
wouldn't be a bad idea if there were something to
distinguish good men from bad." But there can be no
such thing because the traits of both appear in
both.

Robinson, on the other hand, the type of the
outlaw, shows nothing in the way of compassion.
Courtial, likewise an outlaw, is a hard-hearted
scoundrel in every way but two: first, he has imagination, and second, he develops a profound fondness
for Ferdinand. As I have said before, Ferdinand's
vision and character are the sole points of reference in *Death* and *Journey*. I do not agree that
Courtial functions as a general beacon of hope or
humanity. The sympathy with which he is treated is
the result of his intimacy with Ferdinand. Apart
from that he might have been dealt with quite differently indeed.

As for Ferdinand himself, there are in *Death* and
Journey any number of occasions at which he displays
either compassion or coldness. I do not think that
scraping Courtial's body off the road has anything
in particular to do with compassion. Ferdinand has
developed a strong sense of what needs to be done
and how to go about it. But whether or not that act
is symbolic of a larger compassion is not my point.
I have maintained that Ferdinand's feelings and

perceptions are the only sources of information in these two books. And I have maintained that certain kinds of moral distinctions do not square with Céline's sense of the fluidity of life. It remains to be seen how that fluidity proceeds from Ferdinand's character, from Ferdinand's perception of himself.

I cannot agree that self-hatred or self-disgust is merely a critical projection on Céline's writing. I think, on the contrary, that the theme of self-hatred is developed more thoroughly and explicitly than any other in *Death* and *Journey*. How, in fact, could it be otherwise? As doggedly as he drags each of the world's lies into the light, Céline could not fail to expose the most pernicious lie, the lie of one's own worthlessness. To claim that self-hatred is not a major element in the novels is to underestimate Céline's courage and to ignore massive textual evidence.

Death on the Installment Plan is to a great extent the history of Ferdinand's being taught to hate himself. This, in its simplest form, is what his parents, backed by the Lavelongues and Gorloges, tell Ferdinand throughout the book. And as any child who has had his worthlessness impressed upon him again and again might, Ferdinand succumbs. But he is saved by a natural emotional toughness, and by the mitigating influence of Caroline, Edouard, Courtial and a number of minor characters. Ferdinand's silence, which is of such paramount importance in the English section of *Death*, is just as much an expression of his sense of his own undesirability as it is a means of avoiding personal contact. Or, to put it better, Ferdinand's desire to avoid personal contact is equal parts a loathing for the self and a loathing for the other.

I think, next to Ferdinand, that Nora is the
most important character in the novel. She is the
first person in Ferdinand's life who needs him emotionally. But, having sold himself on his own rhetoric of non-response, Ferdinand is unable to help
her. We cannot know why she is dying of loneliness,
because Ferdinand cannot know. But, when she dies,
Ferdinand comes face to face with the wages of his
own insensitivity. It is then, not as Ott maintains, on the road with Courtial, that Ferdinand
chooses compassion. As awful as the self-loathing
of this child may be, the responsibility of having
sealed off his own heart is more awful still.

It is extraordinary, and significant, that after
his return from England Ferdinand never once, explicitly, reflects on Nora. I think that the last
three-hundred pages of *Death* are one long, unac-
knowledged meditation on her death. The form of
Ferdinand's awakened sensitivity is his willingness
to support a personality (Courtial's) in the process
of disintegration. His assumption of practical
responsibility for Courtial, his open confession of
self-loathing, and his emergent manhood are of a
piece. The suicide of Courtial is a doubling of
Nora's suicide which allows us to see how far the
child has come from the one to the other. In the
wake of Courtial's suicide Ferdinand tells his uncle
"I'm no good . . . I'm a fraud . . . I only made
everybody unhappy!" His self-hatred is on his lips
and his heart is open, because he learned once and
finally, in England, not to close it.

The theme of self-hatred is dealt with in the
most direct language in countless passages of *Journey to the End of the Night*. "As you grow uglier
and uglier and more repulsive, playing this game as
you grow old, you can't even conceal your unhappi-

ness any longer, your failure; and in the end your face has become only an ugly expression which takes twenty, thirty or more years to come up from your stomach onto your face." After learning of Alcide's niece, Bardamu calls himself "a useless ass, loutish and vain." In New York he is convinced of his own "personal emptiness," and tells himself "You really have no goodness in you." Again, Bardamu's brutality toward Lola is as much an expression of self-loathing as loathing of the other. To what degree Céline the writer hates himself is absolutely not to the point. The point is that there is no artificial moral distinction between Ferdinand and the rest of the world, no compassionate outlaw marked off with a star on his forehead. He is of course capable of compassion, but always Ferdinand's complicity in the organic corruption which surrounds him is laid before us in the clearest terms.

There is within Ferdinand's character a great dialectic tension between self-disgust and world-disgust--that is as close to a definitive statement as I can make about these books. This tension is at the heart of Céline's vision and technique. The two halves of the vision are put beautifully in *Journey to the End of the Night*: "(. . .) when one's weak, the thing that gives one strength is stripping those one fears of the slightest prestige that one may still tend to accord them. One must teach oneself to see them as they are, as worse than they are, that is; one should look at them from all points of view. This detaches you, sets you free and is much more of a protection than you can possibly imagine. It gives you another self, so that there are two of you together" (59). Later in the book, Céline says that "All that you need to do, and what you always need, is to take a very careful look into your own heart and see what you yourself have sunk to" (209). Trotsky, who sees Céline with great clarity, acknowledges the two urges when he speaks of Céline as wanting "to tear away the prestige from everything that frightens and oppresses him," and as "the moralist . . . repelled by his own image." Céline did both, was both, at the same time, naturally, passionately, a genius.

THREE CONTRIBUTIONS TO THE READING
OF CÉLINE

Gerald J. Butler

1. THE FEELING FOR WOMEN IN CÉLINE AND HIS AMERICAN
   IMITATORS

When Céline's Ferdinand arrives in New York, he
notices something that strikes him as peculiar about
the crowds. "The sexes seemed to stay on different
sides of the street. The women looked only at the
shopwindows, their whole attention was taken by
handbags, scarves, and little silk doodads, displayed very little at a time, but with precision and
authority. You didn't see many old people in that
crowd. Not many couples either."[1] There is no
communication between the sexes, but down below, in
the public toilet, "Men among men," we see "free-
and-easy intimacy" and "a joyous shitting communism"
(169). We have seen this situation one way or
another many times in American literature. And
Céline's American imitators or "counterparts" like
Henry Miller or Jack Kerouac have not imitated Céline in his fictional treatment of women. As can be
seen by a comparison of *Tropic of Cancer* and *On the
Road* with *Journey to the End of the Night*, women for
Miller and Kerouac have been kept on the opposite

side of the street. It is as if they have not even seen women, intent as they both are on some presumably higher illumination than women can give them.

There really are no fully characterized women in Miller's book, though there are one or two caricatures, like the Russian "princess." For the most part, the women that Henry moves among and that he and his friends couple with almost at random are just, as he calls them, "cunts," and finally even less than that--*things*--

> I took a look around but didn't see anything worth while. What I wanted was something fresh and unused--something from Alaska or the Virgin Islands. A clean fresh pelt with a natural fragrance to it. Needless to say, there wasn't anything like that walking about. I wasn't terribly disappointed. I didn't give a fuck whether I found anything or not. . . .[2]

His wife, Mona, is mentioned by name throughout the book, but aside from one description of her sleeping with him in Paris, in which the most striking fact given is that her hair is "crawling" with bedbugs (18), and in spite of occasional protestations of how Henry loved her, including his assertion that "For seven years I went about, day and night, with only one thing on my mind--her" (160), there is little more of her in the book than any of the other "cunts." Nor is Tania, to whom he says he is "singing" (2), much more of a tangible presence in the novel than Mona. Certainly no woman in the novel *matters* very much to Henry in terms of his actions or feelings or thoughts. "That's what I tell every cunt I grab hold of," he says "--*leaving in the morning!*" (18) [Miller's emphasis]. Whores are "a cluster of vultures who croaked and flapped their dirty wings, who reached out with sharp talons and plucked you into a doorway" (38). Or they are "barnacles" (118). His vision of most if not all women does not seem very different from that of his friend Carl, who decides "It's less annoying to masturbate" (263), or Van Norden, who tells him "'I'm actually beginning to hate cunt!'" (93).

Van Norden tells Henry how he once trained a flashlight on the genitals of a woman, saying "it looked ghastly," "just a crack there between the legs," so that in sexual desire "you get all burned up about nothing . . . about a crack with hair on it, or without hair" (216). Van Norden says it's better to read a book because "a cunt, it's just sheer loss of time" (127). But Henry also peers into the female genitals to come to similar conclusions, though couched in mystical language: "When I look down into this fucked-out cunt of a whore I feel the whole world beneath me, a world tottering and crumbling, a world used up and polished like a leper's skull" (224). In fact, although he goes on to suggest that it is the duty of the creative "desperate spirit" to fecundate this hole, he calls it "the ugly gash, the wound that never heals," "the open wound," "the festering obscene horror" (225). On the rare occasions that "sex" is rhapsodized in this book, it is seen as an abstraction, divorced from any particular woman; but ultimately, even as abstraction, "cunt" is a terrible obscenity--with, at most, a certain terrible fascination.

What does Henry really love? Not women, not even "sex," but food, and views of places, especially of parts of Paris, and, in spite of his disclaimer at the beginning, Art. At the beginning, he calls his book "a gob of spit in the face of Art" (2), but this assertion hardly explains the continuous admiring references to art and literature, writers and artists, including a four page paean to Matisse (146-150). In fact, the novel does not spit on Art or any of the other usual so-called "higher" things; it really affirms all the old spiritualities --including feeling wonderful about being in Paris, that center of the arts--and reserves its gob of spit for the traditional targets: the body, women, sexual experience.

In other words, what Miller is expressing is the usual call to castigate the flesh--especially the flesh of women--and exalt the things of the spirit. Karl Shapiro, in his introduction to the novel, calls Miller "a holy man . . . Gandhi with a penis" and mentions one of Miller's own essays that ends with a quote from Hindu scripture: "Evil does not exist" (xiv). Indeed, as Shapiro points out, quoting Orwell who contrasted Miller to Céline, Miller finally calls for "acceptance" (x).

In fact, Henry, the alcohol-sodden mystic, the rhapsodizer of Paris and Matisse, is not Ferdinand, but in his ultimate "acceptance" is in direct line to Jack Kerouac and Beat "saintliness." It is significant that Miller wrote an admiring introduction to Kerouac's *The Subterraneans*, and what Shapiro calls Miller's "beautiful clown story"--"The Smile at the Foot of the Ladder"--gives expression to what could well be Kerouacian "Beatitude": "joy is like a river, it flows ceaselessly. It seems to me that this is the message which the clown is trying to convey to us. . . . Here and there . . . we meet with individuals who are untouched, unsullied by the common grief. They are not heartless individuals, far from it! They are emancipated beings. . . . We

say of them that they have died to the world. They
live in the moment, fully, and the radiance which
emanates from them is a perpetual song of joy"
(xxvi-xxvii).

So, presumably, are we to see Dean Moriarty in
On the Road. Dean is "a new kind of American
saint."[3] He tells Sal about God. "These were the
first days of his mysticism, which would lead to the
strange, ragged, W. C. Fields saintliness of his
later days" (121). And this clownish saintliness is
just as "accepting" (and unlike Céline) as Miller.
About one of Dean's disciples Sal says, "He began to
learn 'Yes!' to everything, just like Dean at this
time . . ." (126). And when his disciples, spoken
for by Galatea Dunkel, turn hostile to Dean in San
Francisco, Kerouac wants you to see they are turning
against their Christ, "the HOLY GOOF." "He was
BEAT--the root, the soul of Beatific" (193-195).

And just as "saintliness" pervades both Miller
and Kerouac, they share a common attitude towards
women. Where Miller says "cunt," Kerouac says
"girl," but in context they mean pretty much the
same thing, except that Miller's word is the more
honest of the two. And Miller is not afraid to
express his horrors and disgusts with sexuality, so
that we can at least partly understand his attitude
towards women, whereas we have to accept what Sal
and Dean do without questioning why they do it--
especially the saint Dean--why they must go from
woman to woman in such a rush. But since as "girls"
they aren't even "cunts" it isn't always easy to
know why they bother at all. So much of Dean's
sexual enthusiasm seems phoney, rhetorical:

He darted the car and looked in every
direction for girls. "Look at *her!*" The

air was so sweet in New Orleans it seemed
to come in soft bandannas; and you could
smell the river and really smell the people, and mud, and molasses, and every kind
of tropical exhalation with your nose
suddenly removed from the dry ices of a
Northern winter. We bounced in our seats.
"And dig her!" yelled Dean, pointing at
another woman. "Oh, I love, love women!
I think women are wonderful! I love wom-
en!" He spat out the window; he groaned;
he clutched his head. Great beads of
sweat fell from his forehead from pure
excitement and exhaustion. (140)

What's the difference in this passage between a
glimpse of a woman and a smell of molasses? And can
you really break into a sweat over a smell of molasses? Dean's pursuit of women seems such a part of
his saintly role, such a show that he is putting on
for the benefit of his disciples--and Kerouac does
not seem to understand why, as in the scene in San
Francisco, his disciples finally are not grateful
for the enlightenment their saint has brought them,
"for the sexuality and the life he had helped bring
into being" (194). Nor is there any irony when
Kerouac describes Sal's attempt at a saintly sexual
act:

Then I went to meet Rita Bettencourt
and took her back to the apartment. I got
her in my bedroom after a long talk in the
dark of the front room. She was a nice
little girl, simple and true, and tremendously frightened of sex. I told her it
was beautiful. I wanted to prove this to

her. She let me prove it, but I was too
impatient and proved nothing. She sighed
in the dark. . . . (57)

Truthfully, there does not seem to be the degree of
desire for the woman that even Henry could feel.
What happens seems less than a Miller "lay," and
Sal's--and Kerouac's--"I told her it was beautiful"
--just serves to hide the truth.

The trouble, as Wayne Burns has pointed out, is
that Kerouac can never see that there is no real
difference between the cold, dead, empty way of life
he is fleeing and the way of life he is affirming.
Both the Quiet American and the hipster searching
for kicks are trying to cover up, in what amounts to
only a difference of style, the deadness of their
lives. They live in a society, Burns explains,
which from Coca Cola ads to sex education tells them
to be "uninhibited" but when they respond to "these
ever-present titillations" makes them feel "delin-
quent if not perverted." And the result is the
deadening of their feelings altogether. The closest
Kerouac comes, Burns says, to seeing "the nullity of
the beatness . . . in meaningful perspective against
the larger nullity of Madison Avenue culture" is his
presentation of Sal's affair with Teresa. "In context, however, the sequence comes to very little.
Kerouac cannot see the full implication of its poignancy, or, if he does, he cannot express it. He
fails to see that Sal cannot love Teresa, or any
woman, or man, not even Dean Moriarty."[4] And certainly we cannot take seriously the ending where Sal
is supposed to have found the girl of his dreams in
the one who invites him up for a cup of hot choco-
late--"So I went up and there she was, the girl with
the pure and innocent dear eyes I had always

139

searched for and for so long. We agreed to love each other madly" (306). This is mere rhetorical assertion: it even sounds like parody.

It is not people, women in particular, that Kerouac can love; just like Miller, he wants something that tradition calls "higher" than sexual experience or human relationships. It is *after* Marylou dumps Sal in San Francisco and he is all alone that he reaches "the point of ecstasy that I always wanted to reach" in a mystical experience where he sees "the potent and inconceivable radiances shining in bright Mind Essence" (193). What Scott Donaldson in his introduction to the novel calls Kerouac's transcendentalism linking him to Thoreau and Whitman (xii) and thus to what we can call the whole "great tradition" of American literature and culture, reduces human beings, as individuals, to something pretty small against the Oversoul or All or whatever it may be called, just as the constant driving away from people reduces them to specks in the Void.

What is that feeling when you're driving away from people and they recede on the plain till you see their specks disappearing?--it's the too-huge world vaulting us, and it's good-by. But we lean forward to the next crazy venture beneath the skies. (156)

When they leave Tim Grey, Sal watches him grow "smaller and smaller . . . till there was nothing but a growing absence in space and the space was the eastward view towards Kansas that led all the way back to my home in Atlantis" (267-268). The method of escape from the routine of the Quiet American is, at the same time, a way of killing people off and one's feelings for them. It is speck-making, a sort of mystical experience that at the same time affirms the great empty spaces and accepts, glorifies and glamorizes "American" as unabashedly--perhaps more so--as a patriotic real estate salesman might with a few drinks in him or when making a sale. Or as Henry Miller does with Paris and Matisse.

In other words, the affirmation in Kerouac and Miller is not only another form of American "positive thinking" but also the very cause of their inability to characterize women and present sexual experience in any way but pornographically or, worse, sentimentally. It is as if in these writers vague, emotionally-charged entities like "America" or "Paris" or "Art" or, finally, "God" take over all the feeling, all the Eros, that belongs to individual human beings. As Burns wrote about *The Dharma Bums* while Kerouac was still alive, "Suburbanites in sneakers are suburbanites still, and so long as Kerouac remains blind to this elemental fact, he can never escape from his Ry-Krisp sentimentalities." In order to do so, he would have to "develop a vision of man and experience comparable to that of his chosen master, Céline."[5] The same prescription could have been given to Miller--or to J. D. Salinger or Kurt Vonnegut--though it could only have fallen on deaf ears, certainly in the case of the last one. For the vision of humanity and experience that Céline's American "counterparts" developed was never anything more than a mystical affirmation that ultimately denies both humanity and experience. It is blindness and deadness together.

So that it would have been better for Julia Kristeva, in her recent book *Powers of Horror*, to have chosen Miller or, under his posturing, Kerouac,

141

rather than Céline to represent the modern writer
who makes works that resemble primitive religious
rituals which function, as she puts it in her Lacan-
ian-pschoanalytic terms, "to ward off the subject's
fear of his very own identity sinking irretrievably
into the mother"--his fear of woman, of sexual experience.[6] For Miller and Kerouac and perhaps many of
the modern writers she cites, but not for Céline,
"That other sex, the feminine, becomes synonymous
with a radical evil that is to be suppressed" (70).
And a Miller or a Kerouac can be seen as a mystic
who, unlike the orthodox, "grants himself the fath-
omless depravity" of what he believes to be "sin" so
that "his holiness never ceases to appear to him as
fringed by sin" (126). But Céline does not believe
in "sin," nor is the feminine to him an evil to be
suppressed. For it is *not* true, as Kristeva claims
in her chapter on Céline, "Females Who Can Wreck the
Infinite" (157-173), that his fiction shows all
women as of only two kinds: desexualized and de-
lightful on the one hand and sexual and terrifying
on the other, so that beauty is what wards off the
sexual. In *Journey to the End of the Night*, an
immediate example that controverts her notion is
that of the nurse Sophie, who appears towards the
end of the book. She is both sexual and, in her
sexuality, a miracle of delight for Ferdinand. For
Céline sees well beyond those traditional categori-
zations that Freud called the result of our "psychi-
cal impotence." To miss this fact, to lump Céline
with Artaud or Miller or those whom Kristeva calls
writers of "abjection" (the other side of whose
coin, it goes without saying, is the sublime, the
sacred, the mystical), is to be reading the cliché
of Céline and not what he actually wrote--the same
cliché, really, that his detractors have promulgated

since *Journey* was published: Céline the one disgusted with all human life, Céline the enemy of man,
Céline the man of hate. He should not be grouped
with modern writers of "abjection," but with the
greatest writers of the past, with Balzac, Dickens,
and Tolstoy. And what links him to these writers is
his feeling for women and his sense of the meaning
and significance of relationships with women.

In *Journey*, but especially in his later novels,
there are many women mentioned who are other than
sexual partners of the protagonist and his male
acquaintance, many more than in *Tropic of Cancer* or
On the Road. But Lola, Musyne, Molly, Tania, Madelon, Sophia, all of whom have had sexual relations
with Ferdinand, are especially significant to all
that happens in the novel, unlike the Monas and
Tanias and Marylous and Camilles of Miller and Kerouac. Very often, it is what happens to Ferdinand
with them that determines what he comes to realize
or what he does next--perhaps they more than anything else. And Céline presents even Lola and
Musyne with sympathy and understanding.

Thus, although Lola, the American girl he meets
when he is a young soldier in the First World War,
chills towards him after he tells her he has no
patriotic enthusiasm (54), he has always been aware
of her absurd, bellicose notions and understood and
forgiven them in her. "Lola's heart was tender,
weak, and enthusiastic. Her body was sweet, it was
adorable, so what could I do but take her altogether
as she was? Lola was a good kid all right . . ."
(40). He understands that she is, as it were, what
Ferdinand called himself before he actually went to
the battlefield--a "virgin in horror" (9). So he
can't believe in her "soul." He can believe in her
body. In spite of the amused tone of this passage,

Ferdinand has had what Céline regards as a genuine revelation:

> To me her body was a joy without end. I never wearied of exploring that American body. I have to admit that I was a terrible lecher. I still am.
>
> And I formed the pleasant and fortifying conviction that a country capable of producing bodies so daringly graceful, so tempting in their spiritual flights, must have countless other vital revelations to offer, of a biological nature, it goes without saying.
>
> I made up my mind, while feeling and fondling Lola, that sooner or later I'd make a trip, or call it a pilgrimage, to the United States, the sooner the better. And the fact is that I knew neither peace nor rest (in an implacably adverse and harassed life) until I managed to go through with that profound and mystically anatomical adventure.
>
> So it was in the immediate vicinity of Lola's rear end that I received the message of a new world. (44)

What he, unlike Henry or Dean, feels "mystical" about is the female anatomy. He does not forget that the possessor of a beautiful body may be shallow-minded, like Lola, but neither does he forget that even Lola, no matter how optimistic-American or stupid, is vulnerable to suffering. "It was through dead fashions that Lola perceived the flight of the years. (. . .) The possibility that there would never again be races at Longchamp overwhelmed her.

The sadness of the world has different ways of getting to people, but it seems to succeed almost every time" (46).

Ferdinand is more angry with Musyne's desertion of him than he is with Lola's, and he talks about his accidental meetings with her over the years in scathing terms (63-64). After all, Lola is, at this stage anyway, full of stupid notions, but Musyne, "a very shrewd little angel," is one of his own people, someone he has to take seriously. So her rejection of him must go much deeper than Lola's. Musyne clearly chooses money, in the form of the rich men from South America, over Ferdinand's love. He is made very bitter by that choice. Still he does not blame her personally for the fact that, after all, "There won't be any love to spare in this world as long as there's five francs" between people--an observation he made when, at the front, he saw that even a woman's real grief over her young boy, bayonetted gratuitously by the Germans, pauses to make him a deal over a bottle of white wine (31-32). "For a long time I thought little Musyne was stupid, but that was only because I was vain and she had run out on me" (64). It's merely "conceited" to think that love can so easily wipe out the power of money. "I hadn't found out yet that mankind consists of two very different races, the rich and the poor. It took me . . . and plenty of other people . . . twenty years and the war to learn to stick to my class and ask the price of things before touching them, let alone setting my heart on them" (67). But this knowledge, acquired from Musyne, leaves him full of bitterness, and with it he believes he can detect the unspoken meaning of the kind words of the nurses at the mental hospital where he is a patient,

to be cured of his terror of war, along with the
other terrified enlisted men:

> ". . . Be nice, die quickly . . . and
> let's hope the war will be over soon, so
> we can marry one of your charming officers
> . . . preferably one with dark hair . . .
> And long live the Patrie that Papa's al-
> ways talking about! . . . How wonderful
> love must be when Johnny comes marching
> home! . . . Our little husband will be
> decorated! . . . cited for bravery . . .
> You can shine his lovely boots on our
> happy wedding day if you like . . . if
> you're still in existence, soldier boy
> . . . Won't you be happy about our happi-
> ness, soldier boy? . . ." (74)

But what is behind this bitterness as it never
is (or is never admitted to be) in Miller--and the
bitterness is not even mentioned in Kerouac--is
Ferdinand's adoration of the female body. It is
this adoration which never leaves him. What infuriates him is that he is denied the right, as a poor
man, to touch this beauty, to him the greatest
beauty that there is.
     When he gets to America, he sees that the reve-
lation he received in the vicinity of Lola's rear
end was a true one: Major Mischief's fifteen year
old daughter in a tennis dress is "a promise to make
a man shout for joy" (164). He views the office
workers of New York as "a sudden avalanche of absolutely and undeniably beautiful women":

> What a discovery! What an America!
> What ecstasy! I thought of Lola . . . Her

promises had not deceived me! It was true.

I had come to the heart of my pilgrimage. And if my appetite hadn't kept calling itself to my attention, that would have struck me as one of those moments of supernatural aesthetic revelation. If I'd been a little more comfortable and confident, the incessant beauties I was discovering might have ravished me from my base human condition. In short, all I needed was a sandwich to make me believe in miracles. But how I needed that sandwich!

And yet, what supple grace! What incredible delicacy of form and feature! What inspired harmonies! What perilous nuances! Triumphant where the danger is greatest! Every conceivable promise of face and figure fulfilled! Those blondes! Those brunettes! Those Titian redheads! And more and more kept coming! Looks like I got here just in time.

What made those apparitions all the more divine in my eyes was that they seemed totally unaware of my existence as I sat on a bench close by, slap-happy, drooling with erotico-mystical admiration and quinine, but also, I have to admit, with hunger. If it were possible for a man to jump out of his skin, I'd have done it then, once and for all. There was nothing holding me back.

Those unlikely midinettes could have wafted me away, sublimated me; a gesture, a word would have sufficed, and in that moment I'd have been transported, all of

me, into the world of dreams. But I sup-
pose they had other fish to fry. (167-168)

Compared to this passage, Dean's "love of women"
expressed from the car window in New Orleans is flat
and not convincing. Here the prose itself is ex-
cited, and what Ferdinand sees is specified, and the
rest of the world is not forgotten or denied--he
needs that sandwich, and, above all, these beauties
have "other fish to fry." As do those "miraculous
beings" sitting in the lobby of the "Laugh Calvin
Hotel" that he has to pass on his way to his room.
"Is the poor man's aesthetic torment to have no
end?" he cries (170). "Nearly all a poor bastard's
desires are punishable by jail" (173). "The life of
people without resources is nothing but one long
rebuff and one long frenzy of desire, and man can
truly know, truly deliver himself only from what he
possesses" (178). And when he comes to see Lola
again, to put the touch on her for some money, he is
full of bitterness and even ruthlessness towards her
and succeeds, by talking about her mother's liver
cancer, in breaking through the armor of her fatuous
American optimism for a moment. But even in his
bitterness he can realize that in our world a "poor
woman's ass is her goldmine"--the only one she has--
and means this to apply to Lola as well as Musyne or
the nurses (182). Indeed, what he says earlier
about Madame Herote, who is a kind of symbol of Eros
in the novel (Herote is from *érotique* according to
the glossary supplied by Manheim), applies to them
as well: "Maybe if people are so wicked, it's only
because they suffer. (. . .) Madame Herote's impres-
sive material and amatory success hadn't had time
yet to soften her rapacious instincts" (61).

It is in his bitterness and disappointment and torment that he encounters Molly working in the whorehouse in Detroit. And it is from her that he feels something he never felt from a woman before. "For the first time somebody was taking an interest in me, looking at me from the inside so to speak, taking my egoism into account, putting herself in my place, not just judging me from her point of view like everyone else" (197). Molly is "one of the lovely girls there. (. . .) I remember her kindness as if it were yesterday, and her long, blond, magnificently strong, lithe legs, noble legs" (196). But her beauty, love, and kindness cannot overwhelm him. "If only I had met Molly sooner, when it was still possible to choose one road rather than another. Before that bitch Musyne and that little turd Lola crimped my enthusiasm" (197). Moreover, he says he is "the restless type" and doesn't want to settle down with "a little business" and "be like other people" as Molly suggests. But why would keeping to her necessarily mean *that*? And he calls a "vice" this "mania for running away from everywhere" and guesses he is just driven "by stupid pride, by a sense of some sort of superiority" (197). And would it be easy to admit to himself--in our world--that he has found his "true mate," as Trotsky called her in his great essay on the novel,[7] in a prostitute?

Later, Ferdinand feels great regret for having left Molly and returned to France and, as narrator, even calls out to her if she reads the book to come to him, even if "she's no longer beautiful" (203), just as Céline himself searched for Elizabeth Craig, to whom the book is dedicated. Céline has been called sentimental in his treatment of Molly, but he is more than that. He is illuminating what sentimentality means, showing it as a sort of love coming *after* the event, when it can't be of any use to the person it addresses, a love that dared not risk existing at the time.

> We kissed. But I didn't kiss her prop-
> erly, as I should have, on my knees if the
> truth be known. I was always thinking
> about something else at the same time,
> about not wasting time and tenderness, as
> if I wanted to keep them for something
> magnificent, something sublime, for later,
> but not for Molly and not for this partic-
> ular kiss. (199)

Ferdinand's feelings of "restlessness" and bitterness and "sense of superiority" at this point are
similar to, but not nearly so intense as, the feelings Robinson has that make him run away from
Madelon at the end of the novel--though, of course,
she is not so sweet as Molly. And it is what happens between Robinson and Madelon that Céline said,
in an interview given not long after the publication
of *Journey*, shows the meaning of the story--a meaning he said no one got, not his editor or the critics or anyone:

> Le voilà! C'est l'amour dont nous osons
> parler encore dans cet enfer, comme si
> l'on pouvait composer des quatrains dans
> un abattoir. L'amour impossible
> aujourd'hui. Robinson le cherche comme
> chacun, avec l'argent, cet autre bien
> indispensable. Il finit enfin par trouver
> un coin tranquille, des rentes, une petite
> femme qui l'aime. Pourtant, il ne peut

pas rester là. Il lui faut partir quand
il a le bonheur bourgeois sous la main,
une petite maison, une epouse câlipe, des
poissons rouges. Il se dit qu'il est fou
pour être comme cela. Il s'en va. Madelon le poursuit. (. . .) La petite l'as-
saille. Elle ne comprend rien. Lui, pour
ensortir et sortir de lui-même, voudrait
être heroïque dans son genre. Mais il ne
sait pas comment.

A la fin, dans le taxi, il trouve. Il
dit à Madelon que ce n'est pas elle mais
l'univers entier qui le dégoûte. Il le dit
comme il peut et il en meurt. (. . .)[8] [A
translation is given in the footnote.]

Robinson cannot love and says why--and he is
killed for it. Ferdinand can recognize that Robinson is "heroic," but he himself never gets to that
point. His bitterness and "sense of superiority"
stop this side of death. And he has Molly to thank
for it:

To leave her I certainly had to be mad,
and in a cold, disgusting way. Still,
I've kept my soul in one place up till
now, and if death were to come and take me
tomorrow, I'm sure I wouldn't be quite as
cold, as ugly, as heavy as other men, and
it's thanks to the kindness and the dream
that Molly gave me during my few months in
America. (203)

Just as Ferdinand always retains his adoration of
the female body, unlike Kerouac's or Miller's heroes, or Robinson, so he is not "as cold, as ugly,

as heavy" as they are either. And he can value love--though he makes wisecracks about it--even though he knows the misery that overwhelms it, that it becomes.

It is that knowledge which is expressed, inadvertently, in the singing of the English girls at the Tarapout--"real artists"--an expression, in their case, of "the no-nonsense misery of their lousy country" (313) which of course is like that of all countries. It is heartache, and it is heartache that above all else Céline's novel expresses. That is not a common feeling in *Tropic of Cancer* or *On the Road* or in American literature in general. In *Journey* it is almost on every page, because it is only heartache that can preserve for us the knowledge of what we have lost, what our bitterness and all that has happened to us keeps us from having, what we want so badly.

One of the Tarapout girls, Tania, mourns an absent and now dead lover, in spite of the fact that Ferdinand, after so many kisses of consolation, gets into bed with her. But he tells us--bitterly--it's the man's *absence* that insures her love, just as in the case of Jesus Christ (315). This point applies as well to Molly and Elizabeth Craig: it is loving anyone actually present, Céline wants us to know, that is not so easy to do in this hell, this slaughterhouse where we live. But copulation can be just a kind of reflex. And it is as a reflex that he takes Madelon, standing up, as soon as he sees her. It's as if, for Ferdinand, there's nothing left now but this reflex; at least, he doesn't become lyrical over the bodies *or* souls of Tania and Madelon. But the heartache is still in the novel.

So the heart, Ferdinand's heart, is not dead. And when, working at the lunatic asylum, he hires

the "Slovak" woman Sophie as a nurse, his enthusiasm
begins to return. "But what youth! What vigor!
What muscles! What an excuse! Supple! Springy!
Amazing! Her beauty was diminished by none of that
false or true reticence that impedes all-too occi-
dental converse. Frankly, I couldn't admire her
enough." And he exclaims:

> The era of these living joys, of great
> undeniable physiological and comparative
> harmonies is yet to come . . . The body, a
> godhead mauled by my shameful hands . . .
> The hands of an honest man, that unknown
> priest . . . Death and Words must give
> their permission first . . . What foul
> affectations! A cultivated man needs to
> be rolled in a dense layer of symbols,
> caked to the asshole with artistic excre-
> ment, before he can tear off a piece . . .
> Then anything can happen! A bargain!
> Think of the saving, getting all your
> thrills from reminiscences . . . Reminis-
> cences are something we've got plenty of,
> one can buy beauties, enough to last us a
> lifetime . . . Life is more complicated,
> especially the life of human forms . . . A
> hard adventure. None more desperate.
> Compared with the addiction to perfect
> forms, cocaine is a pastime for station-
> masters. (407)

About Sophie herself he says

> (. . .) We admired her, so alive in our
> midst . . . just her way of getting up

153

from a chair, coming to our table, leaving
it again . . . she charmed us . . .

And every time she performed those
simple gestures, we experienced surprise
and joy. We made strides in poetry, so to
speak, just marveling at her being so
beautiful and so much more obviously free
than we were. The rhythm of her life
sprang from other wellsprings than ours
. . . Our wellsprings were forever slow
and slimy. (407)

His "wellsprings" have been fouled, so that

Though our instinct reveled in her
innate joy, our peevish knowledge of
things of this world rather frowned on it,
that essentially frightened, ever-present
knowledge which cowers in the cellars of
existence, accustomed to the worst by
habit, by experience. (408)

Nevertheless, "Just to look at her did your soul
good. Especially mine." And, moreover, "All that
can be fucked" (408). What he has thought about
Molly--"the only women you cherish in your hearts
are the ones who really loved men a little, not just
one man, even if it was you, but the whole lot"
(338)--applies as well to Sophie; in contact with
her enchantment, he has given up some of his bitterness and "superiority."

To be enchanted all the way, he would be re-
newed, given real youth, the kind of youth he tried
earlier in the novel to explain to Father Protiste:

. . . Youth? . . . You and I never had
any youth!

The poor, it's true, get younger inside
as they go along, and toward the end,
provided that on the way they've made some
attempt to jettison all the lies and fear
and contemptible eagerness to obey they
were given at birth, they're less revolting than at the start. (. . .) The only
real youth, Mr. Priest, is loving everyone
without distinction, that alone is true,
that alone is young and new. Well, Mr.
Priest, do you know many young people who
are like that? . . . I don't! . . . All I
see is crusty old stupidities fermenting
in more or less recent bodies. (. . .)
They're young the way a boil is young, no
more, because of the pus inside that hurts
and makes them swell up." (327)

Sophie's beauty could soften him in the direction of
that true youth that Bébert, the little boy who died
of typhus, possessed, with his "infinite little
smile of pure affection," an affection Céline says
few people past twenty preserve--"the affection of
animals" (209). This would be something quite different than Miller's "clown" or Kerouac's "Holy
Goof" because what Céline calls for is not the "joy"
of one "untouched by the common grief," not ecstasy
or the thrill of finding "It," but something much
more difficult, something that even through Sophie
and Molly, Ferdinand could only hope to do a little
bit, that is, feel a love for the lives of others.

Sophie could pull the novel away from its tragic
drift. As Wayne Burns has pointed out, Céline does
not let her. What she could mean as a character, he

155

argues, is sacrificed by the novelist in the interest of making *Journey* turn out like a conventional
novel. The killing of Robinson by Madelon overwhelms the book.[9] But still, Sophie is there, and
her presence and Ferdinand's reaction to it is
enough to give the lie to the "heroism" of Robinson
that is the epitome of that bitterness and "sense of
superiority" and "heaviness" that the world, with
its five francs, teaches. Love, and sexual delight,
are, in spite of everything, in spite even of the
bitter, satiric scene where Madelon affirms her love
for Robinson with Ferdinand listening (352-354),
worthwhile in the world of Céline's novel. Certainly
in the world of Céline's novel only love and sexual
delight can prevent men from being so "heavy"--that
condition that Merlin Thomas tells us was Céline's
final criticism of his contemporaries: "*Ils étaient
lourds*--They were so dim [lit. 'heavy']."[10]

But Céline's American imitators have not seen
women and the love for women, terrible that Céline
acknowledges that these can also be, as able to do
anything very miraculous. American men who have
written novels, with a few exceptions like Dreiser
in *Sister Carrie*, do not really seem to recognize
the women who are on the same streets--or on the
open road--with them, to wish to go over to where
they are or admit them into their own depths. Perhaps, like good little boys, good little Americans,
they are too afraid.

2. CÉLINE'S *BAGATELLES POUR UN MASSACRE*: THE EXPRESSION OF A FORBIDDEN PASSION

i

It is now, 1980, almost impossible to discuss *Bagatelles pour un massacre*--a crime, it seems, to do anything else than dismiss it. For by now almost everyone, at least everyone who participates in our intellectual life, would agree that the expression of anti-Semitic feelings which is Céline's infamous book is utterly evil or sick, with no more to be said about it.

To put all this another way, the point of view expressed by Jean-Paul Sartre in his little volume *Reflexions sur la question juive* (Paris: Gallimard, 1954) has come to prevail in our intellectual community so absolutely that there is, at least among our intellectuals, not even any longer an issue. And Céline's book becomes therefore a *priori* something not even to consider, at the very best a mere embarrassment to explain away--if one is going to mention it at all--when discussing the works of this writer whose *Voyage au bout de la nuit* and *Mort à crédit* are beginning to be treated by many as modern classics: for how could those two novels, so full of compassion (as they are often described now) be written by--an anti-Semite?

Sartre's own explanation in *Reflexions sur la question juive* is that "si Céline a pu soutenir les thèses socialistes des nazis, c'est qu'il était payé. Au fond du son coeur, il n'y croyait pas . . ." (48). But for this assertion--that Céline upheld Nazi race theories because he was paid, that in his heart he did not believe them--he offers no evidence. Erika Ostrovsky in her *Voyeur Voyant* implies this particular stab of Sartre's--the imputation that Céline was paid--was made because it would be exactly the one that would hurt most. Her own account of Céline's anti-Semitism is a psychological one: she sees it as a kind of sickness, but nevertheless as rising from the depths of this writer, the depths out of which he created his other works. She does not succeed in explaining it. But she deserves credit for not allowing herself to dismiss the problem in Céline as Sartre does with his bare assertion that Céline's pen had been hired.

Nevertheless, Sartre's book well expresses the consensus on anti-Semitism that is becoming universal among thinkers. Towards the end of his book he quotes Richard Wright's famous statement. "'Il n'y a pas de problème noir aus États-Unis, il n'y a qu'un problème blanc,'" and adds: "Nous dirons de la même facon que l'antisémitisme n'est pas un problem juif: c'est nôtre problem" (183-4). It is no longer the Jew that is the problem, it is the anti-Semite, no longer the Jew who must disappear, but the anti-Semite. So it is not just the anti-Semite who is guilty, but *all of us* (who are not Jews) who have not solved the problem: "Il n'est pas un de nous qui ne soit, en cette circonstances, totalement coupable et même criminel; le sang juif que les nazis ont versé retombe sur toutes nos têtes" (165)--the Jewish blood shed by the Nazis falls again on all our heads.

Let us examine the steps of Sartre's argument. In the first part of the book, in which he gives us his famous "portrait of an anti-Semite," he declares that while he can admit that one may have a thought on whether or not wines may be freely imported from Algeria, "L'antisémitisme ne rentre pas dans la catégorie de pensées que protège le Droit de libre opinion" (10): for indeed, anti-Semitism is not a thought at all, "c'est bien autre chose qu'une pensée. C'est d'abord une *passion*" (10). It is not a thought, but a passion--and, to Sartre, a forbidden one. But he goes even further. Not only is it a passion, but one that is not provoked by an object. Thus, "si le Juif n'existait pas l'antisemite l'inventerait" (14) for the anti-Semite *chooses* to hate: he "a *choisi* de vivre sur le mode passionné" (20), he has chosen a passionate rather than thoughtful life, and if there were no Jew, he would invent one *in order to hate him*, for what he wants is to feel the passion of hate. But anti-Semitism is not, Sartre says, only a joy in hating: "il procure des plaisirs positives" (30), and these positive pleasures are those of affirming, for the anti-Semite, that he himself belongs to an élite, "une aristocratie de naissance" (31) which in turn, in the case of a Frenchman, constitutes a *real* France ("France réelle") as opposed to the legal entity and social collectivity called France--a "real France" from which Jews are excluded. And the love of hate is also sexual, according to Sartre: the anti-Semite is sadistic, with the image of "une belle Juive," (56) the beautiful Jewess, common to "la littérature clandestine" and of importance as a sexual symbol "dans le folklore" (57). Sartre finishes his "portrait" of the anti-Semite--that is, the producer of such "folklore," the "real Frenchman"--with these descriptions of him:

> C'est un homme qui a peur. Non des Juifs, certes: de lui-même, de sa conscience, de sa liberté, de ses instincts, de ses responsibilités de la société et du

> monde; de tout sauf des Juifs. (. . .)
> (62)

and

> L'antisémitisme, en un mot, c'est la
> peur devant la condition humaine. L'anti-
> semite est l'homme qui vent être roc im-
> pitoyable, torrent furieux, foudre
> dévastratrice: tout sauf un homme. (64)

Presumably, *not* to be an anti-Semite would be *not* to
have such fears--of oneself, one's freedom, instincts, responsibilities, solitude, of change,
society, or the world: and *not* to crave a passionate existence. Such fears and cravings are not
worthy, considered from Sartre's point of view,
which one can safely say is that of the majority of
intellectuals in the Western World today, of what he
calls "un homme."

Finally, Sartre maintains that our society--
unfortunately, made up of men with such fears and
cravings--historically *created* Jews to do the dirty
work with money forbidden to Christians: indeed,
the non-Jews made them accumulate wealth, as indeed
they caused in the Jews all the traits which the
anti-Semite claims are racial and for which they are
condemned. "Et s'il insiste sur la puissance de
l'argent, c'est pour défendre ses droits de consom-
mateur dans une communauté qui les lui conteste
. . ." (155). So the traits non-Jews object to,
including the love of money, Sartre concedes are
there in the Jews. But they are there *understand-
ably*--as a reaction to what the folk (which claims
to be a *real* nation against the legal entity of
classes and interest groups), men crippled by fears

and passions, have done to them. Finally, it is up
to us--"nous" --to make a revolution so that we can
have a society of men beyond "les erreurs passion-
nées," beyond passionate errors (178), a world-
society that Jews can safely live in, as well as all
the others Sartre calls oppressed--that we ("nous")
are guilty of oppressing.

ii

Now let me give a summary of Céline's book.
I'll give a running paraphrase along with the quotations, but I do not pretend to be his translator.
But what emerges as more interesting than what he
says about Jews is the criticism, direct and implied, he makes about "Aryans." "J'ai rien de spé-
cial contre les Juifs en tant que juifs, je veux
dire simplement truands comme tout le monde, bipèdes
à quête de leur soupe," he says in *Bagatelles* (Paris: Denoël, 1937, p.72): he has nothing special
against the Jews in so far as they are jews, simply
like everyone, bipeds in search of their soup.
"Mais c'est contre le racisme juif que me révolte
. . ." (72)--it is what he calls *Jewish racism* that
disgusts him. And he claims, at the start of the
book, to have come up against it in a way particularly enraging for him.

In the beginning pages, he tells how much he now
loves the dance. "Dans une jambe de danseuse le
monde, ses ondes, tous ses rhythmes, ses folies, ses
voeux sont inscrits!" he tells one Leo Gutman, "Le
plus nuancé poème du monde! . . . Gutman mon ami,
aux écoutes du plus grand secret, c'est Dieu! C'est
Dieu lui-même! . . . je ne veux plus travailler que
pour les danseuses . . . Tout pour la danse! Rien

que pour la danse!" (12) But when he submits his ballet, "La Naissance D'une Fée" (the text of which is included in the book), he is told that "Mr. Rouché a trouvé que c'était pas mal ton affaire, mais il demande la musique . . ." (27); Mr. Rouché cannot look at a ballet without music. But all the great musicians are Jews. Gutman offers to talk his work up to them for him. Then he himself goes to see them and they are very flattering and cordial, but each gives some reason for evading or declining to provide music for his "poème": "Mais cependant un peu long! . . . trop court peut-être! . . . trop doux? . . . trop dur? . . . trop classique? . . ." (28).

He is furious. "Tu ne me judaïsersais pas, dis donc, par hasard?" he asks Gutman (28), who seems hurt and proposes, in the face of this frustration, another idea: that Céline write a ballet for the Paris Exhibition of 1937, which is going to offer "Des ballets de Paris"--and Céline is enthusiastic since he feels he knows Paris. But Gutman tells him that "L'Exposition des 'Arts et Techniques' c'est l'exposition juive 1937 . . . La grande youstricave 37." Not the workers at the exhibition, "Pas les stafeurs, les jardiniers, les déménageurs, les ter-rassiers, les forgerons, les mutilés, les gardes aux portes . . . Non! . . . les remasseurs de mégots . . . les gardiens de latrine . . . enfin la frime . . . les biscotos . . . Non! . . .:" rather, all the big shots, "tout ce qui ordonne . . . qui trance . . . qui palpe . . . architectes, mon pote, grands ingénieurs, contractants, directeurs, tous youtre . . ." (29).

Céline's ballet, with the parodic title "Voyou Paul. Brave Virginie," written specially for the exhibition (again he provides us with the text) is

rejected: only Jewish works will be exhibited--as
"French." "Rien pour les Français alors?" asks
Céline, ". . . Rien pour les enfants du sol?" . . .
and he exclaims "Je n'aurai jamais des danseuses
alors?"--I shall never have the dancers then? Gutman watches him, enjoying the spectacle of his suffering. "Il était sadique," Céline says and asks
him if he knows the effect this has on him and
finally cries out: "Ah! tu vas voir l'antisémitisme!" (40-41)--you're going to see antisemitism!

The rest of the book, some 340 pages more, is an
outburst of hatred occasioned by these rebuffs. His
knowledge, he says, of "les Semites," goes back to
observations he made during his period on the docks
of London (42-3)--observations, he claims--for he
writes from no party point of view: "j'adhère jamais rien. . . . J'adhère à moi-même, tant que je
peux. . . ." (45); especially he denies ever having
any official affiliations with the Soviet Union that
he can be said to have betrayed and which he considers an atrocious country dominated by Jews (45-48).

It is this supposed domination, which he sees
everywhere--"Les Juifs sont nos maîtres--ici, là-
bas, en Russie, en Angleterre, en Amérique, partout!
. . ." (49) that he claims is never mentioned by
other writers. Most significantly--and this is a
point to which he returns again and again--the Jews
control the media of information and entertainment,
the press, cinema, the radio (and the ballet),
throughout the world from Hollywood to Moscow (53).
Thus with "Publicité . . . on fabrique un Joseph
Staline comme une Joan Crawford, même procédé, même
culot, même escroquerie, mêmes Juifs effrontes aux
ficelles" so that "Charlie Chaplin travaille aussi,
magnifiquement, pour la cause, c'est un grand poin-
nier de l'Imperialisme juif"--a Stalin is made by

the same process and people as a Joan Crawford, Charlie Chaplin can be considered a magnificent worker for the cause of Jewish imperialism; the film renders us all "anti-préjugés" and "internationaux" (54) in our outlook.

Céline interrupts his exposition, which has hardly begun, with a scene of a visit to a pal of his, "Popol," an old painter in Montmartre, whom he lets know he has just become an anti-Semite, a really ferocious one, and Popol warns him to watch himself, for he doesn't actually realize how powerful the Jews are. Does Ferdinand think he is Joan of Arc? And especially, Popol says, they control the fine arts--galleries, academies, judges, expositions. And who is going to fight these "dix mille youtres. . . . racistes à mort, insatiables?" The proletariat? "Il est alcoolique et cocu," answers Popol (56-60).

So there is to be no frontal attack on the Jews. The reason the papers of the right, left or center never speak of the Jews except with "dix mille flatteries," of ". . . tres grand artiste israélite . . ." is, according to Céline, that they are all prostituted to Jewish power (61). "Je dois dire qu'avec le Popol on est tout de même tombé d'accord, on a conclu: c'est des vampires!" (65)--he has to agree with Popol. Then Céline's cousin, Gustin Sabayote (from *Mort à crédit*), comes on the scene; Gustin's comment is that the Jews are very intelligent and that Ferdinand will surely end up in prison.

Céline denies their intelligence and attributes all the fame of their artists and intellectuals to publicity and racist prejudice towards their own kind: "si Einstein n'était pas youtre, si Bergson n'était pas coupe, si Proust n'était que Breton, si

Freud n'avait pas la marque . . . on ne parlerait pas beaucoup ni des uns ni des autres. . . ."; in fact, "Que ca soit peinture Cézanne, Modi, Picasso et tous autres . . . films de Monsieur Benhur, musique de Tartinowsky, ca devient tout de suite un événment . . . L'énorme préjugé favorable, mondial, devance, prélude toute intention juive. . . . Toutes les agences juives du monde se mettent au moindre mumure, au moindre frisson de production youtre à cracher des foundres du tonnerre . . . et la publicité parlée, raciste juive, fait admirablement écho . . ." (65-66). And the non-Jews, whom Céline calls "Aryans," are so abject, subjected, drunken, prostrate, enslaved that they cannot tell the difference. The "Aryans" have no more "mystique commune"--no mystic commune--as do the Jews: these "Aryans" have no feeling for each other anymore, and so no regard for their own expressions of feelings.

It is not the Jew as jew, as "biped in search of his soup," Céline says that bothers him: it is Jewish *racism* which excludes everyone else and considers them as animals to be exploited. The Jews stick together against the world--the arts once again provide the example, in the doings of the critics, who condemned him for his *Mea Culpa*, a pamphlet on the U.S.S.R. written after his visit there. The consensus of these critics is that intellectuals and artists must now be guided above all by "sozial denken" (76)--"social thinkin'." Céline shows us a gathering of these "social thinkers" in their hangout, their "cave de la Culture," full of bureaucrats, and not a non-Jew present but himself: the revolution they agitate for will, according to Céline, clearly be in their favor (77-79).

But Céline wants us to know: "je suis pas réactionnaire! . . . pas une minute! pas fasciste!"

(80)--he is not reactionary or fascist. "Moi je me sens communiste sans une atome d'arrière-pensée"; "Je me sens communiste de toutes fibres"--he feels communist in every fiber. What he denies is that what calls itself communist is so at all; "le système bolchevique" he calls "superfasciste." Céline says *his* is the "vrai communisme" (81)--a communism without overloads, Aryan bourgeois *or* Jew. And the reason the "social thinkers" have not produced any communist art, he says, is that they are all of them, to a man, "absolument bourgeois" really, in their hearts and intentions (83).

He proposes an idea on how to avert the next great war: if he were dictator, he would force all the Jews to the front line: there would then be such an outburst of pacifist propaganda that the war would never come off (91). This is no doubt meant humorously, but if so, the point of the joke is that the Jews have all the power of "publicité." The theme that seems to run throughout the book is not just that the Jews have political power but that they have it essentially through their tight, cooperative control of media of the press, publication, information, entertainment, education, all the arts. And this belief recalls the occasion for Céline's whole onslaught--the rebuff from the ballet.

Indeed, everything else in the book is secondary to this theme of Jewish control of the means of communication. The "Aryans" assembled at the medical congresses the Jew Yubelblat so easily controls, are totally unable to communicate with one another, they jabber and fight so much: thus he can run them (96-109). Céline knew this Yubelblat in Geneva, after the war: he even says he came to like him-- "J'avais même pour lui de l'affection" (102) in

comparison to the "Aryans": "Quant aux Aryen, c'est
la détresse . . . Si on leur annonce pas les choses
avec du 'neon' . . . Quel est l'animal, je vous
demande, de nos jouis sot? . . . plus épais qu'un
Aryen? Quel Zoo le reprendrait? . . . ." What Zoo?
"le Paradis? . . ." (103)

The non-Jews are all atomized individuals while
the Jews, with what Céline calls their "racism,"
possess all the means of communication: they possess the power of the lie, "Le Mensonge," which
Céline quotes Lenin as saying is the prime tool of
the Bolscheviks. Thus on the one hand the world is
a "prison pour aryens, directeurs juifs" and, on the
other, Proust, "la 'Miche juive aux Camélias,'" is
elevated to the rank of a Balzac (124-126). The
French, totally out of communication with each other, ashamed of each other, alcoholic and "absolument
stérilisée de tout lyrisme" "n'ont plus de'âme," are
controlled by "la grande propagande juive" (131-132)
which Céline says always represents the Jew as martyr and persecuted idealist. But Céline remarks
that beneath the highest idealist crusades *always*
lie the most indecent motives: "Le matuvuisme le
plus exorbitant, le plus indécent est à la base, au
fond de tous les grands mouvements d'Idées actuels,
inseperable" (139)--which is his comment on the
Spanish Civil War, a war he says is for amateurs,
i.e., one you can quit when you want.

It is directly to the theme of communication,
and specifically of literature, that Céline now
addresses himself. Denoël, his publisher, has asked
him for a report on the crisis of the book in
France. Céline quotes two sets of statistics: one
showing that the French pay, per head, less a year
for books than the people of other western nations,
the other showing that they consume by far the most

alcohol. And it is the Jews, he maintains, that control the wine industry, the 350,000 bistrots--the bistrots and the cinema (142-147). The French "Aryans," that is to say, in Céline's constant apposition, the French workers, are "cons" (152), the least wise proletariat of the nations--such is the basis of "la crise du livre." He then begins an attack on modern French literature, which he calls "onanisme" (163). What is essentially wrong is that it is written by "imposteurs," bourgeois or Jewish (164), who have no style because they have no feeling, all feeling having been muffled in them by the way they grew up and were educated, which was, essentially, *to follow rules.* "Leur destin de petits bourgeois aryens et de petits juifs, presque toujours associés, engendrés, couvés par les familles, l'école, par l'éducation, consiste avant tout à les insensibiliser, humainment" (166). Their French is "de lycée," it is "déconté, français filtré, depouillé, français figé, français frotté (modernise naturaliste), le français de muffle, le français montaigne, racine, français juif à baclots, français d'Anatole enjuive, le français goncourt, le français dégueulasse d'élégance, moulé, oriental, onctueux, glissant comme la merde, c'est l'épitaphe même de la race française. C'est le chinois mandarin"--it is Mandarin Chinese--"le francais idéal pour Robots"--the ideal language for Robots (167), "le parfait journalistique objectif langage Robot"--clichés, proper phrases for the proper roles in the great social farce.

This "proper" French is, according to Céline, of great significance to the Jews, who achieve complete control over the "Aryans" through the annihilation "de tous nos arts essentiels, instinctifs, musique, peinture, poésie, théâtre . . . ," for their task is to replace "l'emotion aryenne par le tam-tam nègre"--the current instrument of this despotism being "sur-réalisme," modernism in literature and the other arts (170-171). It is the ultimate conquest, the ultimate robotization to Céline--to replace *feeling* with the jungle beat--and he says that if you don't want to be "négrifié," then you are called "fasciste" (173). But he claims it is the whole force of modern literature, "bien insipide, objectif, descriptif, fièrement, pompeusment robot, radoteur, outrecuidont et nul," to do it to us, along with the film, music, the radio, the newspapers and alcohol (175). The whole international literary-artistic world of sophistication to him is Jewish (178); no wonder then "Nous sommes en plein fascisme juif" (180). According to Céline, literary standardization, created by "la publicité juive," standardizes us, cutting off from us the possibility of communicating to each other "quelque authentique emotion" (186), for feelings can be authentic only in so far as they are not standard, but individual. He says such standardization is the result of the art-world movements in Bloomsbury and "the Village." "La seule défense," writes Céline, "le seul recours du blanc contre le robotisme, et sans doute contre la guerre, la régression à 'pire que cavernes' bien pire, c'est le retour à son rhythm émotif propre"-- the only defense a white man has against this robotism and doubtless against war too is to get back his own right emotional rhythm (191). This point is the climax of Céline's argument.

Céline identifies the Jews with the Bolscheviks: "Mais le Komitern, c'est le Judaisme même"--the Komitern is Judaism itself (209)--achieving its ends, once again, through emotional massification. Once again the means are through "leur bonne merde

juive, merde-radio, merde-sport . . . , merde al-
cool, merde-crime, merde-politique, merde-cinéma,"
through modern art, whose cubistic technique he
explains as the photographing of any object which is
then torn apart and reassembled as a "puzzle,"
through "Chaplin, Paramount . . . Fairbank . . .
Ulman . . . Cantor . . . ," all Hollywood, which he
says frankly produces pro-Jewish propaganda,
"démocratie, l'égalité des races, la haine des 'pré-
jugés nationaux', l'abolition des privelèges, la
marche du progrès, etc . . ." (221-225), with the
Jew always portrayed as an innocent persecuted one
(225-229).

The book now becomes somewhat fragmentary in
relation to what I have called its main theme.
There is a chapter criticizing the Paris Exhibition
of 1937, which Céline, as pointed out above, considers Jewish dominated; a chapter of specific examples
of Jewish control and of Jews in power in unexpected
places--with the note that this people is only the
last of a succession of conquerors of France (Roman,
Italian, Spanish, and English before them) (243).
Then further chapters of miscellania follow, including: a testimony that Jews really have a "martyr
complex" by a Jew Céline calls "honnête homme"
(255), inconsistencies in the viewpoint of "l'Human-
ité" which he attributes to the need to serve Jewish
interests, a study of Jean Renoir's film "Grande
Illusion" which he sees as an argument that the
millionaire Jew now replaces the old aristocrat in
control over the worker, citations of the so-called
"Protocols of the Elders of Zion," quotations to
show connections between the Masons and the Jews, a
statement--once again--that he has not been bought
by Goering or anyone else, not even Mr. Rothschild
("Tout est possible," he says), an attack on Freud-

ianism as totally presumptuous in pretending to have
"les clefs de l'âme," to be "les juges de nos pensées" of whom we shall have to ask "la permission de
la merde même, pour respirer!" (305-306), a description by Gustin of Jews in the medical profession,
Gustin's observation that all of the noses of even
the French Kings look questionable, Gustin's support
for Hitler because the Jews repel him, and another
encounter with Gutman. The book then concludes with
"un peu de Baedecker," a description of his stay in
Leningrad, of the places his Intourist guide
Nathalie, a devoted little Communist, takes him,
and--of a rebuff of his attempt to get a "poème"
accepted by the Ballets Russes, essentially for the
same reason he met with rejection in Paris. The
last pages of the book are the text of another piece
for dancers: "Van Bagaden, Grand Ballet Mime et
quelques paroles."

iii

The great problem in evaluating this book of
Céline's, and partly perhaps also, in a sense not so
obvious as in the case with *Bagatelles*, his other
books, lies in the fact that Sartre's side won the
Second World War. Fidel Castro once said of himself, "History will absolve me"--but History has not
absolved Céline nor any anti-Semite. Those who grew
up in the United States during that war or after-
wards, in the big cities anyway, were indoctrinated
on all sides, in the school and in the media, with
an ideology of racial tolerance, political liberalism and a definitely philo-Semitic point of view,
and by 1954, the time of Sartre's book, the "Jewish
question" was no longer a question at all.

Such was the voice of public education in America—but at the same time, even in the big northern cities, what can be called the folklore of working-class, non-Jewish whites still said something else: and very much the same thing that Céline says, especially, for instance, concerning Jews in the field of the arts and entertainment in America—also Jews as loan sharks, slum lords, and leftwing political activists. The "folklore feeling," if it may be called that, of these whites is one of hatred, a hatred which the voice of public education, in media and schools, certainly opposed. Anti-Semitism becomes, in relation to the *legal* state, a forbidden passion. And in fact, we have here a fine example of what Freud discussed in *Civilization and its Discontents*: an aggressivity repressed for the sake of the ideal of "the brotherhood of man."

Céline has refused to repress his anger in the name of the ideal of the brotherhood of man. But what of those who do repress it? Does it go away? Freud himself was not at all sure that human beings would be able to stand the sense of guilt such an ideal would seem to demand. We can well wonder ourselves if those who preach ideals of tolerance and brotherhood are indeed friends of the Jewish people, especially if, in their equation of the cause of the Jews with such ideals, they make Jews into the very symbols of repression. May they not be preparing a further holocaust? Frankly expressed prejudice, even hatred like Céline's, may well be less dangerous for Jews—or blacks or any other "minority"—than the idealistic benevolence that casts them in—that prepares them for—the role of martyrs.

3. THE MEANING OF THE PRESENCE OF LILI IN CÉLINE'S FINAL TRILOGY

Lili, the narrator's wife in Louis-Ferdinand Céline's final trilogy,[11] is *there* with him to such an extent that one could almost read these novels as being as much about her life during the end of the Second World War as about the narrator's own. And not only is she at most of the scenes of the novels, undergoing all the sufferings the narrator undergoes, but she is the witness back at Meudon to his telling of these scenes and sufferings. But what is the meaning of this presence that is so much *there* and yet often seems to become almost invisible?

Erika Ostrovsky had this to say:

> A progression may be noted by comparing *Vogage au bout de la nuit*, which contains only some indirect references to the dance and in which the disablement of the principal characters is of a passing nature (Robinson's temporary blindness, Bardumu's war injuries), to the last works, in which the narrator is "75 per cent mutilated" and in which one of the central figures is a double amputee, but the figure of Arlette, Lili, Lucette--the dancer--grows more and more prominent. As the world is progressively torn to pieces, dismembered or devoured by bloodthirsty maenads or more mechanical destroyers, the urgency of the dance becomes even greater. The figure of the dancer--the dancing goddess-- emerges clearer and stronger from the bloody rubble and the destruction. Hers

is the sole remaining matrix, through her
the only rebirth possible.[12]

This is such an evocative statement, and hints
at such an important truth about Céline's trilogy--
at what he sees as "the only rebirth possible"--that
it is hard to want to take issue with it. But it
must be pointed out that in these novels Lili's
dancing has little to do with any of the dramatic
action. We are actually presented only once in all
three novels with a performance by Lili, when she
dazzles the Gypsies in *North* with their own casta-
nets (227). But she does not even seem to be dancing; at any rate, nothing of importance in the novel
issues from her castanet-playing. All her other
performances in these novels are mere practice and
rehearsing, going on when she is absent from whatever scene is happening. That she is a dancer is a
given fact of her characterization and it certainly
has a symbolic significance. But beyond these considerations, her importance to the final trilogy
does not really seem to be as a dancer *per se*. How
then is she important in these novels?

She seems almost invisible. But her near invisibility in fact is part of how she is characterized;
she is the very opposite of the "assertive woman."
The narrator reflects, back in Meudon, in the beginning of the first book of the trilogy, *Castle to
Castle*, on what will happen to her when he dies:
"Lili fighting the world? . . . I can't quite see it
. . . Lili's so generous . . . all generosity . . .
like a fairy! . . . she'd give everything away
. . ." (33); "Lili will be evicted pronto . . . out
on the street . . . I can see it as if I was there
. . . she's incapable of defending herself . . ."
(53); "and you won't see Lili defending herself!

174

. . . no! . . . the exact opposite . . . it's sad
. . . romantic-sad . . . a dancer" (54). She is
also seen in these reflections as helpless against
the world just like the animals they take care of:
"but once I'm gone . . . what about Lili! . . . the
cats . . . the dogs . . . I can't see Lili taking
care of herself . . . she's not made that way . . ."
(61). So contained in her lack of self-assertive-
ness is her generosity, her being a dancer, and her
similarity to animals that live at human mercy--as
if there were a necessary connection between these
three things.

Lili is also the opposite of the "assertive
woman" in what, for the narrator, constitutes her
utter trustworthiness: almost always she does just
what he tells her to do and keeps her mouth shut.
In *Castle to Castle*, when he does not wish her to
see things that might endanger them to know, "'Don't
look at them,' I tell Lili! 'Go back in!'" (247).
But it is especially in *North*, where they are surrounded by people whose motives seem most incomprehensible or terrifying to the narrator, that we see
her obedience and her silence: "And I tell them,
Lili and our friend the illustrious artist [Le
Vigan] . . . to ask me before they say anything
. . . not to put their foot in it! . . . (43); "With
her I don't have to worry, she seldom opens her
mouth, except to Bébert in his bag, a word or two
. . . their private conversation . . . (64) "I say
to Lili . . . 'You go see the heiress . . . you can
dance up there . . . take the cat in his bag . . .'"
(239); "Lili never takes long about anything . . .
the only trouble is she'll ask me what I want in
Denmark . . . I'll tell her to keep it under her hat
and she will . . ." (257); "'And Lili, you go up-
stairs!' I don't believe in haunted houses . . . but

175

I didn't care to leave her alone in our tower cubby-hole . . . with the rats . . . 'Is that what you want?' "Yes!"' (347). In *Rigadoon*, where the terrors that surround them come less from individuals than from the bombs and phosphorous falling from the skies, he orders her about less often than he did in the previous novel—as if she is more capable of doing the right thing in this holocaust than among the people in *North*. But he still tells her what to do, especially when the situation is one where people may be the main threat: "I say to Lili, 'We'd better stay just as we are . . .'" (41); "Lili doesn't wait to be asked twice" (184); "Lili, be careful.' 'Why?' I explain . . ." (218); "'Listen! . . . we've no more papers, no more passports, no more anything! . . . just my arm band!' 'Anything you say, Louis!'" (223). Throughout the novels, she puts her confidence in him completely, and he worries about her and protects her and tells her what she must do.

Yet in senses not meant in the notion of "assertive woman" she can also be said, on occasion, to assert herself. Thus, in *Castle to Castle*, as he is having his fever attack that begins the book, she fusses to take care of him (108, 111, 118), and at Siegmaringen she ministers to the terribly beaten Papillon on her own initiative, in spite of the fury of the crowd against him (217). In *North*, when they are in Berlin, she sets off the antiaircraft defenses by searching for Bébert with her flashlight (80-83). When the *Landrat* makes the cruel joke of pretending to smash Bébert against the wall because he is not pedigreed and is spayed, and so by Nazi regulation has no right to exist, she puts the cat in his bag and walks out of the room, heedless of the authority she may have offended—she even calls the narrator and Le Vigan away from the company (259-260). She worries about the robin, but not the one-armed soldier, able to take care of himself, who owns him (310). In *Rigadoon*, she speaks up when Le Vigan says Bébert originally belonged to him: "'He's ours!' That's Lili . . . I look at her . . . she'd only have done it for Bébert . . . she never says anything . . ." (104). But it is in this novel that she makes her most dramatic assertion--on behalf of the two of them and the retarded children that they take charge of from the tubercular Mademoiselle Odile, who no longer wishes to be bothered with those children. In order to get the children onto a train bound for Sweden, where they will be safe, she takes a desperate action.

> . . . I see this Swedish train isn't
> stopping . . . it's going very slow, but
> it keeps moving . . . it's passing . . .
> with big clusters of people hanging onto
> the doors and couplings . . . lousy luck,
> I'm thinking . . . I stand there like a
> sap . . . not Lili . . . before I can bat
> any eye! . . . she's under the train . . .
> that's right! . . . she's thrown herself
> on the roadbed! . . . and what a scream!
> . . . she that never screams . . . run
> over? . . . not at all! . . . always so
> quiet and soft-spoken! I go down on my
> knees, I crawl . . . I crawl under the
> crowd . . . I sing out: "Lili! Lili!"
> . . . naturally she can't hear me, they're
> all yelling, too loud . . . oh, I've got
> my wits back! better late than never, I
> need them! "Lili! Lili!" . . . the Swed-
> ish train has stopped . . . . (225)

So Lili *will* assert herself for the animals, for the children, for her husband. It is only that she never asserts herself just for herself.

In this respect, she is set in contrast to the angry generalities that the narrator makes about women. Thus when he says in *Castle to Castle* that "young ladies are always glad to betray . . . all young ladies . . . for a little friendliness" (186) or calls bitchery "a secondary feminine characteristic" (190) or declares about flattery that "it's no good treading lightly with politicians! heavy does it! massive! . . . same as with dames!" (274) it is clear that he does not mean them to apply to Lili. When in *North*, living under the power of the violent Inge von Leiden, he says that "women always find some pretext to go looking for gossip" (153), that if you did not look at women as "just bodies" you'd be so bored and irritated "you'd better hang yourself for your own good" (189), that "women and girls feel at home in tragedy, they want more and more! . . . at prayer, knitting by the guillotine, in the arenas, in bed, never enough!" (241), that "women's sexuality never gives up, they don't realize that men . . . even the worst priapic monsters . . . a drop of rain and it all shrivels up! . . . they want it, they want it . . . it's a terrible blow to the ladies when a man can't get it up! take female cats, the way they feel about spayed toms! . . . massacred if they don't run away!" (272), he means Lili to be an exception to all of it. Indeed, when he says to Le Vigan, "I'd drown every one of them to make them stop simpering!'" (294), he says, on the very next page, to the reader, "sweet Lili, so thoughtful . . . all heart . . ." (295). The complaints stop altogether in *Rigadoon*, where the only close and continuous contact he has with a woman is with her.

The generalizations about women that may apply to Lili are never angry ones. He says that when he got lost in the castle at Siegmaringen "Lili or Bébert found me . . . women have an instinct for labyrinths, for ins and outs" (135) and that, in Madame Mitre's splendid apartment, "Lili was happy in this 'Imperatrice' setting . . . all women . . . I couldn't find fault with her" (170). Also in *Castle to Castle*, when he says in reference to the ninety-six year old Madame Bonnard, whom he admires, that "the great feminine mystery has nothing to do with ass," that it is "much more subtle than 'cunts and loving hearts' . . . a kind of background music" (240), he is making a statement that seems to apply as well to Lili. The notion he illustrates in *North* with the story of the Russian sharpshooter girls, who can spot the officer in a group at six thousand feet, that "the female knows! . . . same as with she-dogs . . . who's in command!" (146) could apply to Lili in what the novel would intend in a positive way--*i.e.*, she might know who has authority in a situation, but she takes aim at no one. And while she could not be spared "the cruelty of Nature," as Céline calls it, "the tragedy of all women," we can well imagine that he would spare her from either of the two categories he provides for aging women: "if they hang on, they get to look like madams . . . or if they let themselves go . . . like parish ladies, no good for anything but mourning the dead and laying them out . . ." (254). When he says that "the human animal is an informer by nature, a born fink, he can't change" (203), clearly he is exempting her. Nor would his picture of "love" as "kisses in the dark, wriggling asses, flies wide open, foolish virgins upside down, imploring . . . and what prize obscenities at the end! . . . and wedding

bells! . . . a bucking, belching free-for-all" (229)
describe the love he has with her. The only remote-
ly critical thing he ever says that can apply to
Lili, either by implication or directly, as the text
intends us to see her, is that danger has a certain
appeal to her (*Castle to Castle*, 183; *North*, 80),
but he does not say even this without admiration.
And if it did not appeal to her, she would never
have linked up with him. Nor would she ever have
stopped the Swedish train. Really, she is presented
by the narrator with love and admiration throughout
the trilogy without any qualification.

Her relationship with animals extends this glow-
ing vision of her. She is not only linked to them
through the kindness, the "heart," she always shows
them, but there is the suggestion that she shares
their qualities--qualities the narrator admires. In
North, while the narrator is looking at the bombers
diving overhead, "Lili is much more interested in a
little scene between the titmice" (171). But she is
not just interested in animals; rather, she seems to
be on their wavelength. In *Castle to Castle*, when
he is in his fever at Meudon, the narrator thinks
how Bébert and Lili were at home in the labyrinthine
castle at Siegmaringen: "he [Bébert] and Lili would
meet in one corridor or another . . . they didn't
talk to each other . . . they behaved as if they'd
never seen each other before . . . each for himself
. . . animal waves are like that, a quarter of a
millimeter off and you're not yourself . . . you
don't exist!" He seems to be implying that his
reference to "animal waves" applies to her as well
as to the cat; certainly throughout the trilogy she
shows a great capacity to tune out almost all the
humans she comes in contact with, just like Bébert--
except when they are in helpless need. Continuing

his fever meditation, the narrator thinks about the
"same mystery with Bessy, my dog, later in the woods
in Denmark" and how he loved her in her wildness
(138-139). Then he thinks of how he can't tear
himself away from Bessy's memory, calls himself a
"virtuoso of fidelity," and declares, "I really
loved her with her crazy escapades, I wouldn't have
parted with her for all the gold in the world . . .
any more than with Bébert, though he was the meanest
ripper of them all . . . a tiger! . . . but very
affectionate at times . . . and terribly attached!
from end to end of Germany . . . animal fidelity
. . ." (139). Part of this--"I really loved her
with her crazy escapades, I wouldn't have parted
with her for all the gold in the world"--would seem
meant to apply to Lili as well as Bessy. In his
meditation, he goes from "animal waves" to "animal
fidelity" and applies the term to himself; Lili and
Bébert are on the same wave length; and the phrase
"terribly attached" would beautifully describe
Lili's connection to him--the fusion here of the
strands of his thinking connects "fidelity" with
"animal" with Lili. And at the end of the chapter,
he contrasts Bessy's death agony with that of men:
"Oh, I've seen plenty of death agonies . . . here
. . . there . . . everywhere . . . but none by far
so beautiful, so discreet . . . so faithful . . .
the trouble with men's death agonies is the song and
dance . . . a man is always on the stage . . . even
the simplest of them . . ." (140). A man is, a
woman is--but not Lili. She is literally a perform-
er on the professional stage, a dancer, but like
Bessy and Bébert, she does not *live* "on the stage"
the way the rest of us do: her *life* is not histri-
onics. She remains silent, becomes invisible. So
that while the bitter generalizations about humanity

do not apply to her, the admiring ones about animals do. For instance:

> . . . what's wonderful in the animal world is the way they know everything without telling each other . . . and far far away! At the speed of light! . . . we with our heads full of words, it's terrifying the way we knock ourselves out fuddling and muddling . . . till we don't know a damn thing! . . . or understand! . . . the way we stuff our big noodles! . . . full up! . . . busting . . . no room for more . . . not the slightest mini-wave . . . everything slips by . . . we don't catch it. (*Castle to Castle*, 154)

It seems no accident that the wandering of the couple should end, in *Rigadoon*, in a park in Copenhagen, with them surrounded by rare birds--creatures that approach them in friendship.

Since Céline as novelist thinks so highly of animals--the last novel is even dedicated to them--the implied comparison he makes of Lili to Bessy or Bébert and the attribution to her of the "animal waves" is high tribute to her. In fact, it is for her that he goes on living at all. He considers suicide at the beginning of *Castle to Castle* (32), but he cannot do it because he must go on protecting her (*e.g.*, 53). That his wish for death is a serious one is shown by the famous scene with Charon, where he sees his old friends, Le Vigan and Emile, and really wants to go off with them, but he cannot-- cannot die. "Lili must be plenty worried . . . I'd been gone for hours" (104). Rather than die, he stays with her and brings his friends back in novels that he hopes to sell. And when he is hit with the brick in *Rigadoon*, he keeps conscious by thinking "about Lili . . . and Bébert . . ." (139). And at the end of *Castle to Castle*, Lili's return from an errand in Paris he awaits "on tenterhooks" (341).

Thus, Lili functions in this trilogy much the way that the beloved girls do in Dickens' fiction. The words that Dickens had engraved on the tombstone of Mary Hogarth, the prototype of so many of his heroines--"Young, Beautiful, and Good"--could well be applied to Lili and in the same devoted spirit that Dickens applied them to Mary. Lili is at the center of the protagonist's life, as Little Dorrit comes to be for Arthur Clennam. And, like Little Dorrit, she is even more than that: she is put forth in the novels as a guiding light for humanity. In *North* he says "so many vaginas, stomachs, cocks, snouts, and flies you don't know what to do with them . . . shovelsful! . . . but hearts? . . . very rare! in the last five hundred million years too many cocks and gastric tubes to count . . . but hearts? . . . on your fingers!" (55). But she is "sweet Lili, so thoughtful . . . all heart . . ." (295). A few others in the novels also have hearts, notably Paul Marion, the Vichy Secretary of Information who was condemned to ten years forced labor-- "the only one who had any heart . . . who never forgot us . . ." (*Castle to Castle*, 148)--and the doctor who took them on the Swedish train--"that Red Cross man had a good heart" (*Rigadoon*, 230). And Céline says in *North*, about the hunchback and her father who supply Bébert with fish, that "there are good-hearted people wherever you go . . . you can't say that everything stinks" (129). But, for him, the heart that is most always *there* is that of his wife.

Her function as such a beloved woman in these novels links them to the novels of Dickens and not to those of his avant-garde imitators or "counterparts" like Henry Miller, Jack Kerouac, or William Burroughs. The comparison of Céline to Dickens has been made before.[13] Even her animal qualities, in the positive sense that Céline gives to "animal," do not detract from her comparison to a heroine from Dickens, for Lili's "heart" does not exclude the "animal" but seems to be profoundly connected with it. If that is so, then all the sexuality of human beings that Céline does not at all present in these novels in a favorable light is not an expression of animality in the sense that Lili is like an animal. Rather, the implication, the message for human beings is that they should have real animality above all by having hearts, as Lili does. In this sense, then, hers is "the sole remaining matrix," as Erika Ostrovsky says: "through her the only rebirth possible."

FOOTNOTES

1. L.-F. Céline, *Journey to the End of the Night*, trans. Ralph Manheim (New York: New Directions, 1983), p. 168.

2. Henry Miller, *Tropic of Cancer* (New York: Grove Press, 1961), p. 285.

3. Jack Kerouac, *On the Road* (New York: The Viking Critical Library, 1979), p. 39.

4. Wayne Burns, "The Beat and the Dead," in *Towards a Contextualist Aesthetic of the Novel* (Seattle: Genitron Books, 1968), pp. 87-92.

5. Burns, p. 93.

6. Julia Kristeva, *Powers of Horror: An Essay on Abjection*, trans. Leon S. Roudiez (New York: Columbia University Press, 1982), p. 64.

7. Leon Trotsky, "Céline and Poincaré: Novelist and Politician," in *Leon Trotsky on Literature and Art*, ed. Paul N. Siegel (New York: Pathfinder Press, 1970), p. 192.

8. Interview with Merry Bromberger (*L'Intransigeant*), in *Cahiers Céline*, Vol. 1: *Céline et l'actualité littéraire* (Paris: Gallimard, 1976), p. 31.

> Here it is! It's love of which we do not venture to speak yet in this hell, as if one could compose quatrains in a slaughterhouse. Love impossible today. Robinson looks for it like everyone, along with money, that other very indispensable thing. He finally ends up finding a peaceful corner, an income, a little woman who loves him. However, he cannot stay there. He has to leave when he has the good bourgeois life in hand, a

little home, a cajoling wife, goldfish. He tells himself he's crazy for
being like that. He goes away. Madelon pursues him. (. . .) The little
girl assails him. She understands
nothing. As for him, in order to go
away from her and from himself, he
wishes to be heroic in his way. But
he does not know how.

In the end, in the taxi, he finds
out. He tells Madelon that it is not
her but the entire universe that disgusts him. He says it as he can and
he dies because of it.

9. Wayne Burns, "*Journey to the End of the Night*: A
    Primer to the Novel," in *Understanding Céline*
    (Seattle: Genitron Press, 1984), pp. 28-108.
10. Céline in an interview with Albert Zbinden on
    Radio Lausanne, cited in Merlin Thomas, *Louis-
    Ferdinand Céline* (New York: New Directions,
    1979), p. 240.
11. *Castle to Castle*, trans. Ralph Manheim (New
    York: Penguin Books, 1976); *North*, trans. Ralph
    Manheim (New York: Penguin Books, 1976); *Riga-
    doon*, trans. Ralph Manheim (New York: Penguin
    Books, 1975).
12. *Céline and His Vision* (New York: New York Uni-
    versity Press, 1967), pp. 196-197.
13. Professor Wayne Burns at the University of Wash-
    ington often makes the comparison in his class-
    es. There is also an unpublished Master's the-
    sis by Patricia Sullivan, "Céline and Dickens:
    A Comparative Study" (San Diego State Univer-
    sity, 1978), that compares *Mort à .crédit* with
    David Copperfield.

THE DEATH OF MEMORY: THE MEMORY OF DEATH
Céline's Mourning for the Masses . . .

Jerry Zaslove

> If you have understanding and a heart show
> only one. Both they will damn, if you
> show both together.
>
> —Höelderlin

> However, a work of art expresses an entire
> world only insofar as it forms it. It
> forms a world insofar as it discloses the
> truth of reality, insofar as reality
> speaks out through the work of art.
> In a work of art, reality addresses man
> . . . How and why does a work of art out-
> live the conditions in which it had origi-
> nated?
>
> —Karel Kosik

> You'll have to find things in Journey that
> still exist.
>
> —Céline

Céline was the only modern novelist who recognized that the first World War not only destroyed an epoch but would destroy the capacity of a civilization to remember what war did to our entire century, the century of war. To be able to "find things" in his novels that "still exist" would be a test of the truth of his novel, and also a test of the archeological methods required to find the original conditions. How far away are they? Who remembers and who digs them out?

In the interview in which he speaks of a planned film of *Journey to the End of the Night* Céline said: "What you knew the war by, what the people of '14 knew it by, was the gunfire, from both sides. It was a rolling BLOM BELOLOM BELOM, it was a mill, grinding our epoch down."[1] No other writer between the wars (where we still are) recognized that it was a "sinister music, kind of deep Wagnerian music . . . Music that fits everything. (. . .) Very few speeches. (. . .) Very few words . . ."[2] that needed to reach out and find the new genre creating principle immanent in the suffering of the period. How was it possible to touch the masses without assimilating the masses' victimization in the forms of art itself, the forms of art that mime the victims' own forgetfulness of their history? T.W. Adorno's repeated attempts to define and criticise the historical-aesthetic problem of commitment, and the tension between the disappearance of the subject and the suppression of objective knowledge, is also a response to the music of between the wars. In his essay "Commitment," Adorno criticized Sartre and Brecht, epigones of commitment, without finding in them the artist who expresses the problem without being overwhelmed by it. Not even the modernism of polyvalent artists like Schoenberg prevents shame before the political helplessness of art:

> There is something embarrassing in Schoenberg's composition--not what arouses anger in Germany, the fact that it prevents people from repressing from memory what they at all costs want to repress-- but the way in which, by turning suffering into images, harsh and uncompromising though they are, it wounds the shame we feel in the presence of the victims. For these victims are used to create something, works of art that are thrown to the consumption of a world which destroyed them.[3]

The tensions displayed in Schoenberg are the tensions of modernity itself. Everything exposed and displayed, the creative process of the artist is presented as reality itself. Our authentic horror at modernity turns into the opposite: disdain for the past and absence of knowledge about the past. For a novelist to create characters in this life without people is difficult if not impossible. So modernism steels its disciplined asceticism to include but reject the already disciplined humanity by treating people as "masses" or "movements." A century of surplus production and expanded markets makes consciousness of the masses a requirement of political commitment. A surplus of thought or feeling either becomes an art "style" (as in surrealism) or an instrument of mass literacy, spreading *compromised* images into every corner of culture where, "thrown to the consumption of a world," the victims seek new forms of cultural organization.

In the context of the moral meaning of aesthetic commitment that tormented every artist of any magnitude during the "between the wars" period, Adorno's comment is not merely descriptive or explanatory. It also raises the question, "How and why does a work of art outlive the conditions in which it had originated?"[4] in a particularly challenging form. Not only is historical reality compared to social pathology; hallucination--"turning suffering into images"--becomes a normative artistic, as well as political, reality. Adorno is correct to use Kafka as the one who best addressed the reader's dilemma in the writer's creative dilemma:

> He over whom Kafka's wheels have passed, has lost forever both any peace with the world and any chance of consoling himself with the judgment that the way of the world is bad; the element of ratification which lurks in resigned admission of the dominance of evil is burnt away.[5]

The challenge that I am undertaking in this essay is to speculate about Céline's "commitment" to his own work, that is, to the question of the autonomy of his work in the face of the "element of ratification which lurks in resigned admission" of the political and social, that is mass pathology of the age. As if anticipating that an autonomous literature would, indeed, must be drawn into the political arena, Céline, the most uncommitted of all the novelists to political solutions, becomes the one most immersed in political ambivalences. Following the logic of Adorno's argument, he is the most responsible, the most authentic, the most truthful. The tabooed historical truth of this work and this logic is that, in addressing the terrible ambivalences of the relationship of writer to reader, he discloses the horrible ambivalences of his characters' relationship to their past and their history. In this sense, then, the work of this alleged horrible workman may ultimately be read as the work of the just, the just work, *not* the horrible work that ratifies horror.

Reading Céline in our hyper-dehumanized age requires reliving the historical agonies of his. The implications of this act of reconstruction (as if he *were* an obscure medieval writer!) are both literary and historical. And while it is in that relationship I am primarily interested, it goes without saying that what should follow would be a careful treatment of the nature of the characters in his work. However, Ferdinand's ambivalence toward his mother and father can only be felt and understood if the question of Céline's creative ambivalence toward authority, love and devotion is posed in the way the novel does--as a question of the crisis of literacy in our times, that is our ability to read our own feelings *about* the pathos of modern political responsiveness. While the question of his artistry is ultimately the most important subject, the question of the isolation of "artistry" from complex historical responses must also be faced. That is why his detractors, those who have dismissed him for his political and racialist views, are only in part incorrect. Incorrect on factual and interpretive grounds about his alleged fascism and collaborationism, his detractors are right in sensing that his art and his politics are entwined. But how entwined? While Merlin Thomas' fine study of Céline provides substantial evidence for Céline's innocence of the charges of treason and collaboration, Thomas still finds it necessary to say that Céline was politically naive, if not politically ignorant. Not only do I argue this is not true, or at least more complicated than Thomas' exonoration, I argue that Céline's work expands our sense of commitment into areas difficult to understand from most of the prevailing literary and ideological standpoints.

The implication, seen through the crisis in literacy in our times, is that in an authentic literary culture there can be no such thing as a fascist literature, a fascist novel, or an anti-semitic literature or novel. This would be a contradiction in terms. The literature that is or *becomes* fascist is no longer literature. Literature, paralyzed before fascism or anti-semitism, or their counterparts, turns its back on itself and becomes something else, not literature but its counterfeit, an unfathomable force that reproduces the non-human. Objectively considered this unfathomable force can be found and isolated in the social process; but since the standpoint of the novelist is both immanent and committed in the sense, described by Karel Kosik, of *forming* the world, not passively reproducing it, the novelist, like Archimedes, can objectively move the world only by finding a place to stand: therefore, the question--How and why does Céline's work "outlive" the period, the class, the ideology of its origins?--becomes one of the most important questions we can ask about the contemporary significance of his work.

Given the continuities in the World War ideologies and mentalities it is important to think through the concreteness attributed to the pain and violence in Céline's work. The thin line between "authenticism," or inauthenticity, in modern works, and their *autonomy* divides genuine literacy from non-literacy. Put another way, the ability of a work to "point . . . beyond the work itself, at something that transcends it",[6] determines its meaning and significance. In Céline's case, the combination of pathos, mourning, and consciousness of the masses and their painful life under modernity is not only pointed at, but is experienced and explored through the characters and their inner thoughts. Even more inexplicably, these thoughts are lyrical thoughts, so much so that it can be said that Céline was the last of the lyrical writers, a writer who experiences his past through his characters.

Céline confirms Freud's discovery of the thin line between *Lust, Unlust* and *Schmerz* (pleasure, unpleasure and pain) drawn in the dust settling on the debris of culture and the cultural heritage. To complete Adorno's comment:

> The so-called artistic representation of the sheer physical pain of people beaten to the ground by rifle-butts contains, however remotely, the power to elicit enjoyment out of it. The moral of this art, not to forget for a single instant, slithers into the abyss of its opposite. The aesthetic principle of stylization, and even the solemn prayer of the chorus, make an unthinkable fate appear to have had some meaning; it is transfigured, something of its horror is removed. This alone does an injustice to the victims; yet no art which tried to evade them could confront the claims of justice. Even the sound of despair pays its tribute to a

> hideous affirmation. Works of less than
> the highest rank are also willingly ab-
> sorbed as contributions to clearing up the
> past. When genocide becomes part of the
> cultural heritage in the themes of commit-
> ted literature, it becomes easier to con-
> tinue to play along with the culture which
> gave birth to murder.[7]

While other artists were fleeing into myth,
symbol, religion and party politics or proletarian
vanguardism, Céline fled backward to seek in the
principles and genesis of the novel the idea of
literacy as a form of cultural creation. Literacy
as imaginary social performance struggles to create
historical consciousness by making visible the invisible. Where humanity is annexed to mass culture
literacy disappears into the spectacle, the fatalis-
tic forms of cultural creation. Céline saw how the
needs of literacy change. For him it was no longer
possible to link commitment to the soul of feeling;
the mass soul now existed in the industrial and
cultural reflection in Hollywood. Material production and cultural materialism are tied to the production of literacy--film, symbol, surrealism, ad-
vertising, mass education, the emancipation of the
family into the factory, colonialism drenched in
Coca-Cola liberation. Hope for literacy is now tied
to an audience fulfilled in the nuances of violence.
For Céline, reception of his work must be carefully
measured against this audience's ability to grasp
its own retaliatory powers.

But Céline also understood that literacy needed
"Very few speeches . . . Very few words": his
effort to create a world through self-exposure of
his own idealism within the deterioration of a pub-

lic world illuminates the possibility of being alive in mass culture. He adheres to an aesthetic that is related to the problems of the masses. We see this in his willingness to open the novel again and again to the public world. He does not debase the human, although it may be said he writes of a debased collective life. Through his tendency to personify and objectify the rush of the world toward debasement Céline differentiates between *self*-debasement and world homelessness just as his novelistic counterparts in the nineteenth-century, Balzac, Stendhal, Flaubert (especially in *Sentimental Education*), Dostoevsky and Dickens, also did. The essence of the novel's literacy, unlike poetry, the epic or drama, is that the novel creates a world and by linking it to an emerging audience. Yet the soul-destroying practicality of the novel, its desire to remain in touch with everyday life, also carries with it an ethical principle: to return again and again to doubt, uncertainty, the loneliness and the pathos that accompanies the desire to create and find readers who can participate in one's life. Objectively there is the historical pressure to address an audience that is *being made into anxious recipients*; for both artist and audience are being made into objects not of their own making. In modernity's exhaustion and depletion of literary response there is still Céline's characters' expectations of replenishment and renewal. The dialectic of their death by installments, while fatal to political engagement, is nevertheless committed to making visible the essence of the life of the writer-author-doctor who "stands face to face with a real receptive subject."[8] The French philosopher Merleau-Ponty recognized this principle in the tormented artist, in particular the novelist and painter who makes a work which teaches one to read the nuances, complexities, shadings and changes in the relationship of author to character to reader. Out of self-doubt and the apperception of self-destruction and the awakening of new feelings, the self becomes a life. Put another way, autobiography becomes history as the psychological becomes authentically public: "A painter like Cézanne, an artist or a philosopher, must not only create and express an idea but must awaken in other minds the experience in which it is rooted . . . [t]he truth is that it was *the work which had to be done which demanded this particular life*" [Italics, Merleau-Ponty].[9] In *Death on the Installment Plan* the writer-doctor awakens himself and others to the experience of Ferdinand's criticism of the present.

This need to awaken the war-haunted subject was the pre-condition for the creation and reception, the literacy for the novel, that haunted Céline until his last works. The unforgiveable misapprehension of his work, not to say the confiscation of his meanings in order to link him and the novels to the forces of reaction, remains in this sense indistinguishable from the social meaning of his work, the meaning he saw in his life and work. In the following pages I intend to introduce those aspects of his work and its reception that reveal his deliberate and conscious attempt to create a world that not only personifies the masses at a particular stage of their destruction, but gives them back a form of cultural self-knowledge. I realize that only a longer work can explain why the will-to-create culture is itself politically and historically problematic in the novel form. We would have to know why the novel clarifies cultural crisis by creating profound anti-cultural feelings, profound because

the knowledge that emerges from these feelings is
not a property of any inert "text," but exists in
relation to the reader as a historical subject. The
novel as a form of cultural creation is a phenomenal
experience as well as an historical one. It is
"phenomenal" because it is a response to reality
that cannot be fully recovered; however because it
includes the reader in its world it is by its very
history entangled in enlightenment, idealism, fantasy, ideology, and critique. Further, because modern
readership is entwined with political and ideological manipulation, myth can not be used as a trust-
worthy guide to the phenomenal, or to unpolitical
generalizations about collective response. That is
why it must be emphasized that in Céline's novel,
myth is not the subject matter. If myth exists in
Céline it is only as a living historical, not literary reality; it exists only as the congealed debris
of history out of which the intellect painfully
builds a response to the hierarchically organized
and inhuman cultural forms that torment us. Of
course, modernity is not immune to myth; but myth in
Céline is critically mediated by allegories like the
King Krogold legends that peer out of the saturnine
excesses of a war-torn culture. This is not myth in
the usual sense of the word; for Céline myth is the
now false literacies that still retain the falseness
of their truth to power. The priests, shamans and
warriors who comprise the intelligentsia with its
literacies also own the language in which myths are
drenched. Céline, like Proust or Kafka before him,
seeks to awaken the sleeping subject of myth from
the sleep of reason, and this intention is discern-
ible in *Death on the Installment Plan*. More fraught
with the *past and future* than *Journey to the End of
the Night*, in this novel he attempts to find and

value a specific cultural memory for the amnesiacs about to be trucked off as the gang of consumers of the newly emerging forms of cultural capital. In the novel the *inner* domination that rules modern life is reflected in the public performance of that life by the gods of work, production, commodity and consumption: we see the standard of living is the standard of dying, because public life, like damaged art, continues war by other means. Everyday life is the front line and the bomb shelters the State.

If art also continues life by means other than work, production and capital, it does so by means of culture. But art, Céline recognized, has none of the constituting powers of cultural production. Deprived of autonomy and compassion by society, it only grimaces and mimics production. Writing, unable to live with memory as its historically constituted cultural institution, knocks on the doors of other institutions that deny it entrance. Its knock freezes before the sign: forget the past. To shape Ferdinand's life in this context is impossible, but to speak of a life unshaped to those whose lives are misshapen becomes a labor of art and an affirmation of the pain that has neither "credit" with the right institutions, nor builds approved profit out of cultural capital. Céline's comment that "truth is a pain that never stops" needs to be explained in terms of his negation of culture as we know it; and here lies also his ambivalent affirmation of another culture, one where the truth of unpleasure and the mourning for the legacy of memory from another world criticizes this world.

While he [Brecht] spoke I felt a force acting on me that was equal to that of fascism; I mean a power that has its source no less deep in history than fascism.

-Walter Benjamin
Understanding Brecht

I am asking, what is the subject of Céline's second novel? And answering that the awakening of the masses is the subject matter of *Death on the Installment Plan*. The people as masses that inhabit the novel are seen through Ferdinand who speaks for them. The pathos of the narrator's self-exposure corresponds to the pathos of the individuals, atomized and alone, the solitude of the multitude, whose collective inwardness is determined by the society's mental structures left standing after the war. There is lived reality, everyday life, allowing the state to exist in the self. The notion, addressed in George Lukacs' work, that for "the primitive once upon a time life was individualistic, today humans are,"[10] expresses the deep ambivalence in modern life toward the promised emancipation of the individual. It also expresses the powerlessness of the writer's intellect before the formation of masses. The constructed and guarded social consensus degrades the connections of the present to the past. The past is overwhelmed by the constant externalization and exhumation of intimate life. Whether it is the power of modern life to turn relationships into "the consumption of exchange value," or whether the individual is taught to "empathize with the soul of

the commodity" by accepting the official versions of
need and tragic loss peddled by the spectacle-pro-
ducing society,[11] the commodity itself becomes the
safeguard of "autonomy." The commodity, wrestled to
the breast of the citizen as Private Being, returns
again and again to demonically oppress one's needs
and imagined wants. Céline recognized in today's
citizen the fugitive bourgeois from the French enlightenment who is owned by the state and who becomes adept at watching his inner life emptied onto
the stage of modernity: ". . . the crowds still
being massacred off the Place Gaillon . . . the
buses are still raging . . . the apocalypse goes
on." Inner life is almost completely wrecked in
Ferdinand's stay in England where he learns about
the cost of celibacy and ideal love. He abandons any
hope for intimacy by learning the primary lesson of
the century: So long as "words stay in the dream"
language is pleasant, otherwise the only thing in
the cards was "pure grief," the grief of failed
"intimacies."

Céline's antimodern critique of modernity distinguishes him from artful modernists like Joyce or
Eliot. Their ideologies of cultural despair, only
as complex as failed religion will allow, provides
no vision of cultural creation, no gift of meaning
to those whose memories are held hostage at the
front. In comparison, Céline brings memory into
performance as speech spoken from a new world. As
modernists perhaps only Adorno or Walter Benjamin
can be put in the same category with Céline; however
traces of mourning, pathos, negation and resistance
to cultural amnesia also live in Lawrence, especially in the novels *The Rainbow* or *Lady Chatterley's
Lover*. Traces of memory, writes Adorno, allow the
autonomous work to achieve "a speaking that tran-

scends writing by absorbing it . . . (by) deliver
(ing) human speech from the lie that it is already
human."[12] This "delivering" cannot rest in "writing" or "style." It rests in the social significance of writing, its meaning in the lives of people, not in the meaning of "texts." It is more
useful to think of Céline through the world of the
grotesque where his radical use of memory becomes a
critique of style and ideology. The grotesque was
once the curse and critique of ideological thinking,
but has been assimilated into the very style of
modernism itself. In the works of "post-modernism"
art styles are indistinguishable from the styles of
capitalism's own blind distortions and ignorant
sublimation of people's absent feelings. Where once
alienation in art was misery's way of transferring
violence away from the self and toward the enemies
of the self, now modern culture alienates the meaning of alienation by making it a staple of the
culture industry. Nothing achieved by modern art
cannot be repackaged and redeemed as cultural capital. But the memory of the repressed still lives in
Céline's language because his language apprehends
both the cost of remembering the discontent of living in dreams, and not remembering the public world
of spoken language. Distancing us from the sources
of work, the modern world makes all work hell until
separation and atomization are the alpha and omega,
the weapons and icons, of the factory line society.

Unable to live in the factory society memory
only exists in official history, codified in a literacy found in texts, schools, intellectual systems
and rationalizing bureaucracies divorced from traditional culture. Céline is not only a chronographer
of this process whereby wartime becomes everyday
time, he is the prophet and seducer of *young* memo-

ries that might not already be silenced by the "Blom Belolom Belom" of the cannons. Consequently the novel inherits the culture's danger zone. As "Doctor Ferdinand" heals wounds, he also connects thought, theatre and therapy: the theatre of words disappearing into social iconic pictures that allow us to visualize the cause of our amnesia. Therefore Ferdinand's complexity is also Céline the writer's. Both are artist-healers touching the origins of phantasy in memory and pain. The deepest level of Céline's work must be apprehended as a continuous mode of phantasy where pathos and mourning labor against the "book" and the "state," these modern tools of the intelligentsia that have changed political and imaginative capacity into the psychological and political repression of memory. The Doctor calls to the dispossessed, shelterless and speechless to give them words to enable them to remember the precise images, iconic forms, mute and satiated with modern life, that Céline, out of the debris of war, attempts to reproduce in the feelings of those whose feelings are purchased on the installment plan by patronage, entertainment, industry, conscription, and intellectual barter: your feelings for our minds. No wonder that to understand Céline, as well as his counterparts in the interwar period like Lawrence, Mann, Brecht, Kafka, or Benjamin, we need to explore the ways in which his artistic work reveals the inhuman nature of *intellectual* work, the division of emotional and intellectual labor. For this reason alone he belongs alongside of Marx and Freud who examined the separation of mental labor from physical, or sensual labor, recognizing that the narcissistic, internalized precepts of a civilization, its ideals, not only contribute to the exploitation and imperialization of others' work, but

ennoble exhausting and debilitating work in the name
of art and intellectual achievement. Freud writes
that ". . . art offers substitutive satisfactions
for the oldest and still most deeply felt cultural
renunciations, and for that reason it serves as
nothing else does to reconcile a man to the sacrifices he has made on behalf of civilization."[13] On
the other hand Freud also says, "art heightens his
feelings of identification" with culture, sensing
that our identifying with this *ideological version
of culture* destroys and mutilates genuine culture.
Art does not descend from the world of thought to
the world of sensual relations of individuals. Culture as art, and art as ideals remain stuck at the
level of collective identity where the modern ideal
of liberating the masses is organized by states and
governments into illusions, the pathos of culture.

Production turns the misery of labor into pathos: pathos the mediating element between the hope
that the masses can become a proletariat, and the
myth that the masses can be transformed into a
proletariat without their succumbing to the bureaucracy that is the spirit of the state. The proletariat as a concrete historical force lives or dies
somewhere in this pathos. This knowledge lies behind Céline's metaphor of "installment plan," the
social meaning of work, the substitution of work for
death.

In choosing to concentrate on pathos and mourning in Céline's second novel I am doing so to show
the creative and therefore form-creating, *theoretical* profundity of Céline and his difference from
almost all major modern novelists. Sparing no self-
criticism and refusing to accept that history or
culture were supra-individual, Céline returns the
genre of the novel to its origins in the historical

forces that create masses, those like himself without property or a future. This is a concept of a people whose pastness is made up of the history of their resistance to authority, as well as their receptivity to stories about that resistance, stories that are turned into mistrust, misfortune and lying by, as he says, their simply "working for hire." Torturing his imagination to write a story of characters like his father ("My father tortured his imagination about my future . . .") Céline's own feats of imaginative endurance speak to and about those who cannot speak. This aesthetic mutual aid between writer, characters and readers builds the novel's "aesthetic savings" out of legends, images, photographically bright pictures drenched in our intimate knowledge of Ferdinand's emotional needs. Céline relies on a comraderly intimacy--gifts of language to a "literate" listener who still cannot read the *significance* of Ferdinand's feelings. *Death on the Installment Plan* memorializes his father, his mother, his worker friends and patients, the children and women, helplessly convulsed customers of the salesmen of the world. This world "that ends and begins in 1900" and "gobbles up his brain" with grief and remorse leaves him and the reader afflicted with his mother's memory: "All my father left behind him was his memory and carloads of trouble. Memory is an obsession with her. The deader he is the more she loves him. Like a she-dog that can't get enough." Only intimacy is complicated by an hallucinatory sense of the present; the last century with its aura of people and faces drifts away, and the present is eclipsed by pathology, silence and our sorrow at the bodies lying under the masts of little skiffs. Their silence replaces speech with pictures of grief.

This is not "irony"; it is the pathos of mourning for departed worlds. With the smell of his mother's old lace in his nostrils, he sees his father's imaginary ships cruise by, pathetically but openly vulnerable to the apocalyptical political winds of the century of warfare. Where the entire world goes trampling through his head, Céline sews into the filligree lace of his memory isolation from the past: "Then I was really alone! Then I saw the thousands and thousands of little skiffs returning high above the left bank . . . Each one had a shriveled little corpse under its sail . . . and his story . . . his little lies to catch the wind with." To talk about things no one remembers is the deepest opposition that can be felt. "Old memories stay with you . . . but they're delicate fragile . . ." he says, as the novel continually slips gently in a voyage to the past and away from this century of war that keeps him from *exposing their lies*.

Memory is, then, the organizing feeling, if not the most important principle of composition in Céline's creative process. Memory possesses our imagination of people owned and censored by the ear-splitting roar of petty-bourgeois life. He recognizes his absolute hatred of what was done both to his memory and to the unliberated, shriveled little corpses who have sold themselves in the marketplace; this memory is recreated and is acted out, performed, in such a way that all the inner notes of a tyrannical music play on his ambivalently quixotic conscience. The pseudo-proletarianized public world is later appropriated by the character Courtial, who is the unwitting preserver and perpetuator of the petty-bourgeois values that the novel as truth about Ferdinand ultimately enacts and discredits. We see in Courtial the character who prophetically stands for the crackpot intellectuals who begin to dominate European public life and whose values (for example Sartre's) Céline struggled against. Céline's repudiation of the intellectual literary establishment and the supremacy of the intelligentsia is even foreshadowed in Courtial, who like Céline dismembers the world to save it, not just criticize it.

In Céline's work the intellectual world is thus dismembered too. Intellectual values and thoughts are understood to be part of the *decreating* capitalist world. Because no reader can respond to a work of art by forming ideas about the work without participating consciously in the conditions brought to life by the work itself, Céline knows that works as tormented as his own will not survive unless they become a concrete historical memory. He abhorred aesthetic or political understanding that only reproduced the conditions of its existence. The social reality that totalizes the past only creates the "necessary" reproduction of the present in institutions. The catastrophic modernization of the psyche testifies to the pain of this kind of progress. Not only did Céline hate this modernization, his particular sense of its abstractness illuminated the way the modernized psyche had become solely defined by political economy, that is work whose real end was not emancipation but was a delusion about the immortality of culture.

Work and political economy as the *only* social equivalent of art? This is now the universal condition where we exchange our already abstracted selves for a culture equally abstract, equally invisible. "The more irrational the world becomes . . . the more abstract my art . . . I am abstract with memories" Paul Klee wrote, thus urging that the concrete depended on our use of memory, and our use of memory and history depended on our conscious understanding of the relationship of creation to work. Against Prometheus' rebellion, creation *and* work are stolen *back* by the gods who create terror but do not work, and who, in Marx's terms, produce alienation and reification and our corresponding dead souls. In his recognition and hatred of progress that was little more than the ruins of the old world repeated in modern dress, Céline throws down his writing before the onrushing locomotive of history and defines the alpha and omega of his hatred as hatred of intellectual abstractions, indeed of the debris of intellectual thought in himself that separated heart from understanding, culture from work. Raging against this division his novel addresses a reader who can never knowingly be on the side of pain.

iii

The continuation of life by other means, including the issues of guilt, ceremonies of expunging guilt, the work of mourning as the reflection of this loneliness of infinity.

-H.J. Syberberg
Our Hitler: A Film From Germany

H.J. Syberberg, the Célinean filmmaker from Germany, influenced by Brecht, Benjamin, Wagner and the history of film, has recently recognized what Céline knew. Céline knew that his competition in the world of art was film, the century's mass entertainment, Fascism enduring in simulated reality and entertainment:

Nor is the movie house of the mass
society the fast food joint and beer garden of the proletariat, which has been
going to the theatre for a long while now,
well organized and well prepared, without
popcorn or slapstick, because the proletariat has learned that culture requires
the entire person before opening up. They
say one should distrust anyone who says
otherwise, that he wants to misuse culture
to sell different things with his ideas,
that he simply wants to get at the specta-
tor's money.[14]

If the novel could recreate "infinity," that is,
give us a picture of what had happened after 1900 to
the masses, those who are bought off by culture, it
would be a responsible genre, the way it was when
Zola stood for integrity in the face of his political enemies. Céline made his political enemies *from*
the stuff of his novels. Mob-man was defined as the
slaughtering weapon of the crazed nation-states of
Europe that after 1900 turned nineteenth century
economic imperialism toward not only more global
expansion, but toward expanding the nation-state on
the continent of Europe itself. The collapse of
Eastern dynasties, the growth of liberal parliamentary democracies, and the swift rise of industrial-
ist states rooted in archaic and even feudalistic
social structures (like Germany) required the mobi-
lization of masses of soldiers and worker armies to
maintain the bourgeois-aristocratic fantasy of a
balance of power. The glorious dreams of a global
supremacy spurred on by the emancipation of the
middle classes during the later part of the nineteenth century was articulated by the now "Euro-

peanized" intellectual's alliance with financier, academician and parliamentary democrat. These statesmen of Europe, the new pseudo-world citizens, provided new visions for a society whose character was fundamentally changing. Whether the aging British colonial administration, or the Prussian conservative bureaucracy, or French militant rationalism, or pure American nationalism was at stake in spreading political ideologies, both the allegiance and redefinition of the organic masses were required. The rise of socialism as an international movement redefined the worker as an individual within a collective identity. Concurrently, nationalism and liberalism used social Darwinist ideologies to redefine the individual out of existence. Here and now the struggle of nations was a struggle for the domination of the *souls* of men. State ownership of the souls of men, a subject of political and cultural theory since Rousseau, Hegel and Marx, was dramatized in the struggle of the European nations to mobilize millions of wage-earners, disoriented peasants and country people, middle-class students and professionals in the common patriotic cause of warfare. Public opinion, communicated through a vast entrepreneurial press whose literacy and values were predominantly middle class, participated in the war's violent purgation of the universal hatred of those ideas and peoples unassimilatable into national ideology. The lost world, no longer capable of being grieved over, was, of course, the world of emancipatory cultural values, where freedom was expressed predominantly through the liberal values of the late nineteenth century. It was a world that had produced national cultures in France, England and Russia, however different in all three. Enlightenment, political-economy, and bourgeois cultural emancipation were defined and integrated in national and urban centres and institutions whose growth required a stable work force, unionized or not. The deepest contradictions in this state of affairs were apparent to critical thought. What was *not* apparent, except to the most clairvoyant and eccentric thinker or artist and then only fleetingly, was that the century of pan-Nationalism, the twentieth century, would become the century of irrational lust for change and disorientation, incipient in the origins of capitalism itself. Capitalism would eventually turn to mass violence and state violence as an extension of its view of progress. The state needed armies to ward off mass movements, just as society needed the state to protect itself against its own contradictions. And suddenly the state needed the masses to form the cultural capital on which a consumer society would be built and maintained.

These very brief generalizations about the Europe of Céline's memory of "1900" would have to be explored in precise detail to achieve a proper historical representation of the context and meaning of his work. No such study exists in English and without one Céline's reception is incomplete.

Céline remains, consequently, "unread" just because his work takes on, consciously and unconsciously, the entire social transformation of Europe after 1900. Naturally this is done through fictional means, but it is done, fictionally, through his own historical experience of the psychological and *visual* concerns of the nineteenth century artist that futurism, surrealism and expressionism either questioned or abolished. The modernist critique of inwardness that also led to the fetish of objectivity, behaviourism, and disorienting styles only

210

provoked Céline to refine his indifference to "modernism" all the more carefully. For Céline to use the novel form represented his response to life itself, precisely because his indifference to modernist aesthetics was formed out of his care about the people and readers who were outside of modernism's dehumanized, artistic fragmentations, but were still *inside* modernity's dehumanization and perceptual violence. Céline's indifference, the mask of toughness and anomie, answers to the banalities and pathologies of the emancipatory ideologies of the century which asked the individual to pay in more and more commitment to modernity. His answers, mediated through the voice of pathos and mourning that tenderly echoes the redemptive potential of these ideologies, are heard in the nuances of hope attached to the grief over the failure of hope. This is the essence of his compassion, the opposite of indifference in his work, whose genesis is in his second novel.

If the context in which to place Céline is the crisis of European society and culture since 1900, this must not be understood only in terms of a static social background. His sense of history is too animal, too keen. The *literary-historical* background of his work reflects a long, active legacy: of Villon, Rabelais, Montaigne, Cervantes and Diderot--the legacy of radical humanism that is the heart and soul of the continuing historical struggle of the genre of the novel against hierarchy, the state and the rational language of intellectuals. The aesthetic phenomenon we call "the novel" was for Céline synonymous with "lived reality," that is, with culture itself. His rage against inauthentic writing represents his awareness that a transformation in writing the novel corresponds to a transformation in the entire structure of society, as well as a transformation of our view of history transmitted through cultural institutions. Morbidly aware of how society inherits the past and transforms itself by denying the past, the labor of creating the novel embodies this process. Furthermore, because under modernity the "emancipation" of science from reason and philosophy has led to the supremacy of the violent cults of technology and business, the emancipation of art from feeling and visualization surrenders art to mass culture, the icon-producing image machines of our manipulated fantasies. The genre of the novel reveals the history of forgetfulness. It shows us the "mask" of the bourgeoisie which has inherited, but suppressed, the tradition of the grotesque. Already in the authority-hating humanist tradition of carnival, as represented by Rabelais, or in Balzac's or Stendhal's presentation of personal, life-narratives in forms that challenge the bourgeois state and its official history, we see Céline's sense of the present as non-human history prefigured as the history of forgetting. In his hatred of forgetting lies the awareness that in making the masks of the bourgeoisie is also the making of the masses crushed with work, and whose essence will remain unintelligible until a novel (like his own) takes on the responsibility of giving to forgetting a form that allows "reality to address man." In a particularly important passage Ferdinand-Céline says:

> If you haven't been through that you'll never know what obsessive hatred really smells like . . . the hatred that goes through your guts, all the way to your heart. . . .

Nowadays I'm always meeting characters
who complain, who bristle with indignation
. . . They're just poor bastards that
aren't getting anywhere . . . jerks . . .
dinner-table failures . . . that kind of
rebellion is for weak sisters . . . they
didn't pay for it, they got it for nothing
. . . they're drips.

Where did they get it from? . . . no
place . . . the *lycée* maybe . . . It's a
lot of talk, hot air. Real hatred comes
from deep down, from a defenseless child-
hood crushed with work. That's the hatred
that kills you. There'll be more of it,
so deep and thick there will always be
some left, enough to go around . . . It
will ooze out over the earth . . . and
poison it, so nothing will grow but viciousness, among the dead, among men.

Céline can not be understood without understanding his historical sense, the history of work and
labor, therapy and healing, science and degradation
of reason taking place in the first half of the
twentieth century. Not only does this place Céline
in the proper context with comparable revitaliza-
tions of the novel in the past, along with the use
that popular memory teaches for understanding the
radical literacy of the novel, it defines Céline's
work in terms of the readership most likely to
understand him. Not that this reader can be identified and isolated. Rather criticism must identify
the immanent circumstances that would make it possible for a reader to understand the deepest impulses,
and therefore the imaginary and historical condi-

tions that make a reading of Céline contiguous with
his critique of hate and horror.

Céline, as Marx, recognized the contiguous relationship of culture to labor. He sees the laborer
as bought soul. The bourgeoisie amassed wealth and
emancipated the forces of production, but out of
this, as Céline says, "nothing will grow but viciousness, among the dead, among men." Céline understood the power of hate as no other twentieth
century writer. The *Communist Manifesto*, that hymn
to change urging the proletariat to reinherit its
creative powers, also contains pathos and hate.
Marx also saw that "all things solid melted into the
air" only to produce promethean industrial wealth on
top of the sensuously complex changes within every
aspect of culture. Céline saw this process in two
sides: the collapse of the old world into the
bourgeoisie, and then into the declassed masses.
Accepting the call of impressionism's painterly
*re*composition of all things solid melting into the
air, he gives us the *feelings* of how this "melting"
turns sensual reality into warfare and destruction.
The spectacle character of modern life and the mentality that supports it prohibits and yet mediates
all attempts to establish a perspective of real
labor or creation from which to view the simulta-
neous decline *and* renewal of growth and power.
While the state undermines our ability to think
coherently about the necessary relationship of military to the relations of production in the Western
industrial world, the art of the modern period reproduces a melting perspectiveless perspective
through the reproduction of a world devoid of feeling about the painfully swindled masses. For example, a readership fulfilled in such masochism will
find Orwell's *1984* genuine, unable to distinguish

Orwell's middle-class despair and distaste for the "proles" from visions like Céline's that explore the intimate history of a character's response to the "mass" in himself. There is no affinity between Ferdinand's compassion for people and Winston Smith's sordid desire for self-obliteration.

Immersed in anonymity the masses *learn* to see their reflection in a world without memory of their immersion in themselves. This immersion in a history without memory happens not only because of the growth and accumulation of wealth in the new nation-states; it happens because history requires, at the same time and adjacent to that growth, the destruction of the values, creations and class experiences of those who are conscripted into warfare. The monstrous swindle perpetrated by the bourgeoisie is even reproduced in the electoral politics that represents ideology to the bourgeoisie as the struggle with an historically illusory "people," the proletariat, who will ultimately vanish at the end of history. Instead, factory culture becomes the elusive utopia, history as a stage without actors or people. It is the legacy of *this* history that people with orders shoot the other on sight. A culture without a theory of cultural labor value, or, put another way, without a theory that tells how to transform labor into creative and emancipatory culture, will not provide us with real readers of Céline. Yet because there is no end to this history, the true reader of Céline may still be found where the link between aesthetic enlightenment and social domination is still remembered. Perhaps today only outside of North America is this likely. The true reader of Céline will have to see the connections between mourning for the absent protagonist of history, and disloyalty to intellectually

popularized ideas of the people. In the interwar
period Céline tried to define this readership, yet
the interwar mania insisted on defining loyalty to
the nation in degrees of one's admiration of and
treachery to the masses; this mania may have driven
him mad. It certainly drove him to make political
comments where, as Merlin Thomas says, in displaying
his unaltered "mistrust of political solutions to
human misery," he appears reactionary. His mistrust
was "total and absolute," Thomas says, and the po-
lemical side is seen in the following letter to Elie
Fauré, written in 1935:

> The sad thing is that *there is no "peo-*
> *ple"* in the touching way you use the word,
> there are simply exploiters and exploited,
> and each one who's exploited dreams only
> of becoming an exploiter. He doesn't
> understand anything else. The heroic,
> egalitarian proletariat *does not exist.*
> It's a *pipe-dream*, a nonsense, hence the
> uselessness, absolute and sickening of all
> those derisory images: the blue-overalled
> worker, hero of tomorrow--the wicked capi-
> talist with gold watch chain. One is as
> big a shit as the other. The worker is a
> failed bourgeois. Nothing touching about
> that: senile and dishonest tear jerking![15]

The true reader of Céline will have to find out
where mourning for the lost people is not a form of
passivity, but is an active, imaginary component of
hatred for the modern senility that shows in the
state's usurpation of the past. This is the legacy
of the grotesque that objectifies *self-derision* in
his verbal phantasmagoria.

Céline's novel plunges into this century of grudges with a passion for verbal phantasmagoria that, as Thomas suggests, borders on a kind of inverted quixotic polemic against *anything* that might contribute to the coming war. This same Céline later described communism as "above all a poetical vocation,"[16] condemning scientific communism as slavery. To understand this aspect of Céline is beyond the scope of most of us today, perhaps this writer included. Yet to forgive his "politics" is only possible by understanding his almost ascetic self-identification with the *plight* of the masses, not their cause. My own understanding of him is that he never committed himself to the Fascist side of the human spirit--the "politics of cultural despair" that created the aesthetic and intellectual, and therefore cultural conditions for the rise of Fascism--but he pursued the *intellectual and emotional origins of Fascism* back to their beginnings in the symbolic "1900" and the onset of the secular religion of mass movements. The nationalization of the masses that the Fascists demanded from culture can be traced to the roots of the bourgeosie's emotional and aesthetic offensive war against modernity, and to the intellectual as well as political transformation of this war into a political war against individual emancipation. In this regard Céline tells the same story in *Death on the Installment Plan* in a way that haunts us with its truth about everyday life. While he reproduces the rhythms and tensions of a world that is constantly changing, he shows a world that resists "transcendence" by advocating freedom only for the sake of toil:

It seemed to me that there were two ways of telling stories. The classic,

217

normal, academic way, which consists of
creeping along from one incident to the
next, twisting, turning on the surface, if
I may say so, into all sorts of jerks,
hesitations, restarts for better or for
worse (. . .) the way cars go along the
street . . . and then, the other way,
which means descending into the intimacy
of things, into the fibre, the nerve, the
feeling of things, the flesh, and going
straight on to the end, to its end, in
intimacy, in maintained poetic tension, in
inner life, like the *metro* through the
inner city straight to the end, once the
choice is made, it's essential to stay in
the same conviction, in the same intimate
tension, once and for all, in the intimacy
of life, to seize the story in this fash-
ion.

This creative credo not only defines his writing, it
also defines the imaginary meaning of the "inner
life" of the world he lives in--the metro of political ideologies running over the citizens of the city
and utterly destroying their capacities to resist.
It shows his awareness of how the imaginary world is
destroyed by culturally anti-transcendent vocabularies that run over any feeling for intimate thought.
It is a commitment to take on the enormous task that
he admires in Rabelais, Zola and other writers, like
Barbusse, who not only wrote but created their own
worlds. This is a commitment to turn culture inside
out so what appears to us as life, intellect,
ideals, is recognized and mirrored as death, violence and banality. It is also a commitment to a
kind of intimacy no Fascism could tolerate.

That's the presence of death for you when
you do all their talking for them.

-Céline
Death on the Installment Plan

If Céline recognized his "epoch" in his own
life, he also learned the meaning of "this life
meant art." He paid a high cost for writing his
life on the installment plan. The cost of being
separated from society and the need to maintain that
separation can be reckoned by the language of his
novels and his struggle to prevent memory from being
ultimately overwhelmed by pathology, self-criticism
and fantasy. There at the margins of life he con-
templates the risks of searching for his own audience. This is not a risk of "style" or ritual, say
like Artaud. It risks a world built against social
acceptance, because he understands that the writer's
crime lies in having to rob society of its ideals.
Ferdinand, like the heroes of Rabelais, becomes a
gigantic figure. His *thought* is expressed in a
socially saturated, iconic language that opens pictures of the world to the reader. As a figure of
"lived reality" Ferdinand opens doors to the dying
worlds, and grows older by revealing and even phi-
losophizing on the meaning of death. While dismiss-
ing all attempts to humanize him, he persists in
absorbing the world of pain no one else can stomach.
The world attacks his bowels, groin, gut, head and
prick but he takes vengeance on no one ("it does no
good and makes things worse"): "My thoughts stagger
and sprawl, I'm not very good to them . . . madness
is hot on my trail I can fight back" he says early

in the novel. But it is not until his idealism runs
its course, until it has been suppressed, that he
learns through Courtial that in the "torrent of
things and people" there is no way to stop people
from entering his life:

> I wanted to jump out on them . . . to
> plant myself in front of them . . . and
> make them stop where they were . . . Grab
> them by their coats . . . a dumb idea
> . . . and make them stop . . . and not
> move anymore . . . stay where they were,
> once and for all . . . and not see them
> going away anymore . . .

Ferdinand does not always see the social forces that
obliterate his friends, but his desire to "stop them
where they were," while expressed idealistically,
nevertheless also expresses his awareness that his
idealism is painful--"a dumb idea"--and must be
cured and overcome. He cannot see the full complexity of this until the force of his entire life is
brought home to him through the death of Courtial,
the crazed and lovable Leviathan who plays out idealism's curse to the bitter end. Courtial teaches
Ferdinand the lesson, that he, Ferdinand, cannot be
separated from the life he is leading. By the end
of the novel the plague of Ferdinand's past that
appears to consume the entire countryside has become
a *personally experienced* historical sense of the
plague of capitalism. The combination of hope,
superstition, charlatanry, magic and invention that
Courtial represents as his private belief sums up a
public picture of man-the-worker. Everything appears to Ferdinand ready to explode into violence,
and it is this propensity to provoke violence

through work that produces a system that gives the world its power.

At this point in the novel Ferdinand's thoughts about impending disaster are like both prayer and curse. Starved for more feeling but full of compassion, he recognizes the truth of the feeling that loyalty and trust, his deepest instincts, mark him as a criminal. Only at the end of the novel, as the novel attempts to face his memories of Courtial, does the profound meaning of his separation of feeling from people become clear. "Where are those from whom we all work?" asked a nineteenth century philosopher. What and where is this *we*? we might ask in reply. The answer is in part given by Ferdinand's memory of Courtial's sayings about "intelligence":

> Once you've looked at a thing, you ought to remember it forever . . . Don't force your intelligence . . . it's reason that gums everything up . . . Give your instinct a chance . . . Once it gets a good look the game is won . . . It'll never deceive you . . .

So while Courtial "bounces" through Ferdinand's memory, the fantasy of a tender culture of hope is consigned to Ferdinand by Céline. In this way Céline creates a Prometheus for modern times. While he salvages a perverse idealism out of Ferdinand's memories, he attempts to replace the idealism with a deeper reality about the complexity of Ferdinand's love of people. Ferdinand's greatness is two-fold. On the one hand he represents the author's own feelings "drenched in muteness and invisibility"[17] showing his utterly interior existence. On the other hand, shelterless and exposed to the urban, public world and the anonymous stars above, Ferdinand speaks the lives of others with his life. And in doing so Céline presents a basic theoretical, perhaps even ethical question central in the history of the novel: What is ". . . the legitimacy of taking the same approach to one's life as to another's life, to one's own self as to another self"?[18] Ferdinand is always exactly what he says he is, but the nature of the world he lives in breaks him down, separates him from his memories, deprives him of self-consciousness and makes him consider the legitimacy of others' power over him. Ferdinand's struggle, like Céline's, both in his writing novels and in his tormented and troubled pamphlets, is the struggle to "exteriorize" or make public what the world is trying to make abstract, idealistic. By rendering the world "legitimate" through Ferdinand's critical outlook an exchange takes place between the character Ferdinand and the world of production that illuminates the nature of the historical exchange of people for objects in Céline's "epoch." This is not a longing for the "*Volk*" or the primitive. It is a longing to protect the familiar against the state. It is the Doctor-writer's longing to protect the critical development of Ferdinand *and* the world he needs to address Ferdinand to.

Céline knew it would become necessary to find a context for this exchange of literary character and world, of Ferdinand for Courtial and what Courtial represents. Céline's furious professions and assertions about his "style"--that is his claim that he is only a stylist and every other writer is empty and stupid--is remade in the critical reception that sees Céline as a poet of delirium or horror, as in the post-modernist Julia Kristeva, where his writing is described as "Black mysticism of transcendental collapse":[19] an approach to Céline through style that only assimilates him to the fashions of intellectual despair and to indulgence in the ugliness and insensitivity of the very historical context that his novels set out to repudiate. It is not the style we should be talking about in Céline--this after all has been the burden of French writing since the academy and Catholicism banished the reality of literary transcendence--but the human substance and the exteriorization of the inner world onto the complexity of historical circumstance.

Although Céline's vision is not fully accessible through an analysis of his "style," perhaps elements of style reveal qualities of his mind. In this sense his writing eclipses style by reaching the origins of modern literacy in the evolution of speech and thought; he accomplished this by building a conceptual bridge between the book and the state, indeed by recognizing that novels cannot be reduced to the ideological systems controlled by the intellectuals themselves. As one of the last emotionally literate men, he, like Kafka before him, saw writing, as we know it, becoming circumscribed by the intellectual and social specializations in the state culture. Explored within his "petty-bourgeoisie" vision he sees the capitalist entrepreneur taking economics (that is business) into all manner of life. The merging of the frightened, terrorized working class with big business and the military *within* the aesthetic-cultural outlook of reactionary cultural entrepreneurs outlines the framework or truth-content of Céline's vision, but his political standpoint in that vision is not limited to political labelling; yet it is full of class consciousness. The class that owned nothing and knew nothing

became the big class that rounded up Europe into a
Fascist nightmare, the class nightmare that Céline
had been living through in his first two novels. He
saw a new class, whose pseudo self-creation and
self-glorification combined with the *intellectual*
self-rationalization of the entrepreneurial techni-
cal-military class, and their political outlook,
shadow all his nightmares. Ferdinand learns that
power and prestige is determined by the ability to
organize society. Social organization in turn required the organization of the masses and the dis-
tribution of services parodied in Ferdinand's cohort
of kids who learn the meaning of obedience. Céline's mourning and bitterness over the loss of
thought and feeling is directed at a new enemy: the
autonomous, artist-intellectual who now, complicit,
furthers the decline of traditional classes from
traditional cultural associations into bureaucracies, and specialized technologies and trades--to
become generalized and universalized into the political party where, now, the intellectual enters the
historical drama by shedding the bourgeois costume
in order to be ready for self-discipline, sacrifice
and leadership. In order to link the book to the
state.

Céline saw this as a process of domination on
the installment plan, and saw that the measure of
all cultural creation would soon itself be measured
by a new kind of necessity. Either the masses had
to become expert at being experts or be subjected to
the pathos of being non-intellectuals and being led
by new authorities. His historical imagination
created a profound critique of this process. The
subjugation of art and feeling to the domination of
political identity--racial, political, religious,
Jewish, Vatican or existentialist--required the

subjugation of everything to economics and state culture. The novel, for Céline, illuminated this demonic turn of ideological thought in modern times, and insofar as the novel criticizes the formation of masses and the manipulation of the masses by intellectuals it places itself in direct opposition to both the state-owned culture and the state-owned reader. To imagine oneself in the life of another. To imagine one's novel in the life of the reader. To expose the creation of mass consciousness by showing needs not based on market values. To create phantasmagoric time--the time of immediacy and memory--allows the reader to see and hear impressions. This is real time, not time based on installments. All that is solid melts into the impressionist pictures that unnerve and unbalance. What for Céline was the struggle against the modernization of the psyche is the Doctor-writer's expression in the prologue about his own struggle to remember his "patients." His struggle mirrors the struggle of the masses, a new force depeopled into sorrowing victims who live amid the ruins of the once memorable past. Their sorrow transforms their minds into social spectacle, into the transformation of the past into nothing but a present of work, consumption and war. This is the price Ferdinand pays for the transformation of *his* critical memory into a self-consciousness without a past.

While complaining that his language would be understood only by a few, it is clear that he hoped that his novels would be felt by many. Speech, everyday life, the history of memory as the memory of history, the ascetic, pleasure starved prose that creates a surplus of meaning--this is the paradoxical "pain" that is the grief of truth that never stops. Truth, like memory, always comes back: the critique of the soul of the state is simultaneously a critique of the state of the soul. And the state ensures that the commodity transcends itself by becoming the soul of the masses for which the masses have given up their lives and their stories:

> Here we are, alone again. It's all so slow, so heavy, so sad . . . I'll be old soon. Then at last it will be over. So many people have come into my room. They've talked. They haven't said much. They've gone away. They've grown old, wretched, sluggish, each in some corner of the world.

But we the readers know they have said much more than we or they want to know. "Old, wretched and sluggish" is not only their defense against the modernized psyche, it is the opposite of his prose. His prose will cure this disease; it will awaken the dead. Consequently "the grief that comes in the mail" (their letters) needs a letter in return. By return mail. And that is his novel, written to the grief-stricken, of which he is one among the many. His writing to them is also a way of saying that their presence, if they could read their own thoughts, would *complete* the meaning of his novel. It would enlighten it. Knowing, but not fully accepting that these potential readers have "changed their souls, that's a way to be disloyal, to forget, to keep talking about something else . . .", Céline reminds himself throughout the novel what a quixotic crusade he is on and how fragile his own memory is. They "change their souls" to change their thoughts; they allow their thoughts to be changed for them; for to be in intellectual solidarity with the thought-makers is a betrayal of the human. Céline wants to get inside their heads where the mystifications of culture exist, where the unending source of cultural capital is stocked for the leaders of reality. In this way his novel shows how reality and ideology are the same. The more Ferdinand remembers *how* this process came about and how intimate and personal meanings are reduced to mere traces, the more Ferdinand is sure the culture will pretend it all never happened.

Therefore, Ferdinand's struggle is to survive unpleasure, or what Freud called *pain (Schmerz)*, a pain that is for both Céline and Freud inextricably linked to grief and sorrow. The world's sorrow is embodied in Céline's incessant talk, and the poultices of words that heal the yet unfelt wounds in our souls are meant to "talk for" those who are mute but inwardly raging. "That's the presence of death . . . when you do their talking for them," Ferdinand says looking at Courtial's corpse. But this means "talking for them" *in life as well as death*. In its way Courtial's death transforms Ferdinand's self-inflicted memory of family and friends from the putrid little memory society makes it, into a gigantic, immortal oration speaking to all potential amnesiacs.

. . . the vanishing point of human endurance.

–Harold Rosenberg
Act and the Actor

Ferdinand's talk, like Céline's prose, projects meaning; that is, as in Dickens, it animates and personifies objects. This vision of people always talking has a social significance. As the production process turns people into things, language struggles against that process. While appearing to perform by itself, the talk locates itself in real people suffering alone their own unnarrated grief. Language thus given over to an impersonal force imitates the changes dominating our modern lives: the spatialization of time in factories; the excavation of space in unlivable corners of cities; the destruction of language by middle-class speech. As I have said, his demonic, carnivalesque, pathetic grotesque with its laceration of the social order can hardly be reduced to style, or, in modern critical vernacular, "scription" (scripture?), or "discourse" as Julia Kristeva calls it in affirming Céline's "journey without project, without faith, to the end of the night."[20] What earlier criticism found abhorrent in Céline's world, namely his lack of faith, modern chic criticism embraces. She attributes to Céline a language of evil that insults his subject matter by describing Céline's intention as, "to reshape the subjectivity that stirs within."[21] This claim for "subjectivity" is embodied in a claim for language that refers to no person, that is to Anyone. Infantile linguistic criticism enfeebles the subject's imagination by depreciating and dissolving the historical dimension of the work into Language that is "an organizer of enunciation far more-deep-seated than syntactic structurations."[22] Here modern criticism sacrifices Céline's mind, his acute referential qualities, his critique of ideology, his concrete awareness of the politicization of everyday life to a process that T. W. Adorno has called the suppression of the intellect by the intellectual:

> But the castration of perception by a court of control that denies it any anticipatory desire, forces it thereby into a pattern of helplessly reiterating what is already known. When nothing more may actually be seen, the intellect is sacrificed. Just as, under the primacy of the autonomous production process, the purpose of reason dwindles away until it sinks into the fetishisms of itself and of external power, so reason itself is reduced to an instrument and assimilated to its functionaries, whose power of thought serves only the purpose of preventing thought. Once the last trace of emotion has been eradicated, nothing remains of thought but absolute tautology.[23]

Not only do I believe this describes much modern criticism, it describes the cultural conditions that Céline foresaw. Entangled in Céline's thought is a prophetic criticism of those who today dismiss him or praise him. The deformation of feeling that he named is the pathos of a history without a subject to be sure. But this subject is given a history by Céline, and the reason he pushes language to the "vanishing point of human endurance" is to test and bear witness to the readers' masks, and the inhuman labor process that produces these masks through the cycle of expansion-concentration-of-wealth-crisis of-wealth-and-acceleration-of-collapse fundamental to the warfare state and the police mentality that governs it. This is real "syntactical" work, not Kristeva's "structuration." And in his recreation of the soul of the process, and the props and figures that are required to maintain the process, there is a truth that even Céline could not have predicted: the end of literature in the shadow of Auschwitz, Hiroshima, Viet Nam, Lebanon: because writing cannot bear autonomy within the destruction of the world itself. Against this fear no writer can believe in taking risks. Therefore Céline's use of the grotesque, mourning, pathos and sorrow as resistance to war will appear archaic, pessimistic or unpolitical. His is the voice of the writer between the wars who could still turn to dance, painting, politics, and the tradition of writing itself to evoke, whether in hostility or goodwill, a literacy in which pain and fear could be understood and felt, discussed and located. His stories are for people trapped in the cities and give us the appearance of a barely literate fable. They present a folklore of capitalism, a guidebook for all the fellow travellers of the capitalist ethic, and a dictionary for those beloved who are travelling elsewhere, the emotionally literate.

Céline illuminated the *false* autonomy of the uncommitted political past when he reassembled the legendary feelings of a folklorical heroic protest in his beloved King Krogold comic-strip romances in *Death on the Installment Plan*. In the hallucinatory world outside of the not so figurative bomb shelter there is modernity and destruction of the never-achieved intimate. In the real, private world of the bomb shelter there is King Krogold fighting the muddy and thick novels of modern times with his "beautiful legends" that simulate resistance, sexual desire and romance. While Ferdinand's vision of the world erupting into revolution is fed by his feelings of sorrow over lost fables, we also see his feelings of anger for the women of the world who, in the person of Mireille, "knew all about capitalism long before she even began to menstruate." Ultimately the suffering of women is the first suffering that Céline-Ferdinand identifies with. Giving birth to the world and being screwed by the world, *that* is the incurable affliction of being modernized. Even worse is never having time for one's own fantasies, as if there are too many words in our language for misery, theft, denial, repudiation, too many words disguising King Krogold's terrible hold over us. Ferdinand names this process by showing how it feels to be accused. Yet the narrator's self-accusations are a trick to throw us off the trail of his retreat from the front-lines of death. Once he discovers there are no front-lines, that in fact our shelter-lessness and homelessness have been caused by a world that has abandoned *us*, not we, *it*, then the neutral mask of innocence, the innocence of pure sexless feeling, looks backwards toward the world that subtracts us as too much increasing interest from the ruins of the accumulating cultural capital. Not even Hegel could have created a more vivid picture of a living abstraction as Céline's iconic, that is socially meaningful interrelation of speaking subject and listening reader.

Freud, writing in the torment of the first World War, in "Mourning and Melancholia" (1917), discussed "mental pain" as a form of mourning. He thinks about war from the point of view of cultural pathology, of "the inability to mourn." Freud's investigations into "ideological" motives as the cause of human misery and cultural complicity in misery continues in his reflections on why we are unable to live radically discontented, rather than die fulfilled in despair. Freud writes:

> The essential thing, therefore, is not whether the melancholic's distressing self-abasement is justified in the opinion of others. The point must be rather that he is correctly describing his psychological situation in his lamentations. He has lost his self-respect and must have some good reason for having done so. It is true that we are then faced with a contradiction which presents a very difficult problem. From the analogy with grief we should have to conclude that the loss suffered by the melancholic is that of an object; according to what he says the loss is one in himself.[24]

This loss *in* oneself is the loss of a real world, not the fantasized loss of an absent one. Yet the presence of the absent world is so vivid that our very character is formed by it. Mental pain is the knowledge that one cannot raise the dead past of culture or the public world in which we develop our consciousness. We withdraw the libido bit by bit and installment by installment. It is a slow gradual process. Suddenly the awareness of death in the world around us merges into mourning for the people around us, they too fading away. The door to memory is closed whenever the modern world closes itself to this mourning. By choreographing mourning and melancholia into Ferdinand's inner life, Céline's novel fictionally represents the final chapter in the destruction of the enlightenment intellectual's hope for clarity of purpose toward liberation and feeling. Put another way, we can say that the tradition of radical erotic humanism that began with Rabelais, and which continued the long tradition and struggle for individuation, finally runs out when the hopes for the free individual fail after 1914. The intelligentsia is culpable for its failure to understand this process: for turning critical mourning into narcissism and defeat. For Céline this was a failure of France's intelligentsia. The intelligentsia, of course, had the most to lose, having betrayed the world of enlightenment in the first place.

I would like to end this journey of circling around and around Céline by referring to an incident from Freud's life used by Russell Jacoby in his book *The Repression of Psychoanalysis, Otto Fenichel and the Political Freudians* (1983). Jacoby describes the exiling and ultimate integration of psychoanalysis into modern life. It is another chapter in modernity's loss of memory. He opens the book by retelling how on March 12, 1938, Freud "jotted in his diary 'Finis Austriae' as the Nazis marched into Vienna." In the midst of Nazi troops marching into Vienna and "transports carrying Austrians arriv[ing] at the Dachau concentration camp" an "ailing Freud" leaves for London via Paris. Jacoby writes:

> As a final condition for his release, the Gestapo demanded that Freud sign a prepared statement affirming that he had

been well treated. He signed, appending
the ironic sentence, 'I can heartily recommend the Gestapo to anyone.'[25]

If one understands Freud's unwillingness to leave
Vienna, his historical home and the home of his
work, one understands the sense of *historical* pathos
and tone of mourning in the irony. It is irrelevant
whether Freud would have liked Céline.[26] It is only
relevant that they recognized the same enemy: the
ideological nature of thought and the tendency of
society to turn reality into ideology. The question, in retrospect, is whether in leaving the world
behind to his "Anyone," the last link to the nineteenth century liberal and emancipatory dream of a
social contract based on trust and the written word,
to which everyone could append a signature, had been
broken and left in the ruins of Europe. Everyone
was now Anyone. These ruins, after 1914 and again
after 1939, confirm what Freud not innocently wrote
in 1908 when he compared the imaginative writer and
the day-dreamer ("The Poet and Day-Dreaming"): "I
believe that the greater number of human beings
create phantasies at times as long as they live.
This is a fact which has been overlooked for a long
time, and its importance has therefore not been
properly appreciated."[27] "The writer," Freud says,
"softens the egotistical character of the day-dream
by changes and disguises, and he bribes us by the
offer of a purely formal, that is aesthetic pleasure
in the presentation of his phantasies."[28] The
"briber" allows us "to enjoy our own phantasies
without reproach or shame" but there is a price to
pay for the loss of these phantasies which become
for the reader, in the propertyless and homeless
world illuminated by *Death on the Installment Plan*,

the final payment of the reader's spirit for *their* fantasies; Céline wrote in 1936:

> Since Zola's day not only have man's enshrouding nightmares come into the open, but they have been given official status. As our rulers wax in power, they become fiercer, more jealous, more stupid--and better organized. What can one say to them? We are beginning to speak a different language . . .[29]

It is the nature of that "we" which Céline opened up and which "we" continue to deny.

In this essay I have attempted to describe a context for Céline that would enable him to be read. Some may resent a metacritical approach. Others will see in my emphasis on the "masses" the rehabilitation of a "communist" interpretation. There is no doubt in my mind that Marx's influence on this view of cultural creation is significant. At the same time there is no doubt that Céline's work would form the cornerstone of a modern anarchist esthetic. Céline's tortuous attempt to make peace with himself over his hatred of intellectual complicity in war, the failure of redemptive ideologies to reach the intimate feelings, the breakdown of parliamentary systems, the nationalization of the class struggle and the continued preparation for war--these modern developments form the modern unconscious. Céline's work struggles with what Arnold Hauser called "the superego in society": "The superego is for psychoanalysis personified society: the organ of the strongest bond and of the most powerful revolt of people in relation to one another . . . it is a force which is always the source only of duty, pain, and sorrow, which burdens the subject with an apparently intransigent force--the unconscious."[30]

At the very least one must acknowledge that this force or burden must be seen in its socio-political context. Unless this context is explored, even if the conclusions drawn are different from the one presented here, the meaning of Céline's work will be misrepresented and misconstrued. Claims about his aesthetic significance will remain hollow. At the same time, unless his role as a novelist is understood through the epistemological-ethical nature of a revolution in form, his relationship to the cultural crisis of his time will not be distinguishable from his various counterparts. Equally important, the continuity of his early work with his later, post-World War II work will not be recognized, and his early work will be displaced, either falsely honored as "pre-fascist," or tolerated as pre-his "mental" collapse. Finally, his radical humanism distinguishes him from others like him who despaired over the culture, or ignored the culture entirely. This radical humanism was not worn like a label, and was in part unconscious. It was achieved by changing the entire shape of literacy and reception, and will have to be seen in the context of other writers whose legacy of literacy goes against the best wishes of civilization itself.

FOOTNOTES

1. Louis-Ferdinand Céline, "Interview," *Writers at Work: The Paris Interviews* (New York: The Viking Press, 1967), p. 98. All quotations from the novel are from the Manheim translation; because this essay assumes familiarity with the whole novel no page references are given.

2. Céline, "Interview," p. 99.

3. T. W. Adorno, "Commitment," in *Aesthetics and Politics*, ed. by Fredric Jameson (London: New Left Books, 1977), p. 189.

4. Karel Kosik, *Dialectics of the Concrete: A Study on the Problem of Man and the World* (Boston: D. Reidel Publishing Co., 1976), p. 77.

5. Adorno, "Commitment," p. 91.

6. Kosik, p. 80.

7. Adorno, "Commitment," p. 189.

8. Arnold Hauser, *The Sociology of Art* (Chicago and London: University of Chicago Press, 1982), p. 438. The discussion that follows here is indebted to Hauser's remarks on reception and dialectics: pp. 375-446.

9. Maurice Merleau-Ponty, "Cézanne's Doubt," in *Sense and Nonsense* (Evanston, Illinois: Northwest University Press), pp. 118-119.

10. George Lukacs, *A Modern Drama*, cited in Georgy Markus, "The Soul and Life: The Young Lukacs and the Problem of Culture," *Telos*, number 32, Summer 1977, p. 111.

11. This is a reference to the discussion about the relationship of myth to history and the commodity character of art in the exchange on this subject in: T. W. Adorno and Walter Benjamin, "Letters to Walter Benjamin," and "Reply," in Jameson, *Aesthetics and Politics*. I have written

on this subject in "The Literacy of the Spectacle: The Legacy of Walter Benjamin and the Production of Performance," in *Essays on Performance and Cultural Politicization*, "Open Letter,"
Summer-Fall, 1983.

12. T. W. Adorno, *Minima Moralia* (London: New Left
Books, 1974), p. 102.

13. Sigmund Freud, *The Future of an Illusion* (New
York: Anchor Books, 1964), p. 18.

14. Hans Juergen Syberberg, *Hitler, A Film from
Germany* (New York: Farrar, Straus, Giroux,
1982), pp. 11-12.

15. Merlin Thomas, *Louis-Ferdinand Céline* (London:
Faber and Faber, 1979), p. 136.

16. Thomas, p. 157.

17. Mikhail Bakhtin, *The Dialogic Imagination* (Aus-
tin: University of Texas Press, 1981), p. 135.
The point, hardly understood by rhetorical,
new-, and structuralist critics who have adopted
Bakhtin, is that this great Russian heretical
critic makes the novel, and therefore its world,
a genetically anti-hierarchical genre:

> From the very beginning the novel
> was structured not in the distanced
> image of an absolute past but in the
> zone of direct contact with inconclu-
> sive present-day reality. At its core
> lay personal experience and free crea-
> tive imagination. Thus a new, sober
> artistic-prose novelistic image and a
> new critical scientific perception
> came into being simultaneously. From
> the very beginning, then, the novel
> was made of different clay than the
> other already completed genres; it is

238

a different breed, and with it and in
it is born the future of all literature. (Bakhtin, p. 39)

18. Bakhtin, p. 133. Bakhtin discusses the role of
the novel in expressing the breakdown of the
public world. The pathos of Céline's vision is
that he cannot really affirm the old world, but
in posing the question of its loss he establishes contact with the unlivable world of the
present. Suggestive comparisons could be drawn
between Céline and Dostoevsky, Gogol, or Balzac
in the following sense:

> The tragedy of Gogol is to a very
> real extent the tragedy of a genre
> (taking genre not in its formalistic
> sense, but as a zone and a field of
> valorized perception, as a mode for
> representing the world). Gogol lost
> Russia, that is, he lost his blueprint
> for perceiving and representing her;
> he got muddled somewhere between memo-
> ry and familiar contact--to put it
> bluntly, he could not find the proper
> focus on his binoculars. (Bakhtin, p.
> 28)

19. Julia Kristeva, *Powers of Horror: An Essay on
Abjection* (New York: Columbia University Press,
1982), p. 206. This is an awful book, but will
undoubtedly be praised for its wisdom. It is
the final apotheosis of despair falling into
servile religion. She says of the writer, of
all of literature, of the mind--"no matter what
its socio-historical conditions might be"--that

everything is apocalyptic, abject horror. Céline is reduced to stunning literary punk-rock.
20. Kristeva, p. 186.
21. Kristeva, p. 187.
22. Kristeva, p. 193. She is so concerned about
deep "messages" from regions hidden by God that
she makes no reference to Céline, the human
being, who turned his hatred against the Fascists. Céline's anti-semitism is treated as a
form of "political commitment . . . like, as a
matter of fact, any political commitment . . . a
security blanket" (p. 136). This simple-minded
view of politics and Céline, while dressed up in
Nietzschean prose, is even less analytical about
Céline's demogoguery than he is about himself.
In any case, she dismisses as trivial the view
that "His novels are realistic out of social
constraint . . ." and takes literally his own
view of his works as embedded in "style," diminishing and eliminating their narrative element,
their *history*. But most revealing, as with so
many of the interpretors of Céline I am aware
of, is her obsession with attributing filth,
violence, madness, orgy, inhumanity and disgust
to Céline. She does not know that these are
human feelings in the novels; they are not there
as violence, but as emotionally possible responses to inhuman acts and to objectively real
characters, people or events. They are not
ideas, nor least of all representations of "the
inhumanity of the poet" (137), but are lyrical
and ideological forms directed toward and from a
creative sense of life. As tendentious as that
may sound such cultural forms are found in many
lyrical traditions, as well as scientific ones,
both modern and pre-modern. It is sometimes

known as philosophy or metaphysics, where lyri-
cally performed, human feelings are at home.
Kristeva censors this out.

23. Adorno, *Minima Moralia*, p. 123.

24. Sigmund Freud, "Mourning and Melancholia," in
    Collected Papers, Volume IV (New York: Basic
    Books, 1959), p. 157.

25. Russell Jacoby, *The Repression of Psychoanaly-
    sis, Otto Fenichel and the Political Freudians*
    (New York: Basic Books, 1983), pp. 3-4.

26. In March 1933 Freud wrote to Marie Bonaparte
    that he had "looked into Céline's book [*Journey
    to the End of the Night*]": "I have no taste for
    this depicting of misery, for the description of
    the senselessness and emptiness of our present-
    day life, without any artistic or philosophical
    background. I demand something other from art
    than realism. I am reading it because you
    wished me too." Ernest Jones, *The Life and Work
    of Sigmund Freud*, Volume 3, (New York: Basic
    Books, 1957), p. 176. Three months later Freud
    wrote: "It seems to me that not even in the war
    did lies and empty phrases dominate the scene as
    they do now. The world is turning into an
    enormous prison." Jones, Vol. 3, 181-182.

27. Sigmund Freud, "The Relation of the Poet to Day-
    Dreaming," in *Collected Papers*, Volume IV (New
    York: Basic Books, 1959), p. 175.

28. "The Relation of the Poet to Day-Dreaming,"
    p. 183.

29. "Homage to Zola," *New Statesman and Nation*,
    October 1936, p. 509.

30. Arnold Hauser, *Sociology of Art*, p. 673.

ENGLISH LANGUAGE CRITICISM ON
LOUIS-FERDINAND CÉLINE: 1935-1983

William K. Buckley

Céline's amazing impact on the modern novel began with the publication of *Journey to the End of the Night* in 1932. In Europe the response to this novel was immediate, and the detailed study of all his works continues today in both France and Germany. In America, however, in the 1940's and 50's, the power of his early work was first felt only by American novelists and poets, as well as a handful of thinkers. Leon Trotsky's essay on Céline did make an appearance in the *Atlantic Monthly* in 1935 (rept. in *Leon Trotsky on Literature and Art*, N.Y.: Pathfinder Press, 1970),[1] and it is still considered today as one of the best evaluations of Céline's vision in *Journey*. "Céline's power," Trotsky says, "lies in that through supreme effort he divests himself of all canons, transgresses all conventions." W. M. Frohock's "Céline's Quest for Love" (1942)[2] describes Céline's "nihilism" as a vehicle for documenting the "emotional bankruptcy" of modern man. And Irving Howe's "Céline: Novelist of the Underground" (1948)[3] takes a rather comprehensive look at both *Journey* and *Death on the Installment Plan*, calling the author a philistine with genius.

But it was in 1944 that Céline was first mentioned by an American writer: Henry Miller. It was probably through Miller that Ginsberg, Kerouac, and Burroughs first heard of Céline.[4] As late as 1964 Miller was quoted in the *Paris Review* as saying: "Céline lives in me, he will live there forever. That's what is important."[5] And in his *Sunday After The War* (1944), Miller makes reference to the famous Detroit chapter of *Journey*, calling Molly a whitewash, but describing her body triumphing over "the soul of the machine" as the beautiful and surprising thing about the chapter.[6] Wayne Burns explores the relationship between Kerouac and Céline in "The Beat and the Dead" (1959),[7] and explains the sentimental imitation of Céline that Kerouac and so many other of the Beats trap themselves into making. This sentimental love for the French author can be found in Ginsberg's *As Ever: The Collected Correspondence of Allen Ginsberg and Neal Cassidy* (Berkeley: Creative Arts Book Co., 1977). In 1950 Milton Hindus published his *The Crippled Giant: A Bizzare Adventure in Contemporary Letters*, a hardly sentimental description of his visits and conversations with Céline in Denmark, in 1948, during Céline's exile from France.[8] It is the first book-length study of Céline to appear in the U.S., but as Hindus says in the "Postlude," he was not sure whether his book was a work of criticism, a biography, or a critical biography. He was sure, however, that it made up an answer to Céline's anti-Semitism. He gives us support for his book by quoting letters from Henry Miller and William Carlos Williams, and concludes that Céline simply prostituted literature to personal perversions, and enticed "the public into becoming the ear into which he whispered all thoughts, hallucinations and base impulses which the luckless keep locked within themselves for fear of being locked up" (122). The book does not discuss Céline's novels; it remains a description of the collision between two different men:

> Céline went into his usual song and dance about his paganism and how he really felt himself a Greek at heart and loved beauty above everything else. I broke in rudely: "To hell with beauty! What we need is morality, rules of living together." And then I said to M___ ___: "Céline has a Hebraic genius which he's trying to deny all the time, because morality is his principle too." Céline stuck to his point: "To hell with morality! I've got plenty of that myself. Give me beauty." He said that all of art was a translation of the lines of a dancer's leg. (91-92)[9]

Céline criticism in the early 1960's quickly gained momentum. After the author's death in 1961, academics and magazine critics began talking about Céline's life as a doctor, his politics, and his two famous novels *Journey* and *Death on the Installment Plan*. With the appearance of Brée and Guiton's *An Age of Fiction: The French Novel From Gide to Camus* (1957),[10] however, Céline reaction broke into two camps: those who would study, in isolation, Céline's innovative use of *argot* and the "structure" of his novels, and those who would continue to generalize about Céline's comments on our modern lives. Brée and Guiton began to show the signs of concentrating on Céline's "verbal realism," briefly calling attention to Céline's "ungrammatical, spoken

244

language as a narrative technique" (164). In 1962 Milton Hindus published his "Excerpts from His Letters to Milton Hindus" and the whole world of Céline's theory of language and writing was revealed to the American critic, provoking a flood of linguistical studies in this country and abroad.[11] These Céline letters, written to Hindus, and translated by him and Mitchell Smith, cover the years 1947 to 1948, and have become the basis for most American critical discussion of Céline's famous style. They are rich with remarks on style and writing.

The academicized man expresses himself as an engineer, an architect, a technican --and no longer through his feelings. . . . The *trick* is to force a *distortion* into spoken language, so that once it's written down and being read, the reader feels as though someone's actually speaking to him. . . . This *distortion* is really a little harmonic tour de force. . . . Re-sensitize the language so that it pulses more than it reasons. . . . I'm first of all a Celt--daydreamer, bard. . . . What interests me is a direct message to the nervous system. . . . The truth isn't enough for me. I have to transpose everything. If a thing doesn't sing, the soul doesn't know it is alive. . . . Enthusiasm is to let yourself go into delirium. You have to clean off, sweep around it, make it come out into glaring daylight: *you have to be strong.* It's a question of *strength*--to force the dream into reality--a question of cleaning house."[12]

These remarks have become the basis of the critical apparatus used by most American and British criticism in the 60's and 70's. Erika Ostrovsky uses them while comparing Céline to Artaud in an essay about how each author uses language to assault the reader with knowledge.[13] W. M. Frohock uses them to focus on the "classical formula" of *Journey*, calling the plot of the novel the "*homme traqué*."[14] John Fletcher announces that Céline's colloquial idiom "threw a brick into the millpond of French prose," a fine phrase which adequately characterizes the 1932 reaction of the French Academy to the publication of *Journey*. With John Fraser's "The Darkest Journey: Céline's *Death on the Installment Plan*" (1967)[15] academic criticism begins to talk about the themes and structure of Céline's second novel. Fraser studies in detail the opening 36 pages of *Death on Installment Plan*, calling them a "prelude." Rima Dell Reck's *Literature and Responsibility: The French Novel in the Twentieth Century* (1969) devotes a whole chapter to Céline and discusses his early novels, using his letters as sources for interpretation.[16] Reck looks at Céline's "sound," the source of his style, and his word order. On the whole these linguistic studies, and many others in Germany and France, satisfy one's curiosity about what even according to Céline are secondary matters.[17] Much more needs to be said about Céline's vision of our lives.

Thematic studies continued into the 1960's, trying to explain Céline's view of human behavior, and Wayne Booth's *The Rhetoric of Fiction* (University of Chicago, 1961)[18] illustrates the early American academic response to *Journey*. In Booth's brief remarks, we see an intelligence fully aware of Céline's anti-idealism, and hear moral outrage at such a view: ". . . we cannot excuse him for writing a book which, if taken seriously by the reader, must corrupt him" (383). This kind of reaction characterizes a good deal of English language criticism in the 1960's. There are exceptions, notably the remarks of Anthony Burgess, who sees Céline's "pessimism" as "somehow life-enhancing."[19] But in general, Céline's uncompromising view of life beneath decorum continued to be faced, understood, and condemned out of fear. Irving Howe's two-part study of Céline's work, which appeared in the *New Republic* as "Céline: The Sod Beneath the Skin," is often quoted by American critics.[20] His thesis is that Ferdinand, in *Journey*, is a Dostoevskian underground man no longer in anguish about a valueless existence. This view is popular too. Yet it had been stated as early as 1944, by Harry Slochower, in "Satanism in Céline."[21] He said that both *Journey* and *Death on the Installment Plan*, as autobiographical accounts of proletarian life, were more "underground" than those of Joyce, Döblin, Farrell, or Dos Passos, and give us Céline's vision as a kind of inverted humanism, a vision which sees life as both hopeless and capable of compassion.

It seems there is a difference between American critical reaction in the 40's and 50's and American reaction in the 60's: novelists and critics of the 40's and 50's mention Céline's compassionate voice in his novels, but not much mention is made of this compassion in the 60's. The fact that a man could express compassion in his life as a doctor, and in his fiction, express compassion for the Jew Semmelweis in a medical thesis, yet still be a famous anti-Semite in Paris during World War II, was, and still is today, a hard pill to swallow.[22]

Céline studies in the middle and late 60's are influenced by two major publications: David Hayman's *Louis-Ferdinand Céline* (1965),[23] and Erika Ostrovsky's *Céline and His Vision* (1967).[24] Because of these two studies, thematic explanations of Céline's novels remain the dominant characteristic of late 60's research. Hayman's long monograph is only the second extended look at Céline to appear in the U.S. up to this time, the first being Hindus' *Crippled Giant*. And although Hayman does speculate a little on Céline's style, a "secret recipe," as Céline called it, most of the essay concentrates on *Journey*, *Death on the Installment Plan*, and, for the first time, *Guignol's Band*, *Féerie pour une autre fois*, *Normance*, *Castle to Castle*, and *North*. His major thesis is that Céline not only tried to convey "disgust and terror by comic means," but that he hoped, as he told Robert Poulet, "to make his version of the truth shine through absurdities" (40). And part of this truth, according to Hayman, is this:

> The view of life in the novels should not be confused with life. Here Céline is ahead of the moralizing critics who will necessarily find in his work an affront to human dignity. True, he means what he says: the world is a horrible place; we fail to see the horror because our vision is blunted by familiarity; we are courting corruption and waltzing toward the abyss. But his message relates principally to his fears rather than to his knowledge, and his overstatement surely serves to dull

248

the humming in his ears and in ours as well. (28)

We don't hear the firm repulsion of Wayne Booth here, but we still get that hedging from an intelligence which fully understands the power of Céline to strip away our ideals--that stripping which Trotsky faced so squarely in 1932. Erika Ostrovsky's *Céline and His Vision* is the first book-length study of Céline and his fiction. She too notes how Céline shattered the status quo of the French novel with his new syntax, but she also intended to go far beyond all other studies to date. By relying on numerous sources in French, and on Céline's novels, pamphlets, and letters, the book, as a result, is the best American research could offer up until the 1970's. Ostrovsky tries not to flinch or hedge at Céline's descriptions of the human animal, as do Hayman and Booth. "To understand," she says, "to probe beneath the surface of things, even at the price of turning the scalpel against oneself without pity, this is the real quest for Céline, and of his protagonists" (93).[25] Kingsley Widmer agrees with this kind of view of Céline in his "The Way Down to Wisdom of Louis-Ferdinand Céline," but he does not agree with Hindus, Howe, and Hayman that *Death on the Installment Plan* is Céline's best novel.[26] Widmer returns to discussing the merits of *Journey*, and even more than Ostrovsky or Hayman, looks Céline's view of life square in the eye: "Perhaps life, then, is only 'lie, copulate and die.' That remains the innocent truth for a Céline, until proved otherwise" (91). Only in the 1970's and 80's do Americans find more in Céline than this view, for with the Manheim translations of *Castle to Castle* (1968), *North* (1972), and *Rigadoon* (1974), Céline gives us

some possible answers to the question of whether
life is only lying, copulating, and dying.

I don't know if Céline was aware of the growing
interest in him in America and England at this time,
even though he knew that his last interviews were
being published by both *Paris Review* and *Evergreen
Review*.[27] When Robert Stromberg, of the *Evergreen
Review*, walked into the kitchen of Céline's house in
Meudon, we hear:

> "What is it you want? Who is this for?
> I don't want scandal. I've had enough."
> When I satisfied him finally, he settled
> more comfortably in his seat.
> "There is a good deal of interest in
> you in America," I began. He dismissed
> this with a blow of air and a wave of his
> hand.
> "What interest? Who is interested?
> People are interested in Marlene Dietrich
> and insurance—that's all!" (102)

Céline criticism in the early 1970's is not only
characterized by a large increase in long linguistic
explorations, but also by a marked increase in interest in nearly all of Céline's work—his novels,
pamphlets, medical writings, letters, interviews,
and collaboration trial testimony.[28] Three of the
more interesting contributions in 1971-2 are George
Steiner's "Cry Havoc," Rens and Teirney's "Céline's
Last Journey: An Essay After the Publication of
Rigadoon in 1969," and Ostrovsky's *Voyeur Voyant*
(1972).[29] That bitter pill of Céline's paradoxical
nature—tender one moment, anti-Semitic the next—is
slowly being swallowed by a few critics. Steiner
discusses the anti-Semitic qualities of Céline's

writing, and expresses disappointment with Ostrovsky's *Céline and His Vision* for having overlooked
it. He is one of the first critics not only to
point out that one cannot separate Céline's major
works from his pamphlets, in a critical discussion
of the man himself, but also to recognize the influence Céline had on German and American fiction:

> Increasingly, it does look as if the
> novels of Günter Grass, of William Bur-
> roughs, and of Norman Mailer would not
> have been written without Céline's prece-
> dent. Allen Ginsberg expresses a whole
> trend of opinion when he terms Céline's
> *Journey to the End of the Night* "the first
> genius international beat XX century pica-
> resque novel written in modern classical
> personal comedy prose by the funniest &
> most intelligent of mad Doctors whose
> least tenderness is an immortal moment."
> (37-8)

Rens and Tierney's essay is interesting because it
is the first essay to suggest that after reading all
of Céline's novels--and especially *Rigadoon*--perhaps
natural affection "is Céline's answer to the hatred,
malice, shame, and the slackness of the world" (57).
Part of this idea can be found in Ostrovsky's *Voyeur
Voyant*, the first biography of Céline to appear in
the U.S.[30] C. W. Nettelbeck, in *PMLA*, 87 (January
1972), also argues that Céline's work "evolves toward a spirit of regeneration."[31] He states that
Céline's novels--even the infamous pamphlets--are
attempts to celebrate life, and that his basic intention was to transcend the collapse of Western
civilization. Allen Thiher, in *Céline: The Novel*

as Delirium (1972), although he calls *Journey* a negation of the world, stills sees the novel as an "antidote for the evil and destruction" its picaro hero sees.[32] Philip H. Solomon has also used the idea of *délire* to explain Ferdinand as a "lucid super-seer" in *Death on the Installment Plan*.[33] Thiher calls Céline's novels discourses in a *délire* which springs from an awareness of man's misery. But Bettina L. Knapp, in *Céline: Man of Hate* (1974), sees Céline's work as expressions of destructive hatred. No other book, so far in American criticism, looks at so many of Céline's writings, giving both plot summary and commentary on all. What makes this controversial book valuable is its extensive exploration of anti-Semitism in prewar France and in Céline's works and collaboration trial. Her conclusion is that for us to understand our own hates, we must read Céline.

I am aware of only two journals which have devoted their issues to Céline: the *Australian Journal of French Studies*, 13:1-2 (January-August 1976),[34] which has nearly all of its essays in French, and *Recovering Literature: A Journal of Contextualist Criticism*, which has devoted Volume 2, Number 1 (Spring 1973) to *Death on the Installment Plan*, and Volume 3, Number 1 (Spring 1974) to a bibliography of Céline materials for the years 1932 to 1973. James Flynn's "Céline: Beyond the Gesture" (5-35) maintains that it is Céline who attacks the idealisms of honor, justice, love, and irony, and he argues that novels like *Death on the Installment Plan* take a reader past the point of "comment and detachment." A Céline novel, says Flynn, is one which requires a reader to suspend his belief in ideals. Critics have been hinting for a long time at Céline's treatment of human idealism, but this is

the first time in English criticism that an essay
has explored this matter in detail. Gerald Robel's
"Ferdinand and His Family" and Bill Ott's "The Death
of Des Pereires: Possibilities For Compassion in
Céline's World" both explore the fact of compassion
in Céline's *Death on the Installment Plan* by looking
very closely at numerous scenes from this novel (37-
74). And in Volume 3 is my first attempt at a
comprehensive, international bibliography of Céline
materials, entitled "A Bibliography of Critical
Articles, Books, and Commentaries on Louis-Ferdinand
Céline and His Works: 1932-1973."

In the middle and late 1970's, historical, linguistical, biographical, and bibliographical studies
continue. David Hayman discusses two main aspects
of Céline's style--his "lacework" and "emotive subway" (two terms of Céline's own invention)--by looking at *Death on the Installment Plan*, and concluding
that the art of this novel is its narration.[35]
Nicholas Hewitt proposes that the language of the
second novel constitutes a rejection of Ferdinand's
social and ethical world as well as a rejection of
the epistolary novel.[36] Charles Krance argues that
Céline's words plea for reinstating man at the center of existence instead of dehumanizing him with
Judeo-Christian or Marxian abstract truths. He also
defines Céline's "ecstatic" language, and describes
the process of how Céline's fiction achieves
"*délire*" or "extasis."[37] And Stanford Luce published his *Glossary of Céline's Fiction* (Ann Arbor:
University of Michigan, 1979), containing some 4,000
non-conventional French words. Robert Soucy studies
the French Fascist intellectuals of the 1930's and
discovers that Céline's *L'École des cadavres* (1938)
is a work that complains about the "standardization
of modern life, that human beings in the modern

world are now deprived of individuality and creativity by the standardization of their authentic emotions."[38] Perhaps the most comprehensive look at Céline during the 70's, both historically and thematically, is by Patrick McCarthy, whose two contributions, "Céline During the Occupation" (1975)[39] and *Céline* (1975)[40] give us what some have called the best understanding of Céline today. Anthony Burgess supports the biography, as well as the value of Céline, in *Harper's Magazine*, and John Updike does too in the *New Yorker*, in the process giving us *his* evaluation of Céline's influence on American writers.[41] McCarthy's "Céline During the Occupation" is an extensive description of French politics during the Occupation, and an investigation of Céline's political views from 1941 to 1945. McCarthy is at his best in *Céline*, I believe, when he examines the relationship between the novels and French politics from 1932 to 1940. He concludes by saying that in Céline's vision, fear characterizes all of life. Several book-length studies follow after McCarthy: David O'Connell's *Louis-Ferdinand Céline*,[42] interesting for its calling Courtial the "Don Quixote of Science" and Ferdinand his Sancho Panza--and valuable for recognizing *Entretiens avec le Professeur Y* (1954) as Céline's *ars poetica*; J.H. Matthews' *The Inner Dream: Céline as Novelist*,[43] which is one of the first books in American criticism to talk about sex in *Death on the Installment Plan*, although inadequately; and Merlin Thomas' *Louis-Ferdinand Céline*,[44] which I believe to be the best book on Céline in America today. Thomas does not believe Céline to be a nihilist, a rare position in Céline criticism, and he gives us one of the best studies of the major pamphlets: *Bagatelles pour un massacre* (1937), *L'École des cadavres* (1938), and *Les Beaux*

254

draps (1941). He is also one of the first critics to call the trilogy a supreme artistic achievement. Thomas' wit and intelligence shines through his prose, and I believe he reflects the needed complex understanding of Céline. Four essays are published at the end of the 70's too: Kurt Vonnegut's "Introduction" for both *North* and *Castle to Castle* in their Penguin editions, which claims that Céline "discovered a higher and more awful order of literary truth by ignoring the crippled vocabularies of ladies and gentlemen;"[45] Frederick Busi's "Céline: The Wild Man of French Literature",[46] which is one of the few essays to say that Céline's hatreds were more common to general thinking than we want to admit; Philip Solomon's "The View from a Rump: America as Journey and Landscape of Desire in Céline's *Voyage au bout de la nuit*,"[47] which illustrates how Bardamu's idealization of American women cannot be maintained; and Leslie Davis' "Céline and the Débâcle of Idealism,"[48] which sees *Death on the Installment Plan* as a novel that abolishes ideals and leads to despair.

Céline criticism in the early 1980's concentrates on the author's later works. Gerald J. Butler's "Céline's *Bagatelles pour un massacre*: The Expression of a Forbidden Passion,"[49] argues that *Bagatelles* is more of a critique of Aryans than of Jews, and his "The Meaning of the Presence of Lili in Céline's Final Trilogy,"[50] concludes that Céline's message for us is that "human beings . . . should have real animality above all by having hearts." Jane Carson's "Céline: The Fire in the Night,"[51] discusses *Journey, Normance,* and *North* in the light of two themes: picaro traditions and the symbol of fire as representing creativity. She concludes that Céline changes the picaresque element by having the picaro constantly throwing "bombs of awareness" to his public.

Céline research in the early 1980's is characterized by two essays and two bibliographies. *The Times Literary Supplement* has noted how some 80 letters of Céline to his translator John Marks were recently sold at auction—giving us new clues to the Céline of the 1930's, and showing us his help given to Marks on early translations of his first two novels.[52] Leon Roudiez outlines the critical response to Céline's work from 1948 to 1978 in the *Romanic Review*, commenting on the major English, French, and German studies.[53] Roudiez maintains that most critics fail to take all of Céline's work into consideration because of their fear of his pamphlets, a fear which springs from their narrow perspective as "literary critics." He does cite one work which is not as narrow as previous studies: Julia Kristeva's *Pouvoirs de l'horreur* (1980), which analyzes Céline from the perspective of psychoanalysis. Charles Krance published an annotated bibliography, listing some 200 items, concentrating on criticism from the 1950's to the 1960's. He also lists the latest editions of Céline's works, letters, and interviews.[54] *A Half Century of Céline: An Annotated Bibliography, 1932-1982* (New York: Garland Publishing, Inc., 1983) is the most comprehensive, international bibliography in English that I know about. Stanford Luce and I compiled it, and we have included all of Céline's writings, as well as criticism from many languages.

Nearly everyone who writes about Céline exclaims how unfortunate it is that no comprehensive study of him exists in English. They abound in France and Germany. Perhaps Thomas and McCarthy approach a comprehensive look. But what is still needed in

America is a book that is willing to discuss in detail Céline's view of sex, as well as tenderness-- a book to swallow that large and bitter pill of Céline's parodoxical nature before it discusses the language, comedy, or politics of his world.

FOOTNOTES

1. 156:4 (October 1935), 413-20.
2. *Accent*, 2:22 (Winter 1941-42), 79-84.
3. *Tomorrow*, 8:3 (November 1948), 53-56.
4. Ginsberg's *Howl*, Miller's *Tropic of Cancer*, and Burroughs' *Naked Lunch* all show signs of having been influenced by Céline. Kerouac's remarks on Céline can be found in *L'Herne*, 3 (1963), 205. In English see: *Paris Review*, 31 (1964), 137.
5. 31 (Winter-Spring 1964), 137. Alfred Perlès describes Céline's influence on Miller in *My Friend Henry Miller* (NY: John Day Co., 1956). Kingley Widmer's *Henry Miller* (NY: Twayne, 1963) also notes the particularly strong attraction Miller held for Céline's novels.
6. New York: New Directions, 1944, p. 24.
7. Written for the now defunct *Berkeley Review*. Rept. in *Towards A Contextualist Aesthetic For The Novel* (Seattle: Genitron Books, 1968). See also: Emile Boelens, "Céline et la Beat Generation," *La Revue célinienne*, 2 (1979), 19-20.
8. New York: Boar's Head Books.
9. In *Mosaic*, 6 (1973), 57-66, Hindus states that he sees no reason to change his view of Céline stated in the epilogue to his *Crippled Giant*: that despite his great gifts, Céline's anti-Semitism cannot be forgiven.
10. New Brunswick, New Jersey: Rutgers University Press.
11. *Texas Quarterly*, 4 (Winter 1962), 22-38.
12. 26-37.
13. "The Anatomy of Cruelty: Antonin Artaud; Louis-Ferdinand Céline," *Arts and Sciences* (Spring 1967), pp. 9-13.

14. *Style and Temper: Studies in French Fiction,
    1925-1961* (Oxford: Basil Blackwell, 1967).

15. *Wisconsin Studies in Contemporary Literature*, 8
    (Winter 1967), 96-110.

16. Baton Rouge: Louisiana State University Press,
    1969, 191-215. See also Reck's "Céline and
    Wolfe: Toward a Theory of the Autobiographical
    Novel," *Mississippi Quarterly*, 22 (1968-69), 19-
    22.

17. See, for example, Marc Hanrez, *Céline* (Paris:
    Gallimard, 1961); and J. Hokenson, "Céline:
    Impressionist in Language," *Esprit créateur*,
    13:4 (1973), 329-39.

18. See also: Emanuel Kummer, "Wayne C. Booth et
    l'auteur implicite de Voyage," *Australian Jour-
    nal of French Studies*, 13:1-3 (1976), 18-24.

19. *Listener*, 75:1942 (June 16, 1966), 883.

20. July 20, 1963, and August 17, 1963. Rept. in *A
    World More Attractive* (New York: Horizon Press,
    1963), pp. 192-206.

21. *Books Abroad*, 18 (October 1944), 332-7. Rept. in
    *No Voice is Wholly Lost: Writers and Thinkers
    in War and Peace* (New York: Creative Age Press,
    1945).

22. See: Henri Poulain's review of *Les Beaux draps*
    in *Petit parisien*, 23383 (March 17, 1941), 2;
    "Céline cinq ans après" in *Pariscope*, (January
    26, 1965), 19-23; Brissaud's "Voyage au bout de
    la tendresse" in *Herne*, 3 (1963), 226-31; Guil-
    leminault's "Un Petit tour aux enfers" in *Au-
    rore* (September 6, 1976), 10; and Nourissier's
    "Admirez Céline, ne le défendez pas," *Point*, 387
    (February 18-24, 1980), 121-22.

23. New York: Columbia University Press, 1965.

24. New York: New York University Press, 1967.

Review, 44 (1967), 94-99.

25. An interesting critique of Ostrovsky's book is George Woodcock's "Céline Revived," *The Tamarack Review*, 44 (1967), 94-99.

26. *The Minnesota Review*, 8, No. 1 (1968), 85-91.

27. *Writers at Work: Paris Review Interviews, Third Series* (New York: Viking Press, 1967). Robert Stromberg, "A Talk With Louis-Ferdinand Céline," *Evergreen Review*, 19 (August 1961), 102-07.

28. *Modern Fiction Studies*, 16:1 (Spring 1970), 85-100. Contains a bibliography of Céline criticism for the years 1948-1969.

29. George Steiner, "Cry Havoc," *New Yorker* (January 20, 1968), pp. 106-15. Rept. in *Extraterritorial: Papers on Literature and the Language of Revolution* (New York: Atheneum, 1971), pp. 35-46. Jean-Guy Rens and Bill Tierney, "Céline's Last Journey: An Essay After the Publication of *Rigadoon* in 1969," *Antigonish Review*, 2:1 (Spring 1971), 39-59. Paul A. Fortier's "Marxist Criticism of Céline's *Voyage au bout de la nuit*," in *Modern Fiction Studies*, 17:2 (1971), 268-72, is of interest too. He argues that Trotsky's essay on Céline, and Anissimov's preface to the Russian language edition of *Journey* are off the point because *Journey* is not a "fully developed Marxist analysis of the capitalist system." But of course Céline never intended that.

30. New York: Random House. Written in a style which tries to imitate Céline's style. The book is not a chronological treatment, but more of a free association of ideas and opinions and feelings which jump around in their descriptions of Céline's life, from one year to another. Contains an extensive bibliography.

31. "Journey to the End of Art: The Evolution of the Novels of Louis-Ferdinand Céline," 80-89. He has also written an essay which compares Bardamu and Ellison's Invisible Man. See: "From Inside Destitution: Céline's Bardamu and Ellison's Invisible Man," *Southern Review: An Australian Journal of Literary Studies*, 7 (1974), 246-53.

32. New Brunswick, New Jersey: Rutgers University Press, 1972.

33. "Céline's *Death on the Installment Plan*: The Intoxication of Delirium," *Yale French Studies*, 50 (1974), 191-203.

34. Egs.: Philippe Alméras, "L'Amérique femelle ou les enfants de Colomb," 97-109; Paolo Carile, "Editeurs, critiques et public italiens face à Céline," 151-61.

35. "Céline," *Contemporary Literature*, 15 (1974), 257.

36. "Narration and Desolidarisation in Céline's *Mort à Crédit*," *Essays in French Literature*, 12 (November 1975), 59-69.

37. "Céline and the Literature of Extasis: The Virtuosity of Non-Genre," *Language and Style*, 6:3 (Summer 1973), 176-84.

38. "French Fascist Intellectuals in the 1930's: An Old New Left?" *French Historical Studies*, 8:3 (Spring 1974), 445-58.

39. *The New Review*, 2, No. 14 (1975), 37-54.

40. New York: Viking Press, 1976; Penguin, 1977. Extensive, critical review of this book is by Milton Hindus, "The State of the Céline Industry," *New Boston Review*, 3 (Summer 1977), 16-18.

41. "In Support of Céline," *Harper's Magazine* (August 1976), 768-82; "The Strange Case of Dr. Destouches and M. Céline," *New Yorker*, 52:30 (September 13, 1976), 154-61.
42. Boston: Twayne Publishers, 1976.
43. Syracuse, New York: Syracuse University Press, 1978.
44. New York: New Directions, 1979.
45. New York: Penguin Books, 1976.
46. *Midstream* (June-July 1976), 69-72.
47. *Yale French Studies*, 57 (1979), 5-22.
48. *1936: The Sociology of Literature: Volume I: The Politics of Modernism*, ed. F. Barker et al. (University of Essex, 1979).
49. *Recovering Literature*, 8:1 (Spring 1980), 27-42.
50. *Recovering Literature*, 10 (1982), 57-63.
51. *Symposium*, 35:2 (Summer 1981), 117-30.
52. M. J. Tilby, "Céline's letters to his translator," (April 2, 1982), pp. 385-86.
53. "On Several Approaches to Céline," 72:1 (January 1981), 94-104.
54. Chapter on Céline in *A Critical Bibliography of French Literature*, ed. R.A. Brooks and D. W. Alden (Syracuse, New York: Syracuse University Press, 1980), Volume 6, part 1, 743-65.

SELECTED BIBLIOGRAPHY OF CÉLINE CRITICISM IN ENGLISH: 1935-1983

William K. Buckley

1. ENGLISH TRANSLATIONS OF WORKS BY CÉLINE

Journey to the End of the Night. Trans. John H.P. Marks. London: Chatto and Windus; Boston: Little, Brown and Co., 1934. Rpt. New York: New Directions, 1961, and London: Penguin, 1966.

Journey to the End of Night. Trans. Ralph Manheim. New York: New Directions, 1983.

Death on the Installment Plan. Trans. John H.P. Marks. London: Chatto and Windus; Boston: Little, Brown and Co., 1938. Rpt. London: Panther, 1968.

Death on the Installment Plan. Trans. Ralph Manheim. New York: New Directions, 1966.

"Hommage to Zola." *The Literary World: A Survey of International Letters*, 9 (June 1935). Rpt. *New Statesman and Nation* (10 Oct. 1936); *New Directions in Prose and Poetry*, 13 (1951), 60-64.

Mea Culpa and *The Life and Work of Semmelweis.*
Trans. R.A. Parker.   London: Allen and Unwin;
New York: H. Fertig, 1937. Rpt. H. Fertig,
1979.

Guignol's Band.   Trans. Bernard Frechtman and Jack
T. Nile. London: Vision Press, 1950. Rpt. New
York: New Directions, 1954.

"Excerpts from letters to Milton Hindus." *Texas
Quarterly,* 5:4 (1962), 22-38.

Castle to Castle. Trans. Ralph Manheim. New York:
Delacorte, 1968. Rpt. London: Blond, 1969; New
York: Penguin, 1976.

North. Trans. Ralph Manheim. New York: Delacorte,
1972. Rpt. with introduction by Kurt Vonnegut,
Penguin, 1976.

Rigadoon. Trans. Ralph Manheim. New York: Delacorte, 1974. Rpt. with introduction by Kurt
Vonnegut, Penguin, 1975.

2. SELECTED CÉLINE CRITICISM IN ENGLISH: 1935-1983

Brée, Germaine and Margaret Guiton. *An Age of Fiction: The French Novel from Gide to Camus.* New
Brunswick, N.J.: Rutgers University Press, 1957,
pp. 164-69.

Booth, Wayne. *The Rhetoric of Fiction.* Chicago:
University of Chicago Press, 1961.

Buckley, William K. "A Selected Bibliography of Critical Articles, Books, and Commentaries on Louis-Ferdinand Céline and His Works: 1932-1973." *Recovering Literature*, 3:1 (Spring 1974), 5-59.

Burgess, Anthony. "New Novels." *Listener*, 75:1942 (16 June 1966), 883.

Burns, Wayne. "The Beat and the Dead." *Towards a Contextualist Aesthetic For the Novel*. Seattle, Wash.: Genitron Books, 1968, 87-93.

Busi, Frederick. "Céline--The Wild Man of French Literature." *Midstream* (June-July 1976), 69-72.

Butler, Gerald J. "Céline's *Bagatelles pour un massacre*: The Expression of a Forbidden Passion." *Recovering Literature*, 8:1 (Spring 1980), 27-42.

----------. "The Meaning of the Presence of Lili in Céline's Final Trilogy." *Recovering Literature*, 10 (1982), 57-63.

Carson, Jane. "Céline: The Fire in the Night." *Symposium*, 35:2 (Summer 1981), 117-30.

Davis, Leslie. "Céline and the Débâcle of Idealism." *1936: The Sociology of Literature*. Volume I: *The Politics of Modernism*. Ed. F. Barker et al. University of Essex, 1979.

Flynn, James. "Céline: Beyond the Gesture." *Recovering Literature*, 2:1 (Spring 1973), 5-35.

Fortier, Paul A. "Marxist Criticism of Céline's *Voyage au bout de la nuit*." *Modern Fiction Studies*, 17:2 (1971), 268-72.

Fraser, John. "The Darkest Journey: Céline, *Death on the Installment Plan*." *Wisconsin Studies in Contemporary Literature*, 8 (Winter 1967), 96-110.

Frohock, W.M. "Céline's Quest For Love." *Accent*, 2:22 (Winter 1941-1942), 79-84.

----------. "First-person narration (Bernanos, Céline, Giono, Sartre, Camus)." *Style and Temper: Studies in French Fiction, 1925-1961*. Oxford: Basil Blackwell, 1967.

Ginsberg, Allen. *As Ever: The Collected Correspondence of Allen Ginsberg and Neal Cassidy*. Berkeley: Creative Arts Book Co., 1977.

Hayman, David. *Louis-Ferdinand Céline*. New York: Columbia University Press, 1965.

----------. "Céline." *Contemporary Literature*, 15 (1974), 257.

Hewitt, Nicholas. "Narration and Desolidarisation in Céline's *Mort à Crédit*." *Essays in French Literature*, 12 (November 1975), 59-69.

Hindus, Milton. *The Crippled Giant: A Bizzare Adventure in Contemporary Letters*. New York: Boar's Head Books, 1950.

----------. "The Recent Revival of Céline: A Consideration." *Mosaic*, 6 (1973), 57-66.

----------. "The State of the Céline Industry." *New Boston Review*, 3 (Summer 1977), 16-18.

Howe, Irving. "Céline: Novelist of the Underground." *Tomorrow*, 8:3 (November 1948), 53-56.

----------. "Céline: The Sod Beneath the Skin, I and II." *New Republic* (20 July and 17 August 1963), 19-22, 17-20. Rpt. in *A World More Attractive*. New York: Horizon Press, 1963, pp. 192-206.

Knapp, Bettina L. *Céline: Man of Hate*. University, Ala.: University of Alabama Press, 1974.

Krance, Charles. "Céline and the Literature of Extasis: The Virtuosity of Non-Genre." *Language and Style*, 6:3 (Summer 1973), 176-84.

Luce, Stanford. *Glossary of Céline's Fiction*. Ann Arbor, Mich.: University Microfilms, 1979.

Luce, Stanford, and William K. Buckley. *A Half Century of Céline: An Annotated Bibliography, 1932-1982*. New York: Garland Publishing, Inc., 1983.

Matthews, J.H. *The Inner Dream: Céline as Novelist*. Syracuse, N.Y.: Syracuse University Press, 1978.

McCarthy, Patrick. "Céline During the Occupation." *The New Review*, 2:14 (1975), 37-54.

----------. *Céline*. New York: Viking Press, 1976.

Miller, Henry. *Sunday After the War*. New York: New
    Directions, 1944, pp. 23-25, 154-60.

----------. "A Letter on Céline." *Paris Review*, 31
    (Winter-Spring 1964), 137.

Nettelbeck, C.W. "Journey to the End of Art: The
    Evolution of the Novels of Louis-Ferdinand Cé-
    line." *PMLA*, 87 (January 1972), 80-89.

O'Connell, David. *Louis-Ferdinand Céline*. Boston:
    Twayne Publishers, 1976.

Ostrovsky, Erika. "The Anatomy of Cruelty: Antonin
    Artaud, Louis-Ferdinand Céline." *Arts and Sci-
    ences* (Spring 1967), 9-13.

----------. *Céline and His Vision*. New York: New
    York University Press, 1967.

----------. *Voyeur Voyant: A Portrait of Louis-
    Ferdinand Céline*. New York: Random House, 1971.

Ott, Bill. "The Death of Des Pereires: Possibili-
    ties For Compassion in Céline's World." *Recov-
    ering Literature*, 2:1 (Spring 1973), 65-74.

Reck, Rima Dell. "Céline and Wolfe: Toward a Theory
    of the Autobiographical Novel." *Mississippi
    Quarterly*, 22 (1968-69), 19-22.

Rens, Jean-Guy, and Bill Tierney. "Céline's Last Journey: An Essay After the Publication of *Rigadoon* in 1969." *Antigonish Review*, 2:1 (Spring 1971), 39-59.

Robel, Gerald. "Ferdinand and His Family." from "Compassion in Céline." *Recovering Literature*, 2:1 (Spring 1973), 37-64.

Roudiez, Leon. "On Several Approaches to Céline." *Romanic Review*, 72:1 (January 1981), 94-104.

Slochower, Harry. "Satanism in Céline." *Books Abroad*, 18 (October 1944), 332-37.

Solomon, Philip H. "Céline's *Death on the Installment Plan*: The Intoxication of Delirium." *Yale French Studies*, 50 (1974), 191-203.

Soucy, Robert. "French Fascist Intellectuals in the 1930's: An Old New Left?" *French Historical Studies*, 8:3 (Spring 1974), 445-58.

Steiner, George. "Cry Havoc." *New Yorker* (20 January 1968), 106-15.

Stromberg, Robert. "A Talk With Louis-Ferdinand Céline." *Evergreen Review*, 19 (August 1961), 102-07.

Thiher, Allen. *Céline: The Novel as Delirium*. New Brunswick, N.J.: Rutgers University Press, 1972.

Thomas, Merlin. *Louis-Ferdinand Céline*. New York: New Directions, 1979.

Tilby, M.J. "Céline's Letters to his Translator." *Times Literary Supplement* (2 April 1982), 385-86.

Trotsky, Leon. "Novelist and Politician." *Atlantic Monthly*, 156:4 (October 1935), 413-20.

Updike, John. "The Strange Case of Dr. Destouches and M. Céline." *New Yorker*, 52:30 (13 September 1976), 154-61.

Widmer, Kingsley. "The Way Down to Wisdom of Louis-Ferdinand Céline." *The Minnesota Review*, 8:1 (1968), 85-91.

Woodcock, George. "Céline Revived." *Tamarack Review*, 44 (1967), 94-99.

Writers at Work: Paris Review Interviews. Third Series. New York: Viking Press, 1967.

CONTRIBUTORS

Wayne Burns is Emeritus Professor of English at the University of Washington. His most recent book is *Journey Through the Dark Woods*, an account of his teaching career. Currently he is working on a full-length study of Céline which will include the essay on *Journey to the End of the Night* which is printed in this volume.

Bill Ott is presently the Book Review Editor for *Booklist*, a publication of the American Library Association, and works in Chicago.

John Leeds is a writer currently living in Mexico.

Gerald J. Butler is Associate Professor of English at San Diego State University. He is the founding editor of *Recovering Literature*.

Jerry Zaslove is a Professor of English and Chairman of the Department of English at Simon Fraiser University, Burnaby, British Columbia, Canada.

William K. Buckley is Assistant Professor of English at Indiana University Northwest. He is the co-author (with Stanford L. Luce) of *A Half-Century of Céline: An Annotated Bibliography, 1932-1982.*

James Flynn is a writer and socioeconomic consultant. He is presently completing a study of construction workers entitled: *Boomers: Life Histories of Traveling Construction Workers.*